Critical Praise for Michael Yapko's

WHEN LIVING HURTS
Directives for Treating Depression

"Dr. Yapko understands that a humanistic approach is nicely congruent with offering directives when they are needed, and he shares this understanding clearly and compassionately." —*The California Therapist*

"Anyone interested in broadening the range of their management of depression would benefit from reading it." —*British Journal of Medical Psychology*

"...recommended to all health professionals who are interested in improving the effectiveness of the treatment of depression." —*Australian and New Zealand Journal of Family Therapy*

"Dr. Michael Yapko presents eminently useful and practical approaches for the most common problem of depression." —Ernest L. Rossi, Ph.D. Author, *The Psychobiology of Mind–Body Healing*

"Dr. Michael Yapko...presents inventive therapeutic prescriptions that, as an integral part of an overall treatment plan, can help depressed patients find the resources to empower themselves." — Jeffrey K. Zeig, Ph.D. Director, The Milton H. Erickson Foundation

ALSO BY MICHAEL D. YAPKO

HYPNOSIS AND THE TREATMENT OF DEPRESSIONS
Strategies for Change

USING HYPNOSIS IN TREATING DEPRESSION
(4-Cassette Audiotape Program)

TRANCEWORK
An Introduction to the Practice of Clinical Hypnosis

THE CASE OF VICKI
Patterns of Trancework
(Videotape)

BRIEF THERAPY APPROACHES TO TREATING ANXIETY
AND DEPRESSION
(Editor)

ESSENTIALS OF CLINICAL HYPNOSIS
(Brunner/Mazel Basic Principles into Practice Series)
Available November 1994

WHEN LIVING HURTS

Directives for Treating Depression

By *MICHAEL D. YAPKO, Ph.D.*

 BRUNNER/MAZEL, *Publishers* • NEW YORK

First Paperback Edition 1994

Library of Congress Cataloging-in-Publication Data

Yapko, Michael D.
  When living hurts.

  Bibliography: p. 219
  Includes index.
  1. Depression, Mental – Treatment.   2. Psychotherapy,
Brief.   I. Title
RC537.Y36   1988   616.85'27   87-22437
  ISBN 0-87630-757-8 (paperback)
  ISBN 0-87630-485-4 (cloth)

Published by
BRUNNER/MAZEL, INC.
19 Union Square West
New York, New York 10003

MANUFACTURED IN THE UNITED STATES OF AMERICA

10 9 8 7 6 5 4 3 2 1

To Wendy and Richard Horowitz, the best of friends,

and

To my clients and students, past and present.

Through the generosity of your sharing, you have taught me the most valuable lessons about living.

Contents

Introduction

Welcome to a perfect world in a perfect universe. All people agree completely on how to best use the planet's resources. Everyone is well fed, all the people wear nice clothes, and each lives in a comfortable home. There is no crime, no aggression, no prejudice. Each person has the utmost regard for human and animal life, and it would never occur to anyone to inflict damage on living creatures or material properties. Each individual has individual preferences and values, but all are acutely aware of their enormous responsibilities to the world of which they are a part. Family members are loyal and fully committed to each other, and all individuals are raised in happy, supportive homes that instill a great sense of personal confidence and self-worth in each family member. Each individual works hard, is treated fairly in the workplace, and each is well paid for his/her efforts. Simply put, there are no problems *anywhere*.

If you or your clients live in a world that even closely approximates the one described above, you don't need this book. Return it while it's still crisp and clean and spend the money on something else. Perhaps a nice sweater. . . .

If you live in the world I live in, then you already know about the pressures and problems that are an inevitable part of living. (I hope that sounds realistic and not pessimistic.) Is there anyone who goes through life trouble-free? Who escapes the pain of deeply loving someone who then dies? Who always gets the job he or she wanted so badly? Who has never had the experience of being at the wrong place at the wrong time when someone else decides he doesn't need to stop for a "stop" sign?

Whose kids don't mouth off, dress preposterously, and use language from some other part of the universe? Who among us will ultimately get out of here alive?

Stress takes a lot of different forms — some good, some bad. There are many models describing the experience and evolution of clinical depression, but a stressor of one sort or another is the common denominator in all of the various models. *One can't prevent stress, one can only manage it well.* Just as stress is inevitable, so is depression. It, too, can be managed well, and when it is well managed it doesn't hurt as much or as long. Some episodes of depression can even be prevented, but the greater focus in this book is on responding to the experience of depression that is already present in the afflicted individual.

How one intervenes therapeutically in the life of the depressed client seeking psychotherapy is always a major factor in the therapy's outcome. My depressed clients come in *hurting.* They are not intent on having a lot of therapy over a long period of time in order to feel better. In fact, the opposite is usually true. The person wants relief *right now,* although yesterday would be even better. I have enough compassion in me for my clients that I strive to find ways to focus my clinical skills in order to try to generate at least some relief at the earliest possible moment. I also have enough clinical acumen to know that brief interventions will sometimes be complete ones, and other times such interventions will be small steps in a considerably longer therapy process. Whether directives are embedded in a longer term treatment or brief therapy (ranging from only 1-20 sessions), the need to intervene actively and to provide catalysts for learning to interrupt the cycle of depression is the responsibility of the clinician. "Directives" are strategies intended to help the clinician do this. If the depressed client knew what to do to escape the hurt, the client would definitely do those things. The client *doesn't* know what kinds of experiences or perspectives he or she needs, which is why you have the job you do. You earn your living as a problem solver, one who is sensitive, insightful, and supportive, but a problem solver nonetheless.

Depression has so many facets, as you already know or will discover, that it usually takes a better than average problem solver to make a difference. This book represents an effort to make the extremely complex and subjective experience of depression one that can be better understood and more effectively treated. It does not represent a school of therapy in a singular way. Rather, it promotes the recognition of the diversity of human experience such that an emphasis on any one approach will seem obviously self-limiting. Another belief promoted here is that therapy can take a variety of forms, all useful somewhere, sometime, with somebody. The clinical skill is evident in knowing what is most likely to be effective for a given individual. I sincerely hope that the patterns of subjective experience described throughout this work become a basis for better understanding the complicated internal world of the client, for that is the arena in which the clinician will be doing his or her work.

This book is organized in a somewhat unusual way. There is a progression of concepts that provide support for the directives, but the directives are the central focus of this volume. They are grouped according to associated issues and are clearly marked by number. A complete listing of the strategies is contained in Appendix A.

One goal in describing so many different strategies is to illustrate ways to promote experiential learning on the part of the client, since it is experience in the real world that is considered to be the best of teachers. Perhaps an even greater goal, however, is to catalyze clinicians' creativity in generating novel and active ways of facilitating recovery for their depressed clients. I hope this book helps.

Michael D. Yapko
San Diego, California

Acknowledgments

The book you are holding in your hands is a product of a great deal of effort by many people, not only me. I would like to acknowledge those people to whom I am eternally grateful for their help and support. Diane Yapko, Wendy Horowitz, David L. Higgins, Brita Ann Martiny, John J. Koriath, and Raymond A. Fidaleo each provided wonderful emotional as well as literary support throughout this project. Each offered valuable feedback, which I appreciate greatly. Linda Griebel, my highly valued secretary and guardian of my time, deserves special recognition for her efforts on my behalf. Ann Alhadeff, my editor, with each stroke of her green pen, taught me a great deal about patience and how to use an attentiveness to detail to my advantage. I appreciate that very much. And finally, to my family and friends, I would like to say thanks for all the wonderful things you are. You are the most natural antidepressants on the planet.

Perhaps a person gains by accumulating obstacles. The more obstacles set up to prevent happiness from appearing, the greater the shock when it does appear, just as the rebound of a spring will be all the more powerful the greater the pressure that has been exerted to compress it. Care must be taken, however, to select large obstacles, for only those of sufficient scope and scale have the capacity to lift us out of context and force life to appear in an entirely new and unexpected light. . . Difficulties illuminate existence, but they must be fresh and of high quality.

Tom Robbins, from
Even Cowgirls Get the Blues (1976, p. 158)

Part I

Theoretical
Framework

1

When Living Hurts

When Living Hurts is the painful reality of daily life for literally tens of millions of people. There is a very good chance that the reader has directly or indirectly experienced the kind of feelings that make it easy to recognize depression in the way that some of the author's clients have described it:

"A robber in the shadows, stealing my life."

"An invisible, insidious monster."

"A suffocating shroud of pain."

"An evil curse of ongoing agony."

A couple of years ago the author was affected quite profoundly by a most troubling event that can be described here. It involved a psychiatrist who was a most remarkable man. We had never met, but his excellent work was well known to me. He had attended and graduated medical school in his early twenties, and quickly established himself as a highly visible and noted authority on patterns of behavior change (even co-authoring a well-received self-help book on the subject) and also on forensic issues in psychiatry. His range of knowledge, especially for so young a man, was most impressive. Unfortunately, when his personal life went through a period of crisis due to a failing marriage, his superior knowledge of emotional needs and mental health did not serve him at all. He literally asked colleagues for help because of feeling so out of control, but others apparently found the pleas for help too incongruous with his stature to take seriously. He soon ended up taking his own life with a bullet to his head. He was only in his early thirties, with a life potentially full of significant accomplishments ahead of him.

Perhaps it was the unrealistic expectation that mental health professionals should be more adept at handling life's difficulties that caused this event to stand out in the author's awareness. Perhaps it was some other reason, but whatever the reason, sadly his death was only one of about 30,000 suicides that year (Davison & Neale, 1986). Suicide has been called the "permanent solution to a temporary problem" and perhaps represents the most dramatic risk of painful depression. Why did so well-educated and insightful a man choose suicide? How does depression become so painful to so many that death seems a viable, desirable alternative? How does it become so debilitating that it causes ongoing suffering for those who have the courage, motivation, or tolerance to live with it? What do we as psychotherapists *really* know about depression and its treatment?

Much research on depression has been done over the years. The body of scientific literature available on the subject is enormous, a testimony to the pervasiveness of the problem and the serious involvement of those who genuinely want to do something to help. From this research have come elaborate theories about the etiology of depression, and a wide variety of ways to intervene therapeutically. Virtually all of the various theories and treatments are of potential benefit to the clinician for developing a comprehensive understanding of the nature of depression, yet paradoxically all are potentially limiting (and may even be harmful to the depressed client) if the multifaceted phenomenon of depression is viewed and treated from only a single perspective.

The mental health profession officially categorizes depression as a mood disorder, and it is so listed in the *Diagnostic and Statistical Manual* (3rd edition, revised) (American Psychiatric Association, 1987). As will be seen in Chapter 3, there are some specific problems with the diagnosing and classification of depression that can have a significant impact on how the depressed client is treated. Suffice it to say at this early point that the clinical entity termed "depression" is still not fully understood, nor is the treatment of depression consistently effective.

This is not a book about a theory of depression, although it undeniably contains some synthesis of theoretical perspectives. Rather, the emphasis throughout this book is on the *treatment* of the depressed individual. As a clinical psychologist working with depressed individuals and families, the author cannot help but be deeply affected by the many ways depression robs people of the positive possibilities life has to offer. As a human being subject to the same frailties shared by others living with human bodies and minds, the author also experiences the aches and pains of depression. It is a highly pragmatic orientation that dominates this work: What can one *say* and *do* that will have therapeutic value? What tools can be utilized to better facilitate recovery from depression, and catalyze the kind of shifts in the depressed individual's world that will both minimize future recurrences and allow for greater speed of recovery when episodes do arise?

THE NATURE OF THE BEAST

Depression has a long and well-known history, documented from earliest writings and lived out by countless numbers of people (some famous, most not). While specific numbers are hard to come by because of the many cases that go unreported, it is estimated that: 1) a range of 30-40 million Americans now suffer a diagnosable depressive disorder *(Newsweek,* May 4, 1987); 2) at least one in four Americans will suffer a major depressive episode at some point in their lives; 3) only about one-quarter to one-half of those who suffer major depression receive any therapy for their symptoms; 4) women are diagnosed as suffering clinical depression nearly twice as frequently as men (although the actual distribution of depression by gender appears to be even); and 5) depression occurs in all age groups (Kleinmuntz, 1980; Kolb & Brodie, 1982).

The prevalence of depression in a general epidemiological sense is troublesome enough. To compound the matter, it is well known that many cases of depression are "masked," hidden behind a host of somatic complaints or other psychological problems. Thus, the problem of depression *must* be more widespread than general statistics indicate and may be even more widespread than clinicians may realize. If the criteria for a diagnosis of depression are broadened, as will be suggested later, depression may be more accurately assessed for its prevalence, a first step in better knowing the scope of the problem we as a profession face.

The pain of depression is known to some degree by most of us on both personal and professional levels. It seems literally impossible for one to be in clinical practice without encountering depressed individuals routinely. What is the effect of the prevalence of depression? The cost in human lives, suffering, damaged relationships, lost work, and lost personal time, as well as in other areas, is incalculable.

A reference to suicide statistics has already been made. It has been suggested that many of the people suffering depression are channeling their abstract bad feelings into concrete bad physical symptoms. It has also been alluded to that many other psychological difficulties are, in fact, depression in disguise. For example, it seems likely that many of the substance abuse disorders are actually patterns that are primitive attempts to cope with the pain (i.e., anxiety) of depression. Abuse of substances in all their forms are commonly relied on coping mechanisms, which carry mentally and physically unhealthy side effects that may help perpetuate the underlying problem of depression. Treating the alcoholic drinking patterns but not the related depression (when that is the case) is almost certain to generate recurrent episodes of "falling off the wagon." Other dysfunctional patterns which may, at first glance, seem unrelated to depression may actually be closely related. The later discussion of diagnosing depression according to a broader range of criteria may help clinicians address this issue more efficiently.

Depression is generally a self-limiting phenomenon. If one does nothing and simply lets it run its course, for most people it will eventually fade away. The data on the average duration of a self-limited depression are ambiguous, suggesting anywhere between 4 and 10 months. Statistics further suggest that somewhere between 10-20% of those with a diagnosis of depression will develop a chronic condition (Davison & Neale, 1986).

ETIOLOGY OF DEPRESSION

Conventional wisdom would lead one to anticipate that with a problem as multifaceted as depression there would be no single underlying causative factor. Conventional wisdom is not always correct, but in this case it most assuredly is. In fact, there are quite a few theories describing causes of depression. These theories include biological, intrapersonal, and interpersonal views, and each offers extremely useful ways to think about the etiology of depression. It is assumed that the reader is already familiar with these theories, and so each is given only a cursory description here.

Biological Theories

Derived largely from the effects of certain drugs on the biogenic amines, the major biological theories regarding depression hypothesize that depression occurs when certain neurotransmitters (such as norepinephrine and serotonin) reach too low a concentration in certain areas of the brain. Also falling within the biological realm are those links between depression and physical disorders. The following comprise a partial list of biologically based depressogenic phenomena: certain prescription drugs (including reserpine, some oral contraceptives, antihypertensives, minor and major tranquilizers); some drugs of abuse (e.g., alcohol, barbiturates, stimulants, hallucinogens); neurological diseases;

metabolic-endocrine disorders; heart disease; surgery; and diseases of the kidneys, liver, and pulmonary systems (Hollister, 1983).

Depression may be secondary to debilitating illnesses, or vice versa. When depression is observed in tandem with physical illness or dysfunction, it may simply be coincidence, but it may also be a significant finding with strong implications for appropriate treatment. Careful diagnosis is needed in such instances.

The biological framework includes theories regarding the genetic transmission of depression. Studies have shown that a range of approximately 25-40% of depressed individuals have a parent or other first-degree relative with an affective disorder (Clayton, 1983). Owing to the fact that women are diagnosed as depressed twice as frequently as men, some have suggested that depression is linked to an X chromosome transmission, but there is no firm support for this theory to date. Female hormonal influences have also been considered as significant etiological factors (related in particular to the hormonal changes associated with postpartum and menopausal depressions), but firm conclusions in this area have not yet been made. Furthermore, while women may be diagnosed as depressed more frequently than men, the actual distribution by gender appears to be equal. Differences in diagnostic criteria for men and women are thought to be the basis for the larger percentage of women deemed clinically depressed (Davison & Neale, 1986).

Intrapersonal Theories

"Intrapersonal" is the general heading of those theories that emphasize depression as a problem *within* an individual. This encompasses psychodynamic, cognitive, and the "learned helplessness" models.

The psychodynamic model conceptualizes a sense of "loss" as the chief component of depression. Freud (1917) theorized that some individuals become overly dependent on others for maintaining a sense of self-esteem (arising from too little or too much gratification of needs during the oral stage). Thus, when the object of dependency is lost (perhaps through their death or rejection), the individual feels rage that cannot be directly expressed. Rather, it is "anger turned inwardly," and becomes the self-blame and self-hatred that are characteristic of depressed people, according to Freud.

The cognitive model of depression, developed primarily by Aaron Beck (1967, 1973; Beck et al., 1979) conceptualizes depression as a product of distorted thinking. In Beck's model, emotions are consequences of thoughts, and if one is depressed it is because one is thinking in negative and unrealistic ways. The negative belief system may have been established early in life and precede episodes of depression that

arise later. Perception and subsequent activity involve interpreting ongoing events, and if one's perceptions are consistently negative and
demotivating, depression is a fairly predictable outcome. The "learned
helplessness" model of depression, developed primarily by Martin Seligman
(1974, 1975, 1983), conceptualizes depression as the product of a history of faulty learnings regarding personal locus of control. Seligman's
model suggests that when one is subjected to negative events perceived
as outside of one's control, one becomes hopeless, passive, and depressed.

Interpersonal Theories

From a systems perspective, individual pathology is viewed as a reflection of the system of which the individual is a part. Thus, the focus in an
interpersonal model of depression is one emphasizing the involvement
in the therapy of other members of the identified client's social network.
The underlying belief is that depression occurs in a social and interpersonal context and arises primarily from depressogenic relationship
patterns. These may include stressful social role transitions, social role
conflicts, and social consequences of individual choices (Klerman,
Weissman, Rounsaville, & Chevron, 1984).

Strategic psychotherapies that are brief and directive in nature are
generally systems-oriented approaches that typically make use of the
client's everyday social contexts in order to effect change. The systems-
oriented approaches of clinicians such as Jay Haley, Paul Watzlawick,
Virginia Satir, and Milton Erickson are typical of the emphasis on the
antidepressant capability of restoring or elevating a system to its functional capacity.

The various models of depression described so briefly here are each
profound in their own way of conceptualizing the nature of depression.
For the reader unfamiliar with these models, it is strongly recommended
that he or she read the original writings of their developers. Many of the
intervention strategies described later are derived directly from these
models.

In the next section, the range of treatments currently utilized for
depression, which are associated with the above models, are described.

CURRENT TREATMENT PARADIGMS FOR DEPRESSION

Just as there are a variety of ways to conceptualize the origin and
maintenance of depression, there are a variety of ways to intervene
therapeutically in the problem. The various approaches that are currently
utilized are each applied in a manner that is consistent with their

associated theory of etiology. Thus, a biologically oriented framework for understanding the onset of the disorder is treated physically or chemically, the intrapersonal approaches are treated on that dimension, and so on. The following descriptions are abbreviated summaries of the various interventions according to model.

Biologically Based Interventions

The major therapeutic approach in the biological realm is pharmacotherapy, specifically the use of the various antidepressant medications (e.g., tricyclics, tetracyclics, and monoamine oxidase inhibitors). Of these, the tricyclics continue to be the most commonly prescribed, and have as their primary therapeutic function the apparent ability to increase the levels of norepinephrine and serotonin neurotransmitters in the brains of seriously depressed persons. The specific physiological pathways are not fully understood at this time.

Another somatically based treatment used more commonly than most realize is electroconvulsive therapy (ECT). ECT is a highly controversial treatment, which involves the passing of an electrical current through the brain of the depressed individual. The mechanism of action in ECT is not yet understood, but treatment is highly touted by its advocates as a means of disrupting the course of severe depression, allowing the depressed individual to be more calm and receptive to the effects of other therapies. Considered a more extreme form of treatment because of undesirable side effects, ECT is generally used when the depression is so pervasive as to make other approaches untenable. ECT is considered the treatment of choice for psychotic depression. ECT is generally delivered in a series, involving multiple treatments over a period of time.

Other somatically based approaches include the use of vigorous physical exercise to promote physical well-being, reduce fatigue, and enhance self-esteem; the use of light to stimulate the brain; sleep deprivation; and the use of stimulants (such as Ritalin in elderly depressed individuals).

Intrapersonally Based Interventions

Psychodynamically based therapies generally attempt to promote insight into one's depressogenic patterns. Resolving dependency and transference issues, uncovering and expressing suppressed anger and other painful feelings, and analyzing and "working through" one's defenses and fixations are the goals of these longer-term approaches.

Cognitive therapy generally involves promoting an awareness of one's negative thoughts and cognitive distortions, the faulty patterns of thinking and perceiving that cause and maintain episodes of depression. The irrationality, negative selective attention, dichotomous thinking, and other distorted patterns of thinking are well described, along with specific recommendations for ways to counter these patterns, in the cognitive therapy writings of Beck (1967, 1973, 1983), Burns (1980), and others. In essence, cognitive therapy teaches that if one minimizes the inaccuracy of one's thoughts and changes the way one thinks, one can significantly alter one's moods.

Treatment of depression in the "learned helplessness" model involves the gradual shaping of the person's ability to perceive and exercise control over his or her experience. Typically, a hierarchy of tasks is created with an emphasis on building small successes into increasingly larger ones. Specific skills in goal defining and goal acquisition are promoted as being central to maintaining relief from depression. Clarification of faulty perceptions regarding what is and is not within one's control is fundamental in this paradigm.

Interpersonally Based Interventions

Since the underlying belief in the interpersonal models emphasizes that depression is embedded in a social context, those approaches that emphasize healthy communication skills and positive social skills are the primary vehicles for the therapy. Thus, marital therapy, family therapy, group therapy, strategic therapies, and techniques encouraging assertiveness and enhanced communication are the primary approaches. Furthermore, such approaches conceptualize the clinician-client relationship (encompassing an infinite number of interpersonal variables) to be the catalyzing power of the therapy. These approaches are directive and systems-oriented in their observation that the depressed individual is not existing alone, but is involved in a larger network that requires attention as well.

Each of these therapies as well as the many others that are to be described here are successful with certain clients. However, no therapy is completely successful consistently. The goal is to continually develop new approaches and new combinations of current approaches in order to advance the technology of alleviating human suffering in all its forms.

SUMMARY

Clearly the problem of depression is pervasive and has commanded a great deal of attention from the mental health profession. Elaborate models based on biological, intrapersonal, and interpersonal causative factors have been established in the literature, each providing concrete approaches for the treatment of depressed individuals. These models and associated interventions have been described very briefly in an attempt to orient the reader to current perspectives on depression.

The next chapter discusses the characteristics of strategic therapy that underlie the therapeutic patterns described later.

2

The Direction of Relief

According to the available data, only a minority of depressed individuals seek treatment. Why will people endure such discomfort without even attempting to obtain relief? As will be seen in greater detail later, it is the sense of personal helplessness so characteristic of the depressed individual that prevents him or her from actively seeking help. Essentially, the belief is one of "Why bother? No one can help me." Depressed individuals typically experience themselves as trapped in a combination of painful personal and situational circumstances that apparently cannot be resolved through any direct action on their part. Obviously, each person's circumstances are unique, but the underlying belief is generally one that precludes actively taking steps to resolve the situation.

The widespread recognition of the depressed individual's sense of helplessness has been well promoted in the literature on depression. The ever-present threat of suicide is a stark reminder of how extreme the feelings of being hopelessly trapped can get. It is apparent that when the depressed individual is at a low ebb of confidence in the ability to meaningfully influence his or her situation, the paralysis so commonly observed by clinicians is actually a logical consequence. The posture the clinician takes in dealing with the depressed client is thus the most vital aspect of the treatment, even more vital than the specific therapy itself. Taking the position of actively directing the client's experience must be seen as basic to the effective treatment of depression.

Consider the interplay of dynamics between the general nature of depression and several of the more traditional approaches to its treatment. This disorder involves passivity in the face of adversity, apathy in the face of hopelessness, and confusion in place of directionality. Thus, at a time when the client is least in a position to know how to organize and motivate him- or herself, the client may still be required to do so simply because of the type of therapy chosen. For example, in a strictly biological model of treatment, the client may be started on antidepressant medication of one sort or another and may be told, "Let's wait and see whether the medication helps once it reaches its therapeutic level." Psychotherapy may be absent altogether or may be considered of secondary importance to the effect of the medication. Such a posture implies that the client is in a passive role in the treatment process and that any effects of the treatment are generated by biological factors outside of the person's control. The analogical communication in this type of treatment approach is one *confirming* helplessness and illness. Thus, the treatment can inadvertently compound the client's depression by reinforcing some of the most troublesome aspects of the disorder.

If psychotherapy is the primary vehicle for treatment, what are the implications for the use of nondirective approaches or approaches that emphasize insight as vital to the resolution of depressogenic issues? Nondirective approaches may offer the comfort of a supportive relationship but put the burden of responsibility for the therapy's direction on the client at a time when he or she is least able to determine a direction, or to know how to intervene in his or her own issues. To let the client flounder while maintaining a position of denying one's capacity to influence him or her seems irresponsible. It is well established that no therapy can be truly nondirective anyway, since the mere presence of another person alters one's responses (do you do things when you are by yourself that you will not do if even one other person is around?). The issue is not really one of *whether* the clinician influences the client; rather it is *how* and *to what extent* the clinician does so. In treating depression in particular, the need for patterns to catalyze therapeutic influence as rapidly and effectively as possible should be apparent.

Insight-oriented approaches run into certain inevitable limitations as well. The emphasis is on awareness, logic, and understanding, as if rationality can or will prevail. The often-heard statement from clients "I know I shouldn't feel this way, but I do" is one indication of the limits of the intellect in dealing with feelings. Another is when the client says, "I know why and how I got to this point in being depressed; I just don't know what to do about it."

The emphasis on conscious awareness as pivotal to therapeutic success can be limiting for a number of reasons. The conscious mind's ability to have an integrated understanding of "self" is limited since so much of what one experiences takes place at the unconscious level. For as long as there is an unconscious mind, some things will necessarily remain out of awareness. Second, working in the "progress through awareness" paradigm puts the clinician in the position of having to make decisions about which things from the person's unconscious should be conscious. Third, when such decisions are made by the clinician and acted on, the tendency is for the client to "resist" the passing of such information into awareness, effectively delaying or even preventing progress. Fourth, when no such cause-effect insight can be culled from the person's history, an ambiguously defined biological or psychological explanation can be offered with relative impunity. The effect is to further impart to the client a lack of sense of control over his or her own experience. It is true, however, that numerous studies suggest a strong link between genetics, biochemistry, and affective disorders. The question is one of diagnosing such cases, since no reliable diagnostic system for biologically based depression exists yet.

The concept of an exclusively biologically based depression is currently going through a reevaluation by many. The assumption of a unidirectional mind-body relationship in which the body impacts the mind may prove too limiting in the face of mounting evidence for a bidirectional relationship. Taking into account the therapeutic aspects of *experience* may eventually lead psychotherapists to a reduction in the dispensing of currently overprescribed medications. Depending on the severity of the depression, medication or supportive approaches may be employed with the client in order to facilitate a state that is more receptive to the directive approaches described in this book.

The reader must not interpret the observations about the limits of the approaches described thus far as a dismissal of their potential effectiveness. On the contrary, each approach can be effective in its own right. The larger issue of concern here relates to those situations where these approaches may not be deemed viable or are proving ineffective for whatever reason. This concern is particularly relevant when one views depression as a disorder occurring on multiple dimensions within the client, necessitating treatment on multiple dimensions as well. (More will be said about this in the next chapter.) Of special concern is the analogical communication that inevitably accompanies the therapeutic plan. Telling a client on a dimension outside of awareness, and hence conscious scrutiny, that the treatment is one that will "work" without his or her involvement, however slight, is dangerously close to overtly saying, "Your efforts are irrelevant to your condition." Likewise, a reluctance to offer direction or specific tools that may help the client indirectly says, "You're on your own; I can't/won't help you." Such a statement can only isolate the client further and may lead him or her to believe that the problem(s) must truly be insurmountable. The clinician should be selective in the quality of communications delivered on *all* dimensions of intervention.

DIRECTIVE INTERVENTION

Once the clinician has accepted the notion that he or she will be exerting influence on the client regardless of the approach used, it then becomes apparent that different approaches will exert different influences. Typically, the clinician approaches the client in a manner prescribed by the specific theoretical orientation the clinician subscribes to, or at least according to the model(s) of depression the clinician believes best represents the client's experience.

An example of the potential antitherapeutic effects of a routine intervention that is theory-bound may demonstrate the need for a different perspective about treatment in general and the treatment of depressed individuals in particular. A woman in her early thirties sought treatment for a moderate depression of approximately six months' duration. She was sleeping poorly, unable to concentrate on her work as a sales representative, irritable and hypercritical with her two young children, and generally apathetic. Prior to this author's seeing her, she had been in therapy for five months with a traditional insight-oriented therapist who focused her on her negative past family history. During the five months of sessions that were once or twice per week, the focus of treatment was on resolving feelings of loss according to the clinician's belief in the model that depression necessarily involves loss. The woman's anger and guilt over her negative family history were actually compounded by the clinician offering the observation that she was suffering not only the loss of the ideal family she wished she had while growing up, but also the loss of a relationship with her own children due to her depression. The message was, "You are ruining your children, just as you have been ruined." The woman deteriorated rapidly, until the clinician finally recommended that she see a psychiatrist for antidepressant medication and tranquilizers. This recommendation was the final straw, sufficiently angering her by essentially saying, "You are too pathological to be effectively treated by psychotherapy alone." She refused to take the medications and stopped seeing the clinician, who she realized was actually aggravating her condition rather than helping her. She sought a different approach which proved to be immediately beneficial to her in its emphasis on progressive change through realistic problem solving.

By focusing the woman on her feelings of loss, with virtually no emphasis on the positive abilities she possessed to alter her current ways of thinking, feeling, and acting, how could she be absorbed in anything other than the pain of loss? Is *that* therapy? The mistakes in the approach would have been evident to the clinician if the latter had chosen to use ongoing feedback from the client about her lack of progress instead of striving to remain loyal to the model of depression that says depression is necessarily a consequence of loss. The clinician may even have continued to deal with the perceived issue of loss in the client with some therapeutic outcome, but only if the approach were one of building positive future possibilities of avoiding loss or coping with inevitable losses effectively, rather than simply rehashing old hurtful feelings.

Using directive approaches to treatment allows one a broader range of possibilities for intervention in the treatment of depression. There is certainly a broad range of interventions that can be called directive and even strategic, and in this book only a limited number can be presented. Once the clinician learns to *think strategically*, the ability to generate directives spontaneously evolves naturally and then there can be no limit to the creativity of the clinician's interventions. Indeed, fostering the evolution of strategic thinking in order to catalyze more rapid and reliable therapeutic results is the greater goal of this book.

STRATEGIC PSYCHOTHERAPY

What Are We Doing Here?

Strategic approaches have historically been defined as those approaches in which the clinician actively facilitates the course of therapy. It presupposes a willingness on the part of the clinician to guide the client actively in a direction that will ultimately benefit the client. The direction is *not* chosen unilaterally by the clinician, as some mistakenly believe. Rather, the direction is chosen by the client and it becomes the task of the clinician to offer directives (information and experiences) that will catalyze the client's positive movement in that direction. If the client's goal is ambiguous or out of awareness, the first directives may involve catalyzing the clear definition of a goal. Thus, it is an obvious prerequisite of directive approaches that there be a therapeutic goal. The other features of directive approaches discussed briefly throughout the remainder of this chapter all support the goal-oriented nature of therapeutic strategies.

A Question of Realities

Philosophers of all persuasions through the ages have continually reminded us of the subjective nature of reality, perpetually asking the question, "What is real?" It is doubtful there is a psychotherapist anywhere who would deny the observation that "reality" is experienced subjectively. There is an inevitable difference between the physical sensations stimulated by light waves, sound waves, and so forth, and the perceptions derived from the interpretation of experience. Thus, each person must evolve a sense of what the "real" world is based on: one's unique physical skills, the larger social milieu, and one's individual range of experiences. From this, the person develops a range of skills evidenced in meeting life's ongoing demands. The various personality theories and models of human behavior each attempt to define and describe the components and mechanisms of action of the human psyche, and each offers enlightening and restrictive observations.

In the practice of strategic psychotherapy, the deemphasis of reliance on specific theoretical constructs is encouraged, and instead the emphasis is placed on developing a refined awareness for and acceptance of the subjective frame of reference of the client. The client is not viewed as pathological, or sick, but rather as a victim of his or her own inability to have access to the capabilities or tools necessary for effective living. When the individual is empowered with full access to the necessary resources and is competent in their utilization, the therapy is considered complete.

Accepting and utilizing a client's frame of reference is a different approach from the more traditional one in which a clinician instructs the client in the rules and language of the clinician's preferred theoretical perspective. The therapeutic interventions described here are directive in nature and yet are overwhelmingly client-centered in their acceptance and utilization of the client's frame of reference. Thus, the client's language, perspectives, values, goals, needs, and dynamics are all accepted as valid representations of that client's world. The client is considered the ultimate authority on his or her own life; consequently, the clinician is continually adjusting to the client's feedback. The clinician employing these patterns is expected to be flexible enough to meet the client at his or her frame of reference and deliver the therapy from within that frame.

The Relationship Between Clinician and Client

Employing directives in treatment presupposes a very special relationship between the clinician and client. For the therapy to be effective, the clinician accepts that he or she has the capacity to meaningfully influence the client. There is an inevitable dimension of power that exists in *any* human relationship (power is generally defined as the capacity to influence). In the therapeutic relationship, the power is not distributed equally on all dimensions, nor should it be. Strategic therapies require the clinician to actively facilitate the treatment process, and the client is in the position of reacting to the guidance of the clinician and to whatever demands the clinician has of the client. Of course, the clinician reacts to the client's feedback regarding goals, capabilities, and so forth, but the therapeutic moment comes when the client has experienced the directives of the clinician and established new patterns as a result. To catalyze such events, the clinician needs to be comfortable with the capacity to influence, rather than diffusing it with denials of such an ability. Denial is evidenced in patterns such as mirroring and other "nondirective" methods.

The capacity to influence hinges on the degree of rapport between clinician and client. Rapport is a direct consequence of demonstrated ability to relate to the client's world, and thus there is an absolute necessity to know the client's world well enough to know the range of what does and does not seem true, important, and possible to the individual. Utilization of client capabilities otherwise seems impossible.

An integral part of the clinician-client relationship is the clinician's use of context. The therapy session is one context of change, and it is obviously a powerful one when the clinician uses his or her relationship to the client to its fullest capability as a vehicle of therapy. The "real" world of the client, however, is the greater context of change, for it is in the various settings of family, friends, work, and so on, that the person lives out the strengths and limitations of his or her sense of reality. Strategic therapies make abundant use of the many resources available in the client's world in order to effect change. Assignments of varying types can pragmatically utilize the recognition inherent in these approaches that the client's world is a systemic one. The client's strengths and weaknesses (i.e., symptomatic patterns) occur in a *context,* and a variety of influences operate in that context that can inadvertently (sometimes not so inadvertently) perpetuate the problem. Likewise, making therapeutic use of the different dimensions or types of variables related to the problem in order to disrupt it is a goal in designing therapeutic interventions. The general goal of *any* therapy is to build new associations (i.e., responses) in a particular context and to disrupt old ones. Clearly, the strategic approaches are outcome-oriented, and the relationship between clinician and client is a primary vehicle for maximizing the use of context.

Intervention on Multiple Dimensions

In alluding to the systemic nature of the client's world, the point is made that neither the client nor the client's symptoms are isolated or disconnected from the larger context of living. It is obvious from a systems perspective that a problem appropriate for treatment in therapy exists on a number of dimensions (which will be listed and described in the next chapter). Likewise, when a client communicates about a problem, he or she is understood to be communicating on multiple dimensions simultaneously; there is the surface meaning of the problem's description, but there are also the deeper meanings of what the client "really" means. Advanced clinical training teaches psychotherapists to uncover the "real" meanings and their implications, and the process of therapy then becomes one of sharing this awareness with the client by promoting insights. The assumption is that insight will lead to change, enhance perceptions of control, increase self-esteem, and resolve the troublesome issues. Insight-oriented approaches may thus take complex, multiple-level problems and feed them back on a single dimension of awareness.

In employing strategic therapies described in this book, the reader should realize that insight may be helpful at times, but at other times may be antitherapeutic. The variable of insight is challenged as a hypothesized necessary precursor to change. Instead, the idea is promoted that since the client can communicate on multiple dimensions simultaneously (some outside of awareness), so can the clinician communicate on multiple dimensions. The reader can refer back to the antitherapeutic multiple dimension communication of the clinician treating the young depressed woman described earlier. On one dimension, the clinician said, in essence, "Talking about the symbolic loss of your family will help you get better." On another dimension, however, was the message that "You are more mired in pathology than you know and it will take a long time and a lot of suffering before you can get better." Which dimension of communication had the greater impact on the treatment's progress? Granted, these are oversimplified statements, but the point remains that both conflicting dimensions of communication and communications outside of awareness can have dramatic impact on the course of therapy.

Another aspect of this issue regarding conscious and unconscious involvement in therapy is the relationship between thought and action. The key belief in cognitive therapy, a powerful form of treatment for depression, is that depressed feelings are derived from negative and distorted thoughts, and that clear, accurate thoughts are the basis for mental health. The strategic school in pure form suggests that action can precede thought, and thus new experiences will shape one's perspective for better or worse. It is the author's contention that this conflict is a pseudoconflict, i.e., a false and unnecessary one. Clinical experience suggests that each dimension, thought *and* action, can generate healthy responses in an individual, and that the relationship is one of mutuality. Thus, many of the strategies in this book are simply vehicles for stimulating clearer thinking and positive action.

Use of strategic directives and directive forms of influential communication involve a perspective of the unconscious mind that is quite different from the way the unconscious has traditionally been defined. The unconscious has usually been characterized as a primitive entity seething with aggressive and sexual impulses that operate in a destructive manner, and the assumption has been that the more of the unconscious that can be brought under the control of the advanced conscious mind, the better off the individual will be.

In recent years, however, the old models of the unconscious mind have gone through a closer examination. Out of the fields of neurology, neuropsychology, clinical hypnosis, and others has come evidence for a different view of the unconscious, one that characterizes it as more positive, resourceful, and competent to solve problems than was previously thought. With this recognition of the unconscious mind's ability to acquire information, store it, integrate it with other learnings, and utilize it, there is a burgeoning interest in the use of therapeutic patterns that can effect change without the necessity of conscious understanding as a precursor.

Michael Gazzaniga, in his book *The Social Brain* (1985), described a perspective of the brain that may be revolutionary, providing a biological explanation for what those who have been studying and writing on the subject of clinical hypnosis have long observed. In his "modular unit" model of mental functioning, Gazzaniga described how information outside of awareness can trigger changes in mood and behavior, even using the example of a person becoming depressed for no apparent reason simply because the neurological "depression unit" was somehow unconsciously activated. The literature of clinical hypnosis has been describing patterns for promoting unconscious changes for decades, but such approaches were not of general interest until very recently. Out of the recognition for unconscious capabilities may come a wide variety of possibilities for therapeutic intervention.

Employing Directives

Utilizing directives in the course of treatment is a demanding task in more ways than one. Certainly it is demanding of the client, requiring active participation in the therapy on physical as well as psychological levels. It is quite demanding of the clinician as well, requiring the assumption of a larger share of the responsibility for the direction and progress of the treatment.

The utilization of directives is necessary when something needs to happen in a relative hurry, out of fear of suicide or perhaps to build rapid expectations that therapy can help and thus engage the person in treatment. The general task of the clinician involves utilizing the various resources of the client that can facilitate the therapy. In the application of these approaches, there is a different way of conceptualizing and responding to what has traditionally been termed "resistance."

Resistance has historically been considered to be a property of the client that indicates his or her lack of willingness or ability to change. It has generally been responded to with analysis, interpretation, and confrontation. In the systemic model that underlies this work, resistance is viewed as not only an intrapersonal, but also an interpersonal statement. Resistance can be viewed as the client communicating his or her limitations in response to the clinician, effectively stating, "What you are telling me to think or do is not fitting with my sense of reality." Resistance becomes an especially important issue in the use of strategic methods since the client is required to be active in the process and can easily resist by being passive (i.e., refusing to do assignments or carry out tasks). In such instances, the clinician must readjust the strategy. Resistance may arise because of improper timing of the strategy, demanding too threatening a task, demanding too difficult a task for the client's current depressed state, underestimating the negative consequences of the strategy, or presenting it in an unacceptable way to the client.

Directives are best utilized to facilitate the client's integration of learnings so that they may behave congruently in their lives. Such integration can only take place if the strategy is appropriate for an individual client, if it is presented in a positive, motivating way, and if it is forward-looking enough to anticipate the consequences of acquiring new learnings on the multiple dimensions of the client's life. Whenever directives are employed, particularly strategic task assignments, the clinician must be fully prepared for reactions and outcomes other than the ideal therapeutic one that was hoped for. In other words, the strategies described throughout this book, as well as ones the reader may think of, will by their very nature have a possibility of unexpected, even negative outcomes. Unless one anticipates all possible responses, good and bad, and has a viable (i.e., therapeutic) contingency available for all the "what if . . .?" possibilities, the strategies can actually be antitherapeutic. Caution is advised.

SUMMARY

The following is a list of key points regarding the use of directive approaches:

1. Influence is inevitable.

2. Communication is the vehicle of the therapy.

3. Therapy is goal-directed, catalyzed by the clinician.

4. The client is operating on the basis of subjective interpretations of reality, which, in depressed individuals, are generally erroneous.

5. The client is not "sick," but is symptomatic on the basis of inadequate skills in problem solving and a restricted range of responses in a given context.

6. The clinician accepts and utilizes the client's frame of reference.

7. Rapport is a precursor to successful influence.

8. The client's relationship to the clinician is integral to the therapy.

9. Directives make use of contextual variables.

10. Symptomatic patterns exist on multiple dimensions simultaneously.

11. Insight is not necessary for change to occur and may even be antitherapeutic.

12. The unconscious mind is patterned and capable of problem solving.

13. Directive approaches make use of client resources.

14. Resistance may be intrapersonal and/or interpersonal.

15. Directives facilitate integration of positive learnings.

16. Directives may be contraindicated in some instances.

3

The Multiple Dimensions of Depression

Depression is not a singular entity afflicting the individual sufferer. Rather, it is a complex disorder with numerous components on multiple dimensions. The multifaceted nature of depression is precisely the reason that diagnosis and treatment can be so difficult a task for the clinician. Which part(s) of the depressed individual's experience does one focus in on and in what order of priority?

Most clinicians would probably agree that depression involves a multidimensional mix of problematic patterns. Yet, depression is officially classified as a mood disorder (American Psychiatric Association, 1987), a characterization that identifies the emotionally disordered aspect of depression as the key feature of the disorder. There is little doubt that for most of the sufferers of depression the emotional distress *is* the dominant feature in the clinical picture. It also seems true, however, that for some depressed individuals the dimension of mood is a component of lesser significance in the client's experience. In such people, the greater feature of relevance may be the person's thought patterns, situational responses, physical condition, relationship patterns, or other such variables that can each reflect depressive patterns despite the fact that the person does not *feel* depressed or disclose depression as a presenting complaint.

One can question the consideration of depression as exclusively a mood disorder and the widespread acceptance of depression as such. Clinicians seem to acknowledge readily that more people are depressed than the statistics indicate. Furthermore, they recognize that many disorders (particularly substance abuse problems) are rooted in a clinical depression that goes undiagnosed and therefore untreated. It seems only logical that if the current diagnostic system is not working altogether efficiently, allowing clinicians to miss a diagnosis of depression when it is present, a revision in the system is indicated. I am proposing in this chapter that the conceptualization of depression as exclusively or even primarily a mood disorder *may* be misleading in some instances. The consequence is the lack of identification of depression in individuals who are, in fact, depressed, but do not neatly fit the DSM-III-R criteria. Thus, a diagnosis of depression is overlooked in favor of a more dominant pattern, and the depressive patterns are not addressed.

It is rarely useful to point out the limitations of a system without having available another, better alternative. In this chapter, a case will be made for recognizing the multidimensional nature of depression, adding the twist that depression can exist on dimensions outside of awareness that may even include the affective dimension of individual experience. By recognizing the patterns of experience that involve depression even when the mood of the individual does not seem involved in his or her problem, the clinician can more easily diagnose and treat depression.

As a general framework for this proposed dissociative multidimensional model, the basic principle involves assessing the subjective experience of the individual seeking treatment. This means identifying the capabilities of the individual in terms of the quantity and quality of personal resources available. What kind of history (family experience, relationship history, triumphs, defeats) does this person have? What are the focal points of the person's narrative in relating his or her problems? A more specific guideline of patterns to identify will be discussed in the next chapter, so suffice it to say here that the clinician can take a special interest in particular patterns present on specific dimensions of client experience in order to more accurately diagnose and treat depression.

The major point of this chapter cannot be fully appreciated if one is not familiar with the nature of the phenomenon known as "dissociation." Dissociation was briefly mentioned in the last chapter relative to Gazzaniga's "modular unit" model of brain functioning (1985). In the present discussion, dissociation is presented as a *naturalistic* experience and an inherent capability of all human beings. Dissociation refers to the mental ability to break global experiences into their component parts. As one part is highlighted, awareness of another part is inevitably diminished. If one is absorbed in reading this (experiencing an amplified awareness of these ideas and their impact on one's thinking), then one is probably also experiencing a detachment from (or diminished awareness of) the immediate surroundings, perhaps "tuning out" the presence of someone close by or other routine sounds of the environment.

The conscious mind is limited in its ability to be aware. After all, how many things can be in one's awareness at a time? If I am depressed and am especially aware of how badly I am feeling right now, how aware will I be of the situational variables to which I may be responding? If I am focused on my need for your approval by continually adjusting myself to your demands at great expense to myself, how much awareness will I have for my internal feelings of anger or frustration at your withholding approval? If I am preoccupied with working hard, day and night, to save my company from going bankrupt because I am responsible for all my employees' welfare and my family's security, how much awareness will I have for the signs of stress that I am barely managing with an aspirin here or an antacid there? Each of these examples show an ability to "focus here" and "defocus there" relative to ongoing experience. Such "selective attention" is a natural capability of normal mental functioning and necessarily involves a degree of dissociation.

Recognizing that feelings can be dissociated from experience should not be difficult for most clinicians. After all, every cartoon cliché of psychotherapists has them saying to their clients, "You must get in touch with your feelings." If a person isn't in touch with feelings, does that mean he or she doesn't have them? Of course not. This is an example of feelings that are dissociated, but that eventually must be taken into account in treatment.

To acknowledge the role of dissociation as a natural part of the human experience is to say that it is a basic building block in the construction of subjective reality. It may be used constructively to amplify meaningful awareness, and it may likewise be used destructively to suppress awareness of important issues requiring attention. Relative to depression, the reality of dissociation suggests that people can react to things outside of awareness, experiencing alterations of thought, feelings, or behavior with no known etiology. It further suggests that despite lengthy and intensive attempts to uncover such causative factors (in order to develop insights about methods of controlling them), such unconscious and dissociated factors may simply not be recoverable. Thus, the likelihood of an arbitrary explanation of the depression's etiology increases dramatically. Furthermore, in such cases, the failure to uncover causative factors may further compound the depression simply by being absorbed in the virtually arbitrary idea that successful resolution can *only* come from discovering the causative factor(s). Dissociation also suggests that when depression is clearly the problem, factors on other dimensions may be (and almost always are) the focal point of treatment. When depression is not clearly the problem because of the absence of affective disturbance, depressed patterns on other dimensions may be present and significantly influencing the subjective experience of the client. For these reasons, both dissociation and the multidimensional nature of depression need to be better understood by clinicians.

THE MULTIPLE DIMENSIONS OF EXPERIENCE

The following are important questions for the clinician to ask him- or herself in gathering information from the client: What dimensions of the problem seem to most influence the client's subjective experience of depression? Which dimension seems to dominate the clinical picture? Which dimensions seem to be managed appropriately? Which dimensions of experience seem most emotionally charged? Which dimensions seem most removed from awareness?

In reality, every problem exists on multiple dimensions which relate synergistically to maintain the problem. In the case of depression, this is especially true. Identifying the various dimensions and considering the role of each can allow the clinician a broader perspective of the individual seeking help, while offering a greater number of targets for intervention. Instead of imposing the limitations of a particular orientation for treatment on the client, the perceptive clinician can glean information about the client's subjective experience and aim treatment in a more specific direction and in a more methodical manner.

The various dimensions of experience each blend and interrelate in order to provide a sense of cohesiveness in the course of daily living. When depression evolves, there is an imbalance in subjective experience which can be identified and addressed therapeutically in an effort to restore a sense of balance in the client's system. Perhaps the original balance will be restored, or more probably the system will undergo a change in which a new balance evolves. In any event, the various dimensions of experience must work together well enough for the client to reach a satisfactory degree of overall functioning.

The dimensions of experience most relevant to the formulation of a comprehensive assessment of subjective client experience are: physiological, cognitive, behavioral, affective, relational, symbolic, contextual, and historical. These eight specific dimensions encompass the three global areas of intrapersonal, interpersonal, and situational experiences that together comprise the framework for understanding all experience.

The physiological dimension of experience involves those symptoms that exist on the physical dimension. These are listed in Table 1.

The cognitive dimension of experience involves those thought patterns that are symptomatic in the depressed individual, described in Table 2.

Table 1
Depressive Symptoms on the Physiological Dimension

Sleep disturbance (hypersomnia or insomnia)
Appetite disturbance (hyper- or hypophagia)
High fatigability
Marked change in body weight
Sex drive disturbance (hyper- or hyposexuality)
Anxiety
Vague or specific physical complaints with no apparent
    organic etiology
Magnification or persistence of physical symptoms with a
    known organic etiology

Table 2
Depressive Symptoms on the Cognitive Dimension

Negative expectations (hopelessness)
Negative self-evaluation
Negative interpretation of events
Suicidal ideation
Indecision
Confusion
Primarily internal focus
Diminished concentration span
Primarily past temporal orientation
Global thinking style
"Victim" mind set (helplessness)
Cognitive distortions (erroneous patterns of thinking)
Rumination
Perceptual amplification or minimization
Rigidity

The behavioral dimension includes those symptomatic patterns that are evident in the behavior of the depressed individual, described in Table 3.

The affective dimension includes those symptoms that reflect a disruption in the person's emotional state, listed in Table 4.

The relational dimension includes those symptomatic patterns evident in the way the client relates to him- or herself as an individual, and the way he or she relates to others. Symptoms on this dimension are described in Table 5.

The symbolic dimension of experience includes those patterns that expressively represent the inner experience of the client. Not all communications are direct and conscious; rather, much of communication

Table 3
Depressive Symptoms on the Behavioral Dimension

Disturbance in activity level (hyper- or hypoactive)
Aggressive or destructive acts
Crying spells
Suicide attempts
Slow or slurred speech
Substance abuse
Generalized impulsivity
Behaviors inconsistent with personal values
Destructive compulsive behavior
Psychomotor agitation or retardation
"Acting-out" behavior
"Giving-up" behavior
Perfectionistic behavior

Table 4
Depressive Symptoms on the Affective Dimension

Ambivalence
Loss of sources of gratification
Loss of sense of humor
Poor self-esteem
Feelings of inadequacy, worthlessness
Loss of emotional attachments (apathy)
Dejected mood, sadness
Excessive or inappropriate guilt
Feelings of powerlessness
High or low emotional reactivity
Increased irritability, anger
Focus is primarily on depressed feelings
Loss of motivation
Anhedonia

occurs in symbolic form, translating inner drives, wishes, and beliefs into forms that seem to represent inner experience in ways that are acceptable and meaningful to the individual. The symbolic dimension of experience includes those patterns listed in Table 6.

The seventh dimension, the contextual one, involves those situationally specific variables that may combine to catalyze a depressive response in an individual. Generally, these are external factors that the individual responds to with depressive patterns described on the other dimensions. Depression *always* occurs in a context, however, and so the contextual dimension is of vital importance in the treatment plan. The consideration of contextual factors is significant in assessing how gen-

Table 5
Depressive Symptoms on the Relational Dimension

"Victim" relational style
Marked dependency on others
High reactivity to others
Social secondary gains
Social withdrawal, isolation
Social avoidance, apathy
Excessive approval seeking patterns
Self-sacrificing, martyrish patterns
Overresponsible for others
Inappropriate scapegoating of self or others
Passive-aggressive patterns
Diffuse or rigid personal boundaries
Power seeking or avoiding
Incongruent patterns of relating
Hypercritical of others
Narrow range of communication skills (identifying
    and expressing feelings)

Table 6
Depressive Symptoms on the Symbolic Dimension

Destructive fantasies, images
Recurring nightmares
Bothersome images
Symptoms as metaphorical representations of
    inner experience
Interpretation of "meaning" of depression
"Healing" images
Spiritual involvements, interpretations

eralized, and hence chronic, the depression may become. Contextual factors are described in Table 7.

The final dimension, the historical one, involves the specific experiences in the individual's personal history that may have been instrumental in the formation of the depressed patterns. Exploring the client's experiences and the conclusions drawn from those experiences may be fundamental aspects of the therapy. Many therapeutic strategies that are potentially of great value involve making use of historical data, but it is up to the judgment of each individual clinician as to how much history is relevant to the treatment process. The patterns found on the historical dimension are described in Table 8.

While each of the above tables offers a glimpse of the range of patterns that may be observed in individuals experiencing depression, it is neces-

Table 7
Depressive Symptoms on the Contextual Dimension

Generalized, predictable, restricted response in
    particular situations
Depressogenic situational cues (anchors), involving
        • specific people
        • specific places
        • specific objects
        • specific times of day (month, year)
Ambiguity regarding situational demands, responsibilities
Ambiguity regarding situational locus of control
Situational diffusion or rigidifying of boundaries
Situational violation of personal values, ethics

Table 8
Depressive Patterns on the Historical Dimension

History of significant losses
History of aversive, uncontrollable events
Inconsistent demands, expectations, and environments
Narrow range of personal experiences

sary to remember that a person need not have all or even most of these in order to be diagnosed as depressed. The issue here is one of developing an awareness of the many different forms depression is likely to take, and to appreciate that each dimension of experience can represent a current bout with depression or an episode in the making. A closer examination of specific patterns on each of the dimensions that relate to depression is the subject of the next chapter. The next section of this chapter discusses the opportunity the clinician has to more effectively plan and carry out interventions by recognizing and working with the multiple dimensions of an individual's depression.

FINDING A PLACE TO BEGIN

Since the client is experiencing depression on multiple, interrelated dimensions, it may be helpful in the planning phase of the intervention to know on which dimension(s) treatment may be most effectively aimed. Eventually, *all* dimensions will need to be addressed, directly or indirectly, but having a well-reasoned approach at the outset of therapy is especially important since it is at this time that expectations are established, a rapport is built, a timing for the unfolding of therapy is established, and a system of feedback emerges in identifiable patterns.

It may seem obvious that it is a matter of individual clinical judgment as to where the clinician might choose to begin intervening in the client's world. One must assess the presence of any potential for suicide as an immediate concern. One must also rapidly assess the level of discomfort the client is experiencing. How the client describes his or her experience in terms of the associated level of frustration, the quality (intensity and duration) of symptoms, and the expectations of treatment can all provide clues to the clinician as to the likelihood of being able to meaningfully engage the person in treatment. In particular, establishing positive expectations of change is a fundamental requirement for the client to commit to treatment (this aspect is discussed at length in Chapter 6).

The clinician must consider the individual client's personality as the axis upon which treatment will revolve. Therapy can only proceed according to the way the client can absorb new learnings and experiences. What the clinician knows about depression is useless to the client unless the clinician can effectively communicate what he or she knows, making the information usable to the client. Thus, the approaches here are based on the properties of the client (described in the next chapter). It is important to state here, however, that the clinician must make judgments as to which traits of the client are central to his or her experience of depression, and which are peripheral. For example, the clinician may identify the tendency in the client to assume excessive responsibility for others or for the outcomes of events to a self-limiting degree. The clinician may decide that this is a central trait in the client's personality from which numerous depressogenic perceptions and feelings are derived. Thus, the goal evolves to facilitate clarity in the client's views on issues of responsibility. Similarly, the clinician might identify a tendency in the client to socially isolate, but nonetheless the individual has a stable support network of close family and friends. The clinician might judge that social isolation is only a peripheral or lesser concern in the client's problems and may choose to leave that pattern alone altogether, or at least for a while.

Assessing central versus noncentral or even peripheral patterns in the client's makeup may allow the clinician to establish the kind of hierarchy of priorities that is fundamental to establishing an effective sequence for the use of therapeutic directives. This type of approach is reflected in the cases presented in Appendix B.

Established earlier was the recognition that conscious awareness can be dissociated from unconscious experience. Since consciousness is, by definition, limited to what one can be aware of, only a certain degree of the overall experience on all eight dimensions is likely to be in the awareness of the depressed individual. In other words, he or she will only be conscious of aspects of each dimension, or aspects of some dimensions and not others. Which dimension(s) is in awareness and which dimension(s) is not is a significant piece of information for the clinician in its indicating where treatment may begin. There are at least two reasons why it is particularly important to notice from the client's *spontaneous narrative* of his or her difficulties which dimension(s) of the experience of depression is most prominently in awareness. First, this allows the clinician the opportunity to build a stronger rapport based on the ability to demonstrate an understanding of the client's experience. Second, it allows the clinician a greater degree of freedom in making the choice of whether to aim the initial stages of treatment at the dimension(s) of the problem most prominent in the client's awareness, or whether to aim the intervention at dimensions outside of awareness.

The clinician can make this choice on the basis of the immediate ramifications of the symptoms and on the basis of whether intervention on a particular dimension will likely build a momentum of success or a barrier of resistance. If the presenting complaints are life-threatening, then there is considerably less choice about where to begin than if the client's problems are chronic and have been adapted to well.

Here is an example of how this might work. Suppose a client presented the following problems:

> Ever since my wife died in that accident, I just haven't felt right about much of anything. . . . I go to work, but I can't seem to get a handle on anything but how badly I feel. . . . I have a headache almost all of the time. . . my doctor says it's just stress but it still hurts. . . . I sleep only a few hours each night, and though it takes only a few minutes to fall asleep I can't *stay* asleep. I wake up early, maybe two or three hours before I have to and just lay there. . . . I can't date, don't want to date, I mean I'm not even the least bit interested in sex or women, and I'm so damn tired all the time even though my doctor says all the tests show normal. . . . I'm really eating way too much trying to get some energy, but all it's getting me is fat. . . . It's been three years since she died. Could her death still be bothering me?

In this example, the client presents a series of symptom descriptions indicating physical discomfort, sleep disturbance, social withdrawal, fatigue, and appetite disturbance. Clearly the client is describing a strong awareness of experiences on the physiological dimension. The client apparently senses some relationship between his physical experience and the relational dimensions of experience by questioning the relationship of his problems to the death of his wife. Furthermore, a mention of social withdrawal is made but is not focused upon in the presentation.

Once the clinician determines that it is the physical dimension of experience that is dominant in the clinical picture, a choice naturally arises. Is medication for stress headaches and sleep disturbance indicated? Is psychotherapy for the resolution of grief issues indicated? Is assertiveness for getting involved in new relationships a viable place to start? Is supportive therapy for releasing pent-up feelings a better choice? These choices and others the reader may have generated may all be good ones. But how does one know where to begin?

The treatment can be geared to the client's world on the basis of what makes sense to him or her and thus will utilize the client's perspectives, rather than imposing on the client what the clinician deems (usually arbitrarily) "right." The basic rule is one guiding the choice of direct or indirect approaches in communication: The greater the perceived resistance on the part of the client, the greater the need for indirection (Yapko, 1983, 1984a; Zeig, 1980a). In other words, if the client is compliant, responsive, clear about his or her goals, and able and willing to use personal resources actively for change, then indirection is not necessary. If the client is unlikely to respond to direct approaches for whatever reason (e.g., is ambiguous about goals, is unsure of participating in treatment, is unrealistic in expectations), the indirect approaches have a greater likelihood of succeeding.

Using the above example, if the client has a high degree of awareness for the problems on the physiological dimension and, in the clinician's judgment, direct approaches seem unlikely to be effective, then treatment may best be aimed at a dimension that seems to be less available to the person's consciousness (i.e., any of the other dimensions not mentioned in the narrative of the problems). As Zeig (1980a) pointed out, the dimension of the problems most in the person's awareness will likely also have the most defensiveness (i.e., resistance) associated with it. After all, this is the dimension that is the most troublesome and has been addressed the most frequently with any previous attempts at change. Trying to promote rapid change on that dimension will thus be most likely to generate resistance. The clinician can more probably build a momentum of success with the client by beginning treatment on a less involved dimension and then guiding treatment progressively closer and closer to the heart of the problem. "Going for all the marbles at once" is simply not sound therapeutic practice in many instances. With others, however, the clinician *will* need to address the client's presenting symptoms quite directly in order to attain rapport and build trust. Each client must be assessed according to what will most likely establish a positive framework for the progression of therapy.

In practice, this principle of working on dimensions less directly in the person's awareness means offering information and experiences in therapy that amplify awareness of *positive* possibilities for living one's life. Such information or experience can best be introduced at a rate that is acceptable to the individual, being careful not to confront patterns before sufficient rapport is obtained. Likewise, one would not be prudent to intervene before adequate information is obtained about the degree of awareness the individual has for the impact of the depression on the various dimensions of his or her life.

Questions may be easily integrated into the clinical interview that allow the clinician to explore the limits of client awareness for the various dimensions of their problem. Such information enables the clinician to make deliberate decisions about how much of the therapy may be consciously directed, and how much may be directed at the unconscious of the client. The following questions are just a few examples of relevant questions designed to elicit information from the client about particular dimensions of subjective experience. Most of the questions are purposely neutral in regard to dimensions of involvement so as to allow the client the opportunity to spontaneously communicate without an imposed structure.

1. Can you describe your ongoing experience to me?

2. What are you most aware of experiencing that is so troublesome to you?

3. How do you characterize what you are experiencing?

4. What kinds of things have you already tried to do in order to get better? Which seemed to work, even if only a little, and which did not?

5. What factors allowed you to continue your effort?

6. What prompted you to stop trying?

7. What have other people said to you about your situation? What was your reaction?

8. What do *you* think is causing you this distress?

9. What effect is this problem having on your life?

10. What is your understanding of this type of problem?

11. What are your expectations regarding treatment?

12. How did you decide to seek treatment?

13. How would you know if you were improving?

These may seem obvious questions to ask, and they may already be a part of one's clinical interview. This information becomes vital in the formulation of a treatment plan in ways that will be described later in the book.

It may be apparent that with the emphasis being placed on various dimensions of experience involved in depression, each dimension by itself can be a significant factor in the creation or maintenance of a depressive episode. The clinical literature is filled with theories and therapies that have effectively dissociated dimensions of experience from one another by dealing primarily with only one dimension of experience to the outright exclusion or understatement of the role of other dimensions. For example, an exclusively biologically based approach may consider only the physiological dimension of experience, presupposing that when the underlying chemical imbalance is corrected the other problematic patterns will dissipate. Cognitive therapy as an exclusive approach may focus primarily on the distorted thought patterns of the depressed individual, and presupposes that large doses of rationality and an adjustment of the client's belief system will have curative effects. Interpersonal therapy as an exclusive approach presupposes that addressing the depressed person's inevitably troubled relationship patterns will facilitate relief, while behavior modification techniques focus on adjusting the consequences for depressed behavioral patterns. These examples of single dimension focal points could go on and on, but suffice it to say that the unintentional dissociation of dimensions of experience by clinicians can lead to single-dimension treatments which, by their very nature, cannot be uniformly successful in the treatment of depression.

Clearly, each of the approaches has the capacity to be successful; the issue is one of identifying which approaches will be most useful for a given individual. The recognition of which dimension is involved and to what extent based on the client's spontaneous responses to questions such as the ones described earlier can lead the clinician to a more insightful application of purposeful techniques.

SUMMARY

The goal of this chapter is to encourage a closer look at the client's experience in terms of the multidimensional nature of *any* problem, especially depression. The belief is that clinicians who are more able to readily utilize therapeutic techniques that address a broader range of client experience will have more successful therapies than those restricted to single-dimension treatments. Eight dimensions of subjective experience were described, as were symptomatic patterns of depression commonly found on each.

A second concept of significance in this chapter concerns the phenomenon known as "dissociation" relative to the ways one dimension of experience can be "split off" from awareness of other dimensions of experience. The point was made that depressed patterns may exist on dimensions outside of the client's awareness, thereby maintaining a current episode of depression or perhaps predisposing one to later episodes of depression because of the pattern's self-restricting nature.

4

Patterns of Pain

The multiple dimensions of depression previously described indicate the complexity of the problem. An awareness of symptoms on each of the dimensions can allow one to more readily detect the possible presence of depression and, if detected, assess its severity, chronicity, and so forth. This chapter will take a closer look at specific patterns that seem to be closely associated with depression. These patterns are not merely symptom descriptions; rather they are patterns that reflect one's individual style of living, thinking, feeling, and behaving. The patterns described in this chapter may afford the clinician a more spontaneous and naturalistic means for understanding the subjective experience of the client, including the client's strengths and limitations. Identifying these various patterns and their role in the client's experience allows for an easier identification of those specific patterns that are chiefly involved in the formation and maintenance of the depressed condition. One can also identify patterns that can serve effectively as positive resources to organize and make available to the client as a part of the therapy.

The subjective patterns of experience will be presented in a general descriptive style. Furthermore, their general role in depression will be discussed. Several of the patterns have been previously described as diagnostic categories by Zeig (1980a, 1984) and Lankton and Lankton (1983). All of them offer the clinician a practical basis for interpreting the spontaneous presentation of the client according to a framework that focuses on subjective client experience rather than reductionistic diagnostic labels.

COGNITIVE STYLE

The elaborate and effective cognitive therapy model of depression recognizes the role of cognitions in the evolution and maintenance of depression. But rather than focus on the cognitive distortions well described in the cognitive therapy literature (Beck, 1973, 1983; Burns, 1980), the emphasis here is on the general style of the person's thinking that may lead to a susceptibility to cognitive distortions. A person's style of thinking can be described on at least two continua in the author's framework. The first is the "abstract-concrete" continuum, and the other is the "global-linear."

The abstract-concrete dimension involves an assessment of how capable of abstraction the individual is. This is an important piece of information for the development of an intervention strategy, since the more concrete the client is, the less likely he or she is to generalize learning from the specific context under consideration to other similar contexts without assistance from the clinician. The concrete person tends to think along the lines of verifiable reality, in contrast to the abstract thinker who can readily function in a manner that is separate from "objective" reality, responding to hypothetical constructs and theoretical formulations as if they have meaning roughly equal to concrete realities, objects, or experiences. Language is one reflection of style of thought, and by listening carefully to the spontaneous expressions of feelings and ideas of the client, the relative degree of concreteness or abstraction may be evident. Relative to depression, the tendency to be either too concrete or abstract in cognitive style in a particular context can be detrimental. Many of the cognitive distortions described in the cognitive therapy literature are clear-cut examples of concrete thinking, particularly the "all-or-none" thinking that creates a simple but damaging dichotomy in perception where no such dichotomy truly exists.

Research suggests that depressed individuals are more concrete in their style (Burns, 1980). Likewise, the abstract nature of some thinking styles precludes effective living because of the inability to reconcile abstract ideas and feelings with the necessity to make concrete choices on the basis of clearly defined parameters in daily living. Thus, a depressed individual may present a complaint such as, "I've been battling depression for years because I just can't seem to get centered, tap my energy and connectedness to the universe, and self-actualize." What does *that* mean? Does the reader know what that means? The author doesn't. And it's apparent the individual doesn't either, because there is no bridge between such terms and real experience. In such an instance, the immediate goal is to get some concreteness into the person's experience by getting definition to abstractions like "centered," "connectedness," and "self-actualization." For the concrete thinker, the goal may be to foster some ability to think abstractly and discover patterns and generalizations that can take the place of random, disconnected experiences. For the abstract thinker, the therapeutic goal may be to evolve some clear and pragmatically based definitions of valued goals and ideas.

The global-linear continuum related to cognitive style involves an assessment as to whether the individual tends to respond to thoughts or feelings in a way that reflects a lack of organization and prioritizing. This dimension of experience can be evident to the clinician almost immediately simply on the basis of how the client presents his or her difficulties. Are they presented in a sequence based on chronology, degree of difficulty, or some other orderly system? Or are the problems presented in a disorganized "shotgun" approach? Consider the contrast between these two styles of presentation:

1. "I have a number of problems I'm facing, and I know I can't effectively address them all at once. I think *first* I'll tell you about problem X, *then later* we can address problems Y and Z." (Linear)

2. "I have a whole bunch of problems I need to get straightened out and I hope you can help so that I can get X, Y, and Z handled so that I won't be so down on myself." (Global)

A trite but true way of describing the differences between the linear and global thinker is this: The linear thinker may see the trees but not the forest, while the global thinker may see the forest and not the trees. Either style may be related to a depressed mind set in the tendency to be either so detail-oriented that common experiences are overanalyzed (and thus robbed of their gestalt), or so globally reacted to so as to miss individual components that could have signaled a different and more effective response from the individual. In general, however, the depressed individual tends to be a more global thinker who responds to *all* of the circumstances he or she faces with one massive depressed response. The client holds the perception that there are numerous problems to be solved and that collectively they represent an overwhelming and insurmountable barrier to personal happiness. When the client demonstrates an inability to prioritize problems and methodically problem solve, the global nature of his or her thinking is usually evident. This is typical even for linear-thinking individuals when they are depressed. Many of the therapeutic interventions for depression currently in use emphasize breaking down the problems into smaller, more manageable components that can be addressed piecemeal and in a linear fashion.

RESPONSE STYLE

In response to therapy in general, but directive therapy in particular, the style of the client is a major factor in the formulation of an approach. Response styles may be considered along at least two continua: "other-directed-self-directed" and "open-guarded." Together, these two dimensions help determine whether the approach most likely to benefit the client is a direct or indirect one. A flexibility in the clinician's style to be direct or indirect at any given point in the therapy is required, unless a power struggle with the client is somehow deemed appropriate. Directive approaches make use of both direct and indirect methods of problem resolution, appropriate since one cannot be exclusively direct or indirect throughout the treatment process.

ATTENTIONAL STYLE

A person's attentional style can be considered on at least two continua: "focused-diffuse" and "salient-irrelevant." Again, it is a matter of degree, not kind, in assessing how a specific person may be viewed at a given moment in time. The degree of attentiveness an individual demonstrates is a significant factor in determining his or her level of involvement in the therapeutic interaction as well as in the processing of subjective experience. Consider the focused-diffuse continuum. For those individuals who are able to focus their attentions on ideas, demonstrating an ability to stay with an idea long enough to consider its meaning and implications, there is a much better chance for the clinician to introduce information and have it responded to meaningfully. In contrast, the person whose ability to focus is impaired (because of an extreme global cognitive style or perhaps because of anxiety, fatigue, or discomfort) is not so likely to respond with any significant degree of depth to the clinician's communications.

Generally, global thinking and diffuse concentration seem to occur together, and it is also generally true that the depressed client's concentration is diffused by the various components of internal discomfort. Consequently, potentially useful insights or plans of action are scattered as they are responded to by the client, leading to what, on first glance, may seem to be a resistant response of stagnation. Often, the stagnation of the depressed person is not so much a resistant response as it is a manifestation of the limitations associated with the various patterns described in this chapter. In any event, the clinician may be able to identify the attentional capacity of the client by simply observing the client's responses to the interaction. Is the client able to follow the flow of the discussion? Is the client able to selectively attend to the clinician and ignore extraneous variables (i.e., external distractions like ringing telephones, passing planes, and other such routine environmental stimuli), or is the individual easily distracted, even needing to be reminded of what is being discussed? A person's concentration style is immediately relevant to the level of responsiveness to meaningful communication, and it may be a goal early on in the therapy to build attentional focus through such absorbing patterns as clinical hypnosis. Even the most structurally simple induction or relaxation procedure can have a beneficial impact through the reduction of anxiety and the enhancement of ability to focus.

Some individuals have a particularly high need for stimulation, easily losing interest if the level of stimulation is not high enough. Such people can focus for only brief periods of time, and for them it becomes a trade-off of depth for variety. The cycle becomes a vicious one, however, because eventually only a stimulus powerful enough to grab their attention is attended to. Interest tends to wane rapidly, and in the absence of frequent strong stimuli, ongoing experience is viewed as dull and life becomes reduced to intermittent episodes of "feeling alive" amidst an ongoing experience of boredom. In reality, life is not continuously exciting, but for the high-stimulus needs of some individuals anything in between the occasional highs is interpreted and experienced as a low.

Related to the focused-diffuse dimension of concentration is the salient-irrelevant continuum. The concern here is one of whether the client tends to respond to the most central aspects of an issue or to the peripheral aspects. Certainly a degree of avoidance is likely to be present when the client's focal points of attention are only peripheral variables in relation to the problems at hand. It is also true, however, that avoidance may be only one aspect of the problem, when the individual simply lacks the depth to recognize and respond to core issues instead of those that are not. Global and concrete styles can lead one to miss the real issues, and thus can lead to the sort of dubious decisions common amongst depressed persons. An example is, "If I relocate to another city or state, then everything will be fine." More often than not, in such instances all that is accomplished is the transplanting of depression from one geographical location to another. Problem-solving skills in such individuals are generally quite limited, and facilitating the acquisition of such skills becomes a therapeutic goal.

PERCEPTUAL STYLE

In translating the reality of the universe into subjective experience, each person must necessarily amplify or diminish aspects of experience in order to evolve and maintain a concept of reality. Zeig (1984) described the processing style of the individual in terms of tendencies to "enhance" or "reduce" experience. Metaphorically, some people tend to "make mountains out of molehills," while others "make molehills out of mountains." Simply put, some are prone to exaggeration, while others are prone to understatement.

Patterns of both amplification and minimization can and do occur in all individuals. It is a selective process, although not exclusively conscious. In its selectivity, some experiences will be exaggerated, some trivialized. In the case of the depressed individual, the pattern of selectivity is evident in response to the type of information being processed. When the situation offers positive possibilities (e.g., praise, opportunities, support, encouragement), the depressed individual will typically minimize their value and impact. When the situation offers negativism (e.g., obstacles to goals, criticism, discouragement), the depressed person typically exaggerates their value and impact. Small delays in attaining anything desired, less than enthusiastic responses from others, minor hurdles involving institutional protocols, and other such naturally occurring events in life often represent insurmountable barriers to the depressed individual through their exaggeration.

Some depressed individuals seem to recognize the tendency to exaggerate the negative and minimize the positive. Judging this pattern in oneself negatively, an effort may be made to compensate with overt expressions to others or to oneself of exaggerated positivism. However, these are not internalized and so remain more of an attempt to convince oneself of one's value rather than a true recognition of worth.

Addressing the client's selectivity and patterns of perceptual distortions is a basic requirement of therapy with the depressed individual. Many of the patterns of Beck's cognitive therapy (Beck, 1973, 1983) can be useful in doing so, since there is such a close relationship between one's perceptions and subsequent thought and feeling patterns. The depressed client can learn to recognize the distortion process at work in the formation of conclusions about day-to-day experience. As the distortions become routinely challenged and are then replaced with more accurate perceptions, negative generalizations on significant issues can be contradicted or otherwise modified.

As the depressed individual learns to represent experience more accurately (i.e., with less embellishment or minimization), perhaps by taking into account others' perspectives or being encouraged to self-generate numerous alternate views, he or she can learn to consider a range of views on an issue. Having a variety of interpretations or views can allow for responses other than continuing in the familiar pattern of settling on an inaccurate or negative interpretation of events. If the distorted perceptions continue to go unchallenged by the clinician and by the client him or herself, the emotional content of such distorted interpretations will tend to skew perception even further, reinforcing the negative processing style that maintains depression. The person's automatic first response may continue to be negative or exaggerated throughout his or her life, but at the least an effective neutralizing mechanism can be integrated and thus, through self-treatment, he or she can minimize future episodes of depression.

PRIMARY REPRESENTATIONAL SYSTEM (PRS)

The clinician can develop an awareness of the client's preferred or most heavily relied upon sensory modality for acquiring, organizing, storing, and retrieving information. This sensory modality is called the primary representational system, or PRS (Bandler & Grinder, 1975, 1979). Noting sensory-based predicates evident in the spontaneous language choices of the client can allow the clinician to respond to the client by deliberately matching or mismatching those patterns, depending on the desired outcome. Generally, a matching of PRS predicates enhances rapport and thus increases the likelihood of therapeutic influence (Yapko, 1981). The PRS is directly involved in the internal representation of experience, and thus is a significant variable in developing an understanding of the client's experience, which also implies ways to alter the internal representations for therapeutic purposes. The depressed person may describe his depression as a "black cloud that envelops me," or as a "gripping pain that takes the wind out of me." The former describes a visual representation, the latter a kinesthetic one. In general, depression being for many primarily a mood disorder, implies a PRS that is kinesthetic; the client's depressed *feelings* are often the focal point of his or her awareness. The depressed feelings may be experienced in a direct way, or they may be the product of negative visual images or (auditory) negative self-talk. Altering the depressogenic images or self-talk in some way can be one of the goals of treatment.

Related to the concept of PRS is the associated degree of intensity. Is the internal representation a clear one, or is it vague and poorly defined? Generally, the more vivid it is, the greater the degree of emotional reactivity involved. Likewise, when the internal representation is fuzzy and poorly defined, the reactivity is lowered. Creating a different representation and amplifying its intensity can generate a very different and positive internal reaction for the depressed individual.

DEVELOPMENTAL CONSIDERATIONS

Independent of family history, which will be considered next, the clinician may consider several specific dimensions of developmental history of the client. These include the environment in which the individual grew up, the specific stage of development the client is currently in, and what the next progressive stage is that may be attained through the therapy (Lankton & Lankton, 1983).

The environment in which an individual grows up is a general indicator of his or her types of experiences, values, and world view. One who grows up in an urban environment is generally exposed to a wider range of lifestyles and opportunities than someone reared in a rural environment. Likewise, growing up in the suburbs leads to a different range of experiences than growing up in the inner city. With different frames of references evolving out of different environments, the setting for one's development appears to be significant, particularly when the available data suggest that depression is more prevalent in urban environments (Mahoney, 1980). Apparently for some, the range of lifestyle choices is *too* great, and the stress associated with evolving a satisfying personal lifestyle pattern is overwhelming enough to predispose one to episodes of depression. The added stresses of crowding, noise, and other such typically urban phenomena are also likely to play a role in some people's experience of depression.

The particular stage of life a person is at is an obvious factor influencing subjective experience. Each stage has its challenges or tasks to be handled. Depression can and does occur at all ages in the life cycle. It is through noting specific stresses for the depressed individual at the point in their lives preceding the appearance of depression that can lead the clinician to determine whether the problem is more an acute one tied to a particular stage of development, or whether it is a more chronic and patterned problem that is pervasive and not tied to a specific developmental stage.

In any case, the issue at least remains one of personal development, and the clinician must take into account what the next logical stage of personal development would be. There evolves a goal-directedness in so doing and the task of the clinician is to facilitate progress toward the next stage of the individual's evolution. The clinician can ask him or herself such questions as: What skill does the person lack that inhibits him or her? What issue(s) needs to be resolved before this client can move on? What will he or she be able to do that currently does not seem possible? What implication does a progression have for future growth stages? The clinician's beliefs regarding the nature of change, such as whether change is a continuous or discontinuous process, play a major role in the perception of this particular variable.

FAMILY POSITION; FAMILY DYNAMICS

The relationship between the patterns of socialization found in the family of origin and the patterns that continue to operate in individuals throughout life has been well described in the literature. Family roles, rules, mood, expectations, communication patterns, problem-solving patterns, and all the other key components of a family system are instrumental in the formation of one's self-esteem and world view. Family members who have been emotionally withholding or inconsistent in responses, or who have been abusive physically and/or emotionally, can foster a sense of helplessness and victimization in a child early on, leading to depression.

Family position may play a role in the formation of one's personality, although generalizable evidence is ambiguous (Gibson, 1983). At the individual level, however, it is not uncommon that an older sibling is made responsible for day-to-day care of younger siblings. If a strong sense of responsibility is inculcated in one early on, it can be distorted to the point of being detrimental. Similarly, if one is not taught a sense of responsibility, this can surface as irresponsibility or underresponsibility.

In one example of an overresponsible position in the family, the younger daughter became the overburdened, responsible one when her mother became a victim of ARC (Aids Related Complex) received through a blood transfusion. This daughter's responsibility for her ailing mother was most intense and in stark contrast to the older sister who had previously left home. Historically, the older sister had related to the family in a most irresponsible way. In this young girl's case, by being the youngest in the family, her presence at home made her the natural choice to be mother's caretaker. The stress of the excessive responsibilities was too much for her, and she withdrew into a deep depression. Her experience demonstrates clearly how family position can sometimes mean a great deal in terms of the kinds of experiences one has.

DEGREE OF INDIVIDUATION

Each person is continuously faced with the challenge of attaining a healthy balance between living for others and living for self. At any given moment, one is likely to experience the pressure to conform to the needs or demands of others while simultaneously experiencing the pressure to be "true to one's self" and make decisions according to personal needs. The price can be and often is very high: "If I do this for you, I may get your approval but hate myself; if I do this in order to please myself, I may get your rejection." It is easy to appreciate how one may develop an imbalance in the struggle to maintain a sense of self in the face of continuous pressures to conform. When one loses one's self to others and becomes a nondistinct entity—in essence a mere reflection of others to whom one is attached—the personal boundaries that define an individual as an individual are diffused. The term "enmeshment" is an appropriate descriptive label for this kind of experience. In contrast, if one has so separated from others that there is no evidence of any meaningful interaction between them, the term "disengagement" is useful as a descriptive label.

The issue of individuation is an important one for a number of reasons. First, how able the individual is to function autonomously involves critical elements such as how responsible the person feels *to* other people and *for* other people. The pattern of responsibility one evolves encompasses how one handles guilt, decision making, assertiveness, and other such important patterns. Second, degree of individuation determines one's role in whatever system one is inevitably a part of. Thus, the kinds of experiences and demands one is exposed to are, to a significant degree, a reflection of one's sense of self. Third, one's sense of self as a distinct entity determines one's willingness to assert control over one's circumstances, leading to a possibility of distorted perceptions surrounding the issue of control. If the clinician is able to explore the range and depth of the client's involvements with others, as well as assessing the ease with which the person self-discloses, it may become apparent that a problematic individuation pattern exists. Perhaps this person is easily "lost" in others or, conversely, is quite removed from others to the point of being unable to make independent decisions or have close and meaningful relationships. Attaining a balance between functioning well as a competent, independent individual and as a competent part of a social network is a necessary goal of treatment.

AGE AND VALUE PROGRAMMING CHARACTERISTICS

The individual value system one inevitably acquires during the socialization process is a composite of many inputs from diverse sources. It is the author's belief that it is the person's value system more than any other single factor that is the greatest determinant of what one is and is not able to do. The process of learning to make sense out of a potentially overwhelming world of experience involves internalizing thoughts and feelings about what is right or wrong, normal or abnormal, good or bad, and so forth. These are the value judgments that serve to define the limits of experience. As one grows up and is socialized into the family in particular and into society in general, one evolves patterns for maintaining a position in the systems and subsystems of which one is a part. Naturally, systems undergo changes over time, and even those values associated with these inevitable changes are integrated into the person's world view. In particular, values associated with change on a continuum of rigidity-flexibility and values associated with a task-vs.-people orientation are of significance in the treatment of depression.

Morris Massey (1979) described the value acquisition process in terms of cultural norms during different decades of recent American social history. Massey described how personal values at the individual level have been determined in large part by the values that were dominant in society-at-large as the individual was growing up, or "value programming." Massey claimed that 90% of one's values are integrated by around age 10, and 100% by around age 20. Thus, the age of an individual can clue the clinician in to the value-programming experiences the individual is likely to have had in his or her personal history. Massey further claimed that values only change when one experiences an event that is emotionally powerful enough to affect the core of the individual, termed by Massey a "Significant Emotional Event" (or SEE). Therapy may be viewed as the artificial and deliberate creation of a SEE (Yapko, 1985a), in which the identified problematic value is used as either a catalyst or a target in therapy. These processes are described in "The Erickson Hook: Values in Ericksonian Approaches" (Yapko, 1985a).

In the depressed individual, there may be values held that create or complicate the depressed condition. For example, valuing "perfection" as an indicator of self-worth may lead one to evolve obsessive traits that inevitably leave one dissatisfied, since nothing is perfect. In another example, valuing the commitment of marriage may lead one to remain in an abusive relationship and suffer depression as a consequence. The examples of deeply held values that painfully restrict one's life are evident in case examples throughout this book, and it is clear that assessing and responding meaningfully to clients' value systems is a prerequisite of effective treatment.

A number of the patterns described in this chapter are direct consequences of one's values. Can the reader identify the values underlying a strong attentiveness to detail, a marked compliance to authority, an intense orientation to emotion, close involvements with others, accepting burdensome family responsibilities, facing developmental tasks and problems, along the lines previously discussed?

A value that is particularly important in the world of the depressed individual is that of a "task-vs.-people" orientation. Specifically, does the person maintain a value system that makes other people the priority or is the accomplishment of tasks the priority? This value has been studied intensively in the context of organizational settings for its role in the organization's atmosphere and efficacy. At the individual level, this value determines to a significant extent what the client's involvement in the therapeutic relationship will be. A people-oriented client will tend to view a close, ongoing relationship with the clinician as a primary vehicle of the treatment. The task-oriented individual will likely see the clinician merely as an instrument to obtain the objective of relief from depression. Each style has its implications for the self-esteem and social world of the individual. The task-oriented person may continually need accomplishments to bolster self-esteem, whereas the people-oriented person may continually need the approval of others to attain self-esteem, appearing quite nonindividuated to the clinician. In either case, the trap is a negative product of personal values that needs to be addressed in treatment.

The continuum of "rigidity vs. flexibility" is an important one that describes values that determine, at least in part, how the client will respond to therapy. If the client's value system and the patterns derived from it are very rigid, the input of the clinician is inevitably less impactful. Basically, rigidity is a means for self-preservation as one protects what one knows and believes. Rigidity permits stability of perceptions. The more limited one's range of experience, and the more one has been socialized to believe that there are absolute "rights" and absolute "wrongs," the more rigid one will necessarily be. Flexibility as a more sophisticated response comes about when one is willing to accept that others can do things differently and still be "correct" in their actions. Accepting that each person must evolve his or her own "right" way to live and do things takes more flexibility than most people seem to have, unfortunately. By asserting the exclusive nature of one's own correctness, one is able to attempt to control others through guilt, intimidation, or other such negative tactics. When facilitating a greater flexibility in the client is a therapeutic goal, the client is able to learn greater self-acceptance *and* acceptance of others, an important and progressive step for many depressed persons. Furthermore, the issue of absolute right versus absolute wrong is effectively allayed, and the client can ask the more advanced and therapeutic question, "Does what I'm doing *work*, and if not, what *will?*" Evolving values for progress, for what works, and for the acceptance of choices for oneself and for others are all ways of facilitating a greater flexibility in living, and a better quality of life as a result.

Given the high priority assigned here to individual values and their role in functionality, a study of ways of rapidly assessing a client's values and relating to them is encouraged.

DEGREE OF MASTERY OVER EXPERIENCE

Generally described in the literature as "locus of control," the issue of placement of responsibility for one's experience has frequently been the subject of both research and subjective philosophizing (Goldstein, 1980; Rotter, 1966). How one interprets the events of one's life is profoundly influenced by one's sense of control over and responsibility for one's circumstances. Some believe that the experiences one has are all products of conscious and/or unconscious choices and are, therefore, controllable. In its extreme form, this belief says, in essence, "You are responsible for all that happens in your life, your sickness or wellness, your poverty or wealth, and your success or failure are all within your control. If you really want something, you'll find a way to get it."

Others adopt an opposite perspective, which views ongoing experience as beyond one's control and therefore limiting one to a reactive role in response to whatever happens. In essence, this view says, "My life, my destiny is controlled by others or by whatever circumstances I find myself in, and whatever will be will be."

Neither belief in its extreme form is realistic, for ultimately how much one is a "master" or "victim" of experience is determined by the various contexts of life and the perceived relative effectiveness of responses in each context. The more contexts one can respond to effectively, the more generalized the sense of mastery the individual has. However, no one can be totally masterful *everywhere*, knowing all about everything. Situations in which one is totally ignorant can be enslaving, and when one perceives that one's response to a situation has been ineffective or even damaging, self-esteem inevitably suffers, and depression may set in. One of the key symptoms associated with depression is helplessness, described well in the "Learned Helplessness" model of depression (Seligman, 1973, 1974, 1975, 1983). For the depressed individual, and for any person who experiences troublesome symptoms apparently beyond control, there is a significant element of the "victim" mind set underlying the complaints. The person has attempted to make changes but has not succeeded. The person feels utterly helpless to do anything about the problem that might prove beneficial and desperately turns to the clinician to get relief, despite the underlying expectation that "nothing can really help." An important point that reinforces the ideas from the previous chapter is that depression can occur on dimensions outside of awareness and on levels other than just an affective one. This point directly involves the "victim" mind set. Even if the person tends to be masterful elsewhere in his or her life, the "victim" identity is at least present in relation to the symptomatic patterns at hand. At the very least, there is an element of depression and victimization regarding one's problems. How generalized it will be depends on specific dissociative capabilities of the individual, discussed in a later section of this chapter.

The issue at hand for the clinician is the necessity to assess dimensions of the client's sense of control over his or her life experiences. Does the client believe the problem is one that is resolvable in some way? Are the circumstances generating the depression identifiable? Objectively, is there the possibility of exerting some degree of control over the depressogenic circumstances, and if so, to what degree? Or are the circumstances such that *no one* could effectively do anything that would make a positive difference? Furthermore, is this client generally a victim throughout many or most aspects of his or her life? Or is the client generally quite masterful in managing life?

These assessments are pivotal to the interventions of the clinician when he or she helps define the client's role in treatment. For example, a client with a strong sense of being a victim is far less likely to carry out therapeutic directives designed to teach mastery skills such as the ones described in this book simply because being masterful is too inconsistent with his or her "victim" self-image. This is when the clinician typically experiences the well-known rejecting "Yes, but . . ." objections from the client in response to methodologies intending to facilitate relief. Guiding the depressed client from a victim role into one of exerting mastery over experience is a dominant theme in the successful treatment of depression.

A pattern related to the perceived locus of control concerns the issue of blame. As a result of the victim mind set, the client may or may not feel personally at fault for his or her circumstances. Depending on the objective degree of controllability or noncontrollability of events, the issue of responsibility can become clouded. One may inappropriately blame and treat oneself harshly for circumstances that virtually no one could have handled any better. Such a position is common amongst depressed individuals, is experienced as "anger turned inwards," and is characterized by self-recrimination and guilt. This "intrapunitive" response may be contrasted with an "extrapunitive" style (Zeig, 1984), in which others are blamed for one's circumstances, making them fully responsible for all problems while leaving one depressed, but blameless and guiltless. This is another aspect of the crucial issue of responsibility, which, when cloudy for someone, is a factor commonly precipitating depression. Clarification of responsibilities for one's experience and the more important issue of *how* to tell in future experiences where responsibility lies are important goals of treatment.

TEMPORAL ORIENTATION

Each person relates to the construct of "time" in an idiosyncratic way. Depending on one's value system, personal history, and degree of emotional investment, one may be more oriented to one dimension of time than another. For example, some people tend to "live in the past," demonstrating a preoccupation with past experiences at the expense of current and future involvements. Such people focus on what happened at certain points of their personal history, selectively recalling events that can support their current perspectives. Through this type of past orientation, less attention is paid to current circumstances and future possibilities.

Others have a more "present" temporal orientation. This allows for a greater responsiveness to whatever impulses one has, showing little regard for future consequences or previous traditions. The individual can be so "here-and-now" oriented that there is little personal connection to people or circumstances of the past, and the future is something that "just happens, ready or not."

Still others are so future oriented as to have only future goals and opportunities in mind, i.e., the house to be bought, the career to be built, and so forth. When the orientation to future goals is dominant in the person's lifestyle, it can be at the expense of current realities leaving little or no time to "stop and smell the roses along the way."

Each of these descriptions are general characterizations, for no one can "live" exclusively in any one temporal orientation without serious disruption to one's sense of reality. The issue here concerns to what degree the individual is so oriented to one dimension of time that it causes or maintains a dysfunctional state.

With the problem of depression in particular, an individual might be oriented to any of the time dimensions in an imbalanced way to his or her detriment. Generally, however, the depressed individual tends to be more oriented to the past. The depressed individual is likely to have had a personal history of significant losses, aversive and uncontrollable events (Seligman, 1973, 1975, 1983), nonsupportive family members employing dysfunctional communication patterns, and other such

depressogenic variables. The intensity of the individual's emotional
pain may become the focal point of experience and is an emotional
burden the individual attempts to manage. The effect on the present is to
diminish or eliminate awareness for relief-providing alternatives, thus
stabilizing a negative expectation for the future that can become a
self-fulfilling prophecy.

In short, the past is the depressed individual's frame of reference from
which present and future experiences are negatively distorted. With a
negative frame of reference based on a highly charged (and therefore
powerful) past history of learning, the depressed individual may come to
believe that the current experience of pain is all that there is in life, and
that things cannot or will not get any better. This outlook more than any
other is the single underlying rationale for committing suicide. When
the depressed person looks to the future and anticipates only more pain,
suicide can actually seem to be a reasonable alternative. A clinician
telling such a person that "things will get better" or to "look ahead to a
better future" is providing suggestions that are too inconsistent with the
depressed person's past-oriented frame of reference, and thus such
suggestions are likely to be rejected as meaningless (Yapko, 1984a).

Clearly, the depressed individual shows responsiveness to each of the
dimensions of time. While the past orientation seems most typical of
depressed persons, in some instances this is not the case. The present
may dominate and be responded to with an acute awareness of internal
discomfort and victimizing circumstances. Self-flagellation for ongoing
impulsive behavior may fuel one's depression. For others, the future is
responded to with expectations of "more of the same," or conversely,
with unrealistic positive expectations that "When such and such happens, then everything will be all right." The depressed person who
assumes that moving from one geographic location to another will help,
or that finding a different job, getting a college degree, having a new
lover, or some other external change or accomplishment will resolve the
problem, demonstrates a distorted future orientation that precludes
true insight into the dynamics of the depression. The relationship
between depression and imbalanced temporal orientations is a strong
one, with implicit strategies of intervention that involve making shifts to
a more balanced response to the effect of past experience on current
realities and future possibilities.

INTERNAL VERSUS EXTERNAL ORIENTATION

Some people are very sensitive to their own internal experience,
possessing a high level of awareness of their feelings, motives, and

needs. Such people might be described as having a strong internal orientation. When consciousness is directed inwardly, there is naturally less opportunity for awareness of external events. When someone is often preoccupied with internal experience, he or she may do so at the expense of meaningful contact with external experience. Such a person may be accused of being withdrawn, egocentric, insensitive to others, i.e., "off in his own little world."

In contrast, others have a high degree of awareness of others, of subtle changes in the environment, and of external events in general. Such people might be described as having an external orientation. When one is preoccupied with external events or meeting external demands, it is often at the price of not noticing or responding meaningfully to internal experience.

The implications of an internal or external orientation for the etiology and treatment of many disorders may be quite profound. Consider, for example, the individual so absorbed in a highly demanding project that he or she does not notice or respond to the accompanying high levels of stress. The stress may build until it generates physiological symptoms, such as an ulcer or migraine headache, and only then is it noticed. Therapy in such a case might involve learning to recognize and respond to internal cues that indicate stress in order to prevent its destructive accumulation. Such an approach involves building more of an internal focus in order to determine appropriate points at which to apply effective stress management techniques.

Generally, the focus of the depressed individual is an intensely internal one, absorbing the person in his or her subjective discomfort. Most interventions for depression, deliberately or not, utilize a means for "getting out of oneself" and getting involved elsewhere. Many clinicians routinely make suggestions to the depressed person such as volunteering in a hospital or joining in recreational activities. Directive approaches can have a similar injunction to "get out of yourself," but for a broader purpose: to build new frames of reference based on new experiences that can serve as a basis for progress.

Related to an internal or external orientation is the degree of reactivity to internal or external experience, and on what dimension. The term "reactivity" can be used to describe how aware the client is of his or her experience, how responsive the client is to his or her experience and how expressive of those reactions he or she is. Clearly, self-esteem is closely related to reactivity, for if one must inhibit or deny the presence of aspects or dimensions of oneself, then one may be uncomfortable with a significant portion of oneself.

Finding the balance between internal and external responsiveness can only be accomplished when some degree of self-acceptance is accomplished, for no one wants to "go inside" if all that is in there is pain. Likewise, no one wants to be involved with life or with others if this involves only pain. Accepting all of oneself via the reframing of each part (even those parts that were previously viewed to be destructive) as useful in *some* context can allow for a healthy internal focus. Similarly, encouraging the assertion of greater control over one's circumstances can encourage a more healthy involvement with external possibilities.

DISSOCIATIVE CAPABILITIES

One of the most useful capabilities every human being is endowed with to one degree or another is the ability to break global experiences into their component parts. One can then respond to some parts by amplifying an awareness of them, while others are responded to by minimizing them. "Dissociation" refers to this ability to separate components of an experience in order to be able to respond selectively. Another way to describe this particular pattern is in terms of one's ability to compartmentalize experience. Some individuals have a strong ability to experience an event, and it finds its own niche in the person, seemingly separate from other experiences. Others do not have so strong an ability to dissociate one experience from other experiences, and what they experience in one context spills over into other things they experience.

The implications for the depressed person are particularly interesting. In individuals suffering depression, it is common to hear reports of how one minor negative event in a larger positive context can mar the whole experience for the person. For example, the depressed person may meet one person at a party he or she does not particularly like and later report, "That person ruined the whole party for me." In such an instance, one negative aspect of an experience is not compartmentalized, thereby preserving the integrity of the larger context. Rather, the negative feeling associated with one seemingly minor aspect of the global party experience flows through all of the internal representations of the party, effectively ruining it for the individual. Similarly, the client's "whole day is rotten" even though, in fact, the depression of the morning was gone or nearly gone by afternoon. This pattern can be closely associated with several of the cognitive distortions described by Beck (1983) and Burns (1980), such as "all-or-nothing thinking," "overgeneralization," and the "mental filter."

The task for the clinician is to assess the dissociative abilities in clients and to facilitate utilization of those dissociative abilities. In so doing, clients can experience circumstances in their natural, imperfect form without the relatively minor imperfections contaminating the whole experience for them. Working with therapeutic techniques such as clinical hypnosis that involve dissociative patterns and facilitate acquisition of control over dissociative processes can be most useful in this regard.

SUMMARY

Each of the various patterns described in this chapter has a special role in the creation of states of well-being and states of distress. The clinician who is able to detect these patterns in the ongoing experience of the clients he or she treats will have a broader choice of starting points for therapeutic intervention. Briefly, the patterns and subpatterns presented in this chapter are listed as follows:

1. Cognitive style
    abstract/concrete
    global/linear

2. Response style
    other-directed/self-directed
    open/guarded

3. Attentional style
    focused/diffuse
    salient/irrelevant

4. Primary representational system (PRS)
    intensity of representation

5. Developmental considerations
    environment of childhood
    current developmental stage
    next progressive stage

6. Family position; Family dynamics
    roles, rules, atmosphere, expectations,
    communication and problem-solving patterns
    placement in sequence of siblings

7. Degree of individuation
    enmeshment/disengagement

8. Perceptual style
    magnify/diminish

9. Age and value programming characteristics
    task/people orientation
    rigidity/flexibility

10. Degree of mastery over experience
       victim/master
       internal/external locus of control
       intrapunitive/extrapunitive

11. Temporal orientation
       past/present/future

12. Internal versus external orientation
       low/high reactivity
       dimension of reactivity

13. Dissociative capabilities
       low/high compartmentalization

In the following chapters, concrete case examples of presenting problems that reflect disturbances in these subjective patterns of experience are presented.

Part II

Treatment

5

Therapy: Interrupting Patterns of Pain

In the previous two chapters, the multiple dimensions of experience and the subjective patterns individuals employ to relate to ongoing experience have been described. Of particular importance is the underlying recognition that human experience *is* patterned to a large extent and that repetitive mechanisms for responding to life's demands are evident in all persons. Whether we call these patterns of responding "personality," "character," or by some other name, it is important to appreciate the patterning of experience. The ability to detect patterns and assess their relative degree of functionality is the essence of diagnosing. Therapy may be thought of as first the disruption of dysfunctional patterns, at whatever level the clinician and client deem desirable or necessary, and then the subsequent development of different, more functional patterns.

The patterns to be disrupted as the target of the therapeutic process must first be viewed as dysfunctional in some way, thus requiring therapy for the purpose of change. Second, the patterns to be disrupted must also be viewed as changeable, that is, as having the potential for change in response to a meaningful intervention. Are all patterns amenable to change? The debate goes on in some circles, but no one can realistically deny that there are many disorders for which there is no known effective treatment. The clinician must consider this issue at length and in a conservative manner. It is a difficult issue, for certainly each individual must be given the chance to make changes, yet holding out the hope of significant change when none is likely is a cruel building of false hopes.

In considering the process of psychotherapy as a process of pattern disruption and pattern building, several points must be elaborated. First, in the use of the word "patterns," the implication is that one's essence, or wholistic integration of body, mind, and spirit, is totally unique. Each person's subjective world is an idiosyncratic weave of biological predispositions and the effects of socialization. Second, patterns imply a predisposition to act and react in particular ways, although not necessarily predictable ways (since most patterns are unconscious). Third, patterns cannot be fully considered independently of their associated context. A pattern that serves an individual very well in one context may be the source of extreme discomfort in another context. Fourth, a pattern is initially evolved and repeatedly modified as an inevitable byproduct of responding to the experiences to which one is exposed. The implication is that the individual may have no experience with the complements or polar opposites of those experiences to which he or she *has* been exposed. Consequently, there is no personal frame of reference on which to build a better or more realistic response. To the unwitting clinician, such a lack of a response, particularly when the clinician describes or demands the desired response (i.e., the way the client "should" handle things), only to fall on seemingly deaf ears, the client may seem "resistant." However, the client cannot safely be assumed to be resistant. Rather, the clinician can better appreciate that the client simply does not have the frame of reference necessary to produce the desired response, especially on cue. The goal of therapy can then be to build such a frame of reference (i.e., access, organize, and make available the necessary resources of the individual) through experiences obtained directly or indirectly through therapy.

Depression has been described by some as an imbalance. Some represent it as an imbalance at a biological level, others at a cognitive level, others at an emotional level, and still others at a social level. The framing of depression as an imbalance has been a most useful one, in my experience. Each of the patterns described in the previous chapter is simply a way of describing how a given individual tends to act and react to the various possibilities life has to offer. Few patterns, if any, are in and of themselves functional or dysfunctional independent of the outcomes they create. This idea is important in its implication that when a specific pattern is made the target of the therapy for the purpose of disruption, the pattern is *not* extinguished forever. Rather, the pattern is interrupted at a particular time and in a particular place, and a new pattern is catalyzed through the various mechanisms of the therapy. Through the new action itself and its consequences, the individual discovers the possibility of different and better responses. The therapist may be satisfied with a situationally specific resolution or may use such opportunities for a broader teaching of the resolution's implication: change is possible when one seeks out and uses alternatives.

The depressed client in particular is that way because he or she, at some level, feels "stuck" in some hurtful pattern. The astute clinician can readily see where an imbalance is miring the individual and can use the therapeutic process to allow the client to experience alternative ways of looking at or doing things in order to attain balance. The concept of "balance" as a goal of therapy in particular and life in general has been well elaborated elsewhere (Beletsis, 1986; Polster & Polster, 1973; Satir, 1983). Suffice it to say here that when an imbalance is evident, the clinician is in the position of being able to catalyze experience directly or indirectly in a complementary direction in order to intervene therapeutically.

How does change come about? Given that there are currently several hundred recognized types of psychotherapy, there is not much consensus on a response to the question. However, if one looks at the structure of therapy as opposed to the content of a particular model of psychotherapy, there is a strong case for the concept of therapy as pattern interruption and pattern building. When imbalance is the problem and balance the solution, the following intervention structures that comprise the interventions described throughout this book can be most useful:

1. Amplifying a pattern and encouraging resistance to it, catalyzing the shift of momentum in another direction.

2. Making continuation of a particular pattern extremely inconvenient, necessitating the development of a new one.

3. Encouraging the "acting out" of an established pattern's polar opposite, encouraging balance as a result.

4. Using hypnosis to facilitate more rapid and experiential integration of key learnings.

5. Assigning homework and structured experiences to catalyze integration of key learnings.

These patterns are simply listed here but are the core of the many interventions described later.

When therapy involves use of the above structures, interruption of a particular pattern inevitably has consequences on multiple, interrelated dimensions. The patterns of individual experience described in the previous chapter and the various pattern interrupting methods presented in the remainder of this book are each described individually. However, the reader must not infer that they are distinctly separate from each other. In fact, the patterns are closely related to one another, and the clinician who is familiar with these patterns will probably notice them occurring in clusters. In the previous chapter comments were made about where an average depressed individual might be found in respect to a particular pattern. Viewed in clusters, an example would be an individual in a "victim" mode who is also likely to be past oriented, global, and concrete in thinking style, enmeshed with significant others, and intrapunitive.

The danger exists in the therapeutic interaction that if the key dysfunctional pattern(s) is not properly identified, or is responded to inappropriately, the client's condition may deteriorate. In the case example cited in Chapter 2, the client was described as suffering significant depression associated with loss. The therapist treating her did not recognize that she had an overwhelmingly dysfunctional past temporal orientation, and treated her by focusing on the past even more. By reinforcing the client's focus on the past, no concrete future possibilities were constructed. By focusing on issues of loss, she was not empowered to seek new possibilities in current or future relationships. The therapist had unwittingly reinforced the most depressing patterns in the client's life. Predictably, she got worse over time, not better.

Reinforcing the pathogenic pattern(s) unwittingly is clearly a hazard in doing psychotherapy. The therapist who easily accepts abstract goals from the client (e.g., "becoming self-actualized") simply reinforces a hazardous pattern. The therapist who treats solely on the basis of logic and rationality misses the points that symptoms are not the consequence of rationality nor is the unconscious particularly responsive to the laws of logic. The dependency-seeking therapist who unwittingly encourages a client's enmeshment with him or her will appreciate receiving postcards from clients on vacation when they write, "Am having a great time. . . . Wish you were here to tell me why." The clinician must be observant foremost, and careful to build his or her approach around the client's existing patterns and future needs, rather than running the risk of inadvertently reinforcing dysfunctional, unrecognized patterns. This kind of approach to therapy, therefore, is client-centered, demanding that the clinician respond to the needs and limitations of the client, rather than integrating the client into the clinician's preferred, preexisting therapeutic belief system.

SUMMARY

The major premise of this chapter concerns the need to identify and disrupt those client patterns that cause or maintain depression. The major therapeutic goal is to provide strategies that both disrupt old patterns and directly or indirectly provide new patterns that will be more functional to the individual. As described in this chapter, the strategies are intended to teach complements to existing patterns in order to facilitate the attainment of balance in the individual. Often, the strategies are constructed so that the client can *experience* the limitations of the current pattern or the benefits of the new pattern in a nonthreatening, even impersonal way. This is accomplished through the use of contexts that are not particularly emotionally charged but are analogous (in varying degrees) to the "heavy" situations at hand.

The remainder of this book presents the more significant patterns to be dealt with in depressed individuals, with case examples and discussions of related therapeutic strategies.

6

Starting with the Future

The important role of positive expectations in psychotherapy has been well described in the literature. In order for the client to experience positive expectations, there must be a dimension of the individual that is capable of experiencing some degree of orientation to the future. Furthermore, the experiences associated with the future orientation must be sufficient to generate positive thoughts and feelings about the future, as well as provide motivation(s) for positive behaviors. Some degree of ability to orient to the future is present in all individuals, yet this varies markedly with each individual. Perhaps you, the reader, can notice whether you find it easy or difficult to answer questions like these:

1. What do you imagine yourself doing five years from now?

2. How will you feel when you discover that you are no longer bothered by a previously troublesome issue?

3. Can you imagine ways that you can use ideas and strategies presented in this book to help yourself and others in your future work?

Each of the above questions requires that some part of you imagine and experience in some way future possibilities based on the question's implications. Some people will have elaborate expectations, others will have an impoverished response indicating that little or nothing is generated internally as a basis for future possibilities. How does one person experience such rich expectations while another individual does not? One can speculate on the kinds of socialization factors that encourage one temporal orientation as opposed to another. For example, if one were rarely or never encouraged to plan and execute goal-oriented behavior, or if one were outright sabotaged by others in one's plan building, one could easily learn that there is no use in making and working towards goals, because "they never come about anyway." For such individuals, the future seems *entirely* unpredictable, and for them life must always be lived one day at a time.

In the case of the depressed individual, the dominant temporal orientation is usually a "past" one. In other words, the past is the frame of reference for the future, and what the individual does, therefore, is to simply extend past hurts and pain into future contexts. Structurally, such a procedure could be called a "negative self-hypnosis" (Araoz, 1985). By having such negativity spill into future possibilities, the depressed individual effectively creates a self-paralysis. In the eyes of most clinicians, this appears as the "negative expectations" and "hopelessness" that are the common badges of depression.

The lack of positive future possibilities is a key source of the depressed client's apparent inability to become "unstuck." It is also a source of anxiety for the client, since it is truly a conflict-ridden situation. The person is, in essence, in an "avoidance-avoidance" conflict, where the choices all seem potentially negative and hurtful, or else there seem to be no choices at all. Thus, the depressed client may also seem ambivalent to the clinician, wanting to be helped on the one hand, but having no internal frame of reference that suggests anything could change for the better.

It seems a fitting time to digress for a moment in order to reiterate certain points made previously. Thus far in this chapter, the typical depressive symptoms of negative expectations, hopelessness, ambivalence, and apathy have been discussed as features associated with the pattern of a primarily past temporal association. In reviewing the tables of Chapter 3 in which depressive symptoms on various dimensions of experience were described, the reader may now begin to identify how imbalances in the patterns first defined in Chapter 4 will evolve such symptomatic patterns. This is the essence of being able to recognize dysfunctional patterns requiring interruption and reformulation.

Since the depressed individual typically has negative expectations for the future, the clinician can have a number of goals for the client at the start of treatment:

1. Accepting the client's understandings of his or her own situation as a valid representation of the client's world to him or herself (thus enabling the building of rapport).

2. Identifying which dimensions of experience are in the client's awareness and which are not.

3. Assessing which of the subjective patterns are present in the client's experience in a dysfunctional or imbalanced form.

4. Establishing a context for the therapy in which the direct or indirect communications from the clinician to the client strongly suggest the likelihood of positive changes ("building expectancy").

How each individual clinician will go about translating the above steps into actual clinical practice will vary markedly according to individual style. Clearly, in order to accomplish the steps, the clinician will want information from the client that provides a definition of the following: 1) the client's belief system (for reasons discussed in greater detail in the next chapter); 2) personal goals (including their structure, content, clarity, and feasibility); 3) previous accomplishments and methods for having brought them about; 4) previous therapy and its helpfulness or lack thereof; and 5) current experience of emotional discomfort including all related symptomatic problems. From skilled interviewing in these areas, the clinician can gather a great deal of information regarding the client's expectations, conscious and unconscious resources available for the therapy, and the diagnostic patterns' specific configurations in that particular client.

The individual experiencing depression is in a state of distress that is usually quite evident to the clinician from the start. In the presence of the negative expectations and negative interpretations of experience generally found in depressed individuals (Beck, 1983), it seems especially important to be able to demonstrate to the depressed individual fairly immediately that there is, in fact, something that can be done to help him or her. At an early stage of treatment, the clinician willing to employ directive approaches can use a variety of strategies intended to provide some degree of immediate relief from some of the most troublesome aspects of the depressed pattern, particularly anxiety, sleep disturbance, and any demotivating negative expectations regarding the therapy itself.

As was first pointed out in Chapter 2, the various hypnotic and strategic approaches each have the capacity of being applied in either a manner that is symptom-oriented or in a manner that addresses underlying psychodynamics. The use of these approaches does not presume the superiority of one type of intervention over another, since both styles have proven themselves to be most capable of generating meaningful therapeutic changes. Early in treatment, however, the clinician may choose more general, symptom-oriented approaches that can provide relief to the client while more extensive changes are simultaneously being "seeded." In other words, concepts and experiences that will be valuable to build upon later are introduced early, generating a familiarity that makes them more easily accepted later.

More traditionally oriented clinicians often recognize the need for some fairly immediate impact on the depressed client as well, but often choose to use medications as a way of building receptivity. In some cases, medication may be the best way to stabilize an individual sufficiently to allow psychotherapy a chance to succeed. Medication may reduce the severe symptoms that inhibit the client's chance to build a meaningful relationship with the clinician. Furthermore, medication may help the client reach short-term goals that build a positive momentum on which to base further treatment. One must proceed cautiously with medication, however, because of the implicit message that may affirm to the client that he or she is truly helpless to effect personal change. Likewise, the clinician must be careful not to overwhelm the client with an unnecessary elaboration of the extensive nature of the work ahead. After all, the client is likely to already be responding globally to all of his or her problems, even amplifying them to the point of finding them insurmountable. Part of building expectations involves assuring the client that the problems are truly manageable, when approached competently.

Depression, from an intrapersonal standpoint, is a state of ongoing agitation and discomfort, involving anxiety and a perseveration of negative feelings and thoughts. Often, the client is only aware of what seems to be a useless set of symptoms, and relief from the symptoms is the client's goal in seeking treatment. In order to address these immediate concerns, the use of hypnotic patterns can be very effective "pattern interrupters" on which to progressively build more intense therapeutic interventions.

☐ D1 ☐ * Hypnosis for Symptom Reduction

Pattern interruption through hypnosis may be accomplished through even the simplest of hypnotic inductions that leads the client into a state of relaxation. Through "Hypnosis for Symptom Reduction" that accepts and utilizes the client's experience of him- or herself, the client's subjective world is not directly challenged; rather it is used as a basis for promoting the recognition that the client wants to experience him- or

---

*The boxes list the Directive by number for easy referencing. The entire list of directives can be found in Appendix A.

herself differently. Affirming the client's ability to experience comfort despite the problems to be dealt with encourages an interruption of the usual negative perseverations. The trance process might begin as follows:

> You came here for a reason . . . really wanting to experience yourself in a different way . . . and you can *experience yourself differently* . . . in a most comfortable way . . . and there's a part of you that really knows how to *feel good* . . . and maybe it's been a while since you've had the chance to experience it . . . or maybe it just seems like it has been a while . . . but right now there isn't anything you have to say . . . nothing you have to do . . . and so you can . . . take the time . . . to put a comfortable distance between yourself . . . and all the everyday concerns . . . and how soothing it can be to *have all the room you need* . . . all the time in the world you need right now . . . to experience the pleasing sensations of muscles relaxing . . . and parts of your body growing heavier . . . while thoughts are growing lighter . . . and feelings are shifting in ways that can really feel good . . . and you can just let that happen and experience yourself just differently enough to discover that awareness changes, and feelings change . . . and no need yet to think about how deeply a feeling of comfort can go . . . or how very long it can last. . . .

The implicit messages to the client are that a change in experience is possible, that he or she has the ability to relax, think positively, and gain access to relevant learnings and experiences within him- or herself. For the client to discover or rediscover the ability to relax and experience relief from the anxiety associated with depression, even temporarily, can be a most profound experience. Many clients have not been spoken to in so supportive a manner for so long that they can be quite moved by the experience. Tape recording the session and giving the tape to the client can provide a welcome source of support in between sessions.

Use of such simple hypnotic techniques can disrupt the anxiety spiral and allow for the eventual building of self-management skills with self-hypnosis. The client learns that he or she has the ability to make contact with the inner self in a constructive way. Such contact may have previously been avoided altogether because of the assumption that "all that's in there is pain." By making it comfortable to "go inside," the clinician is seeding the possibilities for later recognition that there are many dimensions of self, each with potentially positive capabilities, if developed in a constructive way. When the anxiety spiral has been interrupted and even reduced through the evolution of hypnotic relaxation skills, there is also a very good chance that the client will experience better sleep and a return to other more normal vegetative functions. Less internal discomfort can alleviate the depressed person's reliance on destructive coping patterns (such as excessive intake of alcohol or food), thereby further increasing his or her sense of self-control. (This directive is described in clinical context in Case 3 in Appendix B.)

D2   Reframing: From Useless to Useful

"Reframing" involves transforming what seems to be a liability into an asset by promoting a different perspective. Whenever a change in perception alters one's reactions to or interpretations of an event, a reframing has occurred.

In the case of the depressed individual, he or she may frame the depression as an utterly useless, painful experience existing for no apparent reason. The tendency is then to blame oneself for not only having the problem, but also seemingly having no ability to control it. Such self-blame naturally only compounds the problem.

Reframing at this early stage of treatment may be done with or without the benefit of formal trance induction. The client can be offered a different perspective of depression through suggestions such as the following:

> And you don't like the way you're feeling . . . but feelings change
> . . . perspectives change . . . and it's important to know that . . . be-
> cause each feeling has a different purpose, a different capability . . . the
> ability to love . . . is a wonderful capability that allows for close,
> caring relationships . . . and the ability to feel committed to a par-
> ticular viewpoint allows stability and greater self-awareness . . . and
> feeling bored pushes one to grow . . . and feeling those feelings
> you've called "depressed" is also purposeful . . . even though you
> don't really understand it yet . . . and you haven't really realized just
> yet that those feelings present an opportunity to you . . . an oppor-
> tunity to discover and rediscover yourself . . . your ability to
> change . . . to grow . . . and to outgrow . . . and growing pains are
> only transient . . . and are usually soon forgotten . . . important signs
> of change . . . and then left behind . . . purposeful at one time . . .
> unnecessary very soon after. . . .

The reframing, if desired, may also be accomplished metaphorically, describing the experience of another individual who faced structurally similar circumstances, as in the following:

> And I met a man . . . not unlike yourself . . . who found himself in a
> situation . . . not unlike yours . . . on the outside, he seemed to have

it all . . . a good job, a good marriage and family . . . but on the inside, he knew he was missing something . . . because he felt so unhappy . . . and he really didn't know why . . . at first . . . and he felt sure there was no legitimate basis for feeling badly . . . which made him feel even worse . . . about feeling badly . . . but when he took time just for himself . . . to relax . . . to distance himself from the usual demands . . . and to let his mind drift . . . the way conscious minds tend to . . . he was able to discover parts of himself he'd forgotten about . . . like ambitions from youth . . . memories from childhood . . . and expectations . . . and what seemed purposeless to him at first . . . became a wonderful opportunity to explore . . . and discover . . . parts of himself that he'd forgotten he could enjoy . . . and isn't it wonderful to discover one's needs and abilities . . . and how well he used signs from inside to discover new possibilities. . . .

In reality, depression *is* a warning signal that at some level a change is needed in order to build or restore a healthy balance to the client's world. If the clinician is aware at this early stage of the associated dynamics, he or she can further develop the reframing metaphor to include parallel problems and parallel solutions for the client to consider. Depression may serve as a signal that a relationship requires redefinition, an important decision needs to be made (or remade), an issue needs to be dealt with, a feeling needs to be acknowledged, or some other dimension of experience requires an adjustment. Depression is also a normal and healthy outlet for grief and other significant stresses. Reframing depression as a natural experience laden with positive possibilities can motivate the client to begin thinking about making positive changes as opposed to simply stewing in the juices of discontent. (This directive is described in clinical context in Cases 1 and 2 in Appendix B.)

BUILDING A POSITIVE FUTURE ORIENTATION:
HYPNOTIC AGE PROGRESSION

Age progression as a basic trance phenomenon involves experientially orienting the client to future experience. The process of age progression can be effectively conducted even in relatively light trance states. The client is first oriented to future experiences and then is guided by the clinician in an effort to become experientially absorbed in the experiences. Thus, the client is able to experience feelings, thoughts, sensations, behaviors, interactions, and events that in reality have not yet occurred. If the experience is sufficiently absorbing and impactful, it is integrated as an experience not unlike other experiences which can serve as a frame of reference for initiating desirable changes.

D3   Changes for the Better

The emphasis throughout this chapter is on the need to build positive expectations for the future as a part of any psychotherapy, but particularly with depressed clients for whom the future is often a dark void. The most direct method for doing so involves the strategy of orienting the client to the beneficial consequences of making changes. At an early stage in treatment, the expected changes need not even be specified, but can be described in a general way that only *sounds* specific. Suggestions such as the following might be offered:

> You've described the discomfort that has led you to seek help . . . and you want to feel differently . . . and you really don't know that you can . . . but you'll discover quickly what you've known all along . . . that when you do something differently than you used to . . . the result will also be different . . . and so you can go forward in time . . . so that it's been a while since our work together . . . and you can take a moment . . . to be fully there . . . able to review decisions that you've recently made . . . differently . . . and you can review the positive consequences of those decisions . . . on *all* dimensions within you . . . and what a pleasure to discover that you're so capable . . . of shifting thoughts and feelings . . . and that you can enjoy the relief you worked so hard for . . . and why not look forward to even more changes . . . that feel good . . . as you discover more and more ways of using what you've learned to continue growing stronger. . . .

The client is encouraged to fully experience suggested scenarios in as sensorily powerful a way as possible, with attention being drawn whenever feasible to the inner experiences of relaxation, comfort, pride, satisfaction, and so forth, developing those feelings as best as possible and continually making them available as resources to use. The progression of time occurring in the course of trance sessions can allow the client to *experience* shifts in various dimensions of him- or herself. Thus, useful learnings that normally would require extended periods of time to acquire can be formed at an accelerated rate.

The experience of hypnosis presupposes the presence of dissociation since a trance state is, by definition, a dissociated state. While the client experiences the age progression, the emphasis is on the experience of successful results based on changes *actively* made in one's own behalf.

Through the careful use of dissociation, the client can be temporarily dissociated from the effects of past negative experiences. In essence, this is accomplished indirectly since it is a future orientation that is amplified, relegating the past to a minor role at best in the process. Dissociation, whether in the temporal sphere or some other one, allows the clinician to amplify one dimension of experience in awareness and, in so doing, diminish others. When the usual past orientation is minimized through the absorption of the individual in future possibilities and achievements, current choices (both conscious and unconscious) can be made in a way that is likely to bring them about. In essence, the clinician is facilitating the construction of a "self-fulfilling prophecy." As a result, the client is able to experience a higher degree of confidence that current efforts are worthwhile, a positive source of motivation to continue on the path of recovery. (This directive is described in clinical context in Cases 3 and 4 in Appendix B.)

D4   Extending the Status Quo

Another age progression strategy involves experientially orienting the client to the future consequences of making no changes in his or her life. The progression may involve amplifying the client's awareness of the maintenance of some destructive pattern (e.g., relationship, behavior) evident in the individual's lifestyle, or it may involve experiencing the effects of remaining ambivalent or immobilized regarding some self-help decision. In either case, the client is oriented to some future time in which he or she is encouraged to become experientially absorbed in the intrapersonal thoughts or feelings associated with the context, or with the interpersonal consequences of maintaining current patterns.

Perhaps the most well-known example of this particular therapeutic strategy is the case of Ebenezer Scrooge in Charles Dickens's classic work, *A Christmas Carol.* Scrooge, a cranky, miserly old man was unmoved by Christmas spirit and the emphasis on love for all humanity. One Christmas eve he was visited by three ghosts, the spirits of Christmas Past, Present, and Future. The spirit of Christmas Future took Scrooge to his gravesite and through the streets of his village at the time of his death. So moved was Scrooge by the bitterness and coldness of others' remembrances of him that he experienced an emotional upheaval and a subsequent transformation into a generous, kind man. The age progression to the time of his death and the experience of the negative consequences for maintaining his old ways motivated Scrooge to change. None of the spreaders of cheer he had encountered previously had any impact at all.

It is apparent that some people are motivated more easily on the basis of experiencing positive possibilities, while others are more easily motivated on the basis of avoiding negative possibilities. As another example, some people stop smoking because they genuinely want to look and feel better, while others do not even consider quitting until they are given stern warnings by their physician or until a spot shows up on an X-ray of their lungs. The inability to experience future possibilities to any significant emotional degree is the cornerstone for impulsive patterns, particularly self-destructive ones. The present need to engage in the impulsive behavior is dissociated from the future consequences of having done so. (This directive is described in clinical context in Case 3 in Appendix B.)

D5 Erickson's Pseudo-Orientation in Time

Erickson (1954b) described a strategy involving orienting the client to a future context wherein he or she can assess the quality of life, reflect on any meaningful changes successfully undergone recently, and describe to the clinician what the specific catalysts for those changes were. If suggested amnesia can be successfully employed with the client, the client may then have no conscious recollection of having described useful changes and what brought them about. The client is, in essence, providing information regarding the types of learnings and experiences that he or she needs to have in order to succeed in therapy. The clinician may then use this information to construct therapeutic trances and task assignments.

This particular strategy, when it works, operates on the presupposition that clients already have an idea of what they need to do, but simply may not have the resources available to them that make it possible to do as they would like. The clinician who operates on the commonly held belief that each person has the necessary resources for change knows that his or her job is to provide the context of change, rather than to provide specific advice.

In the following exchange exemplifying this particular strategy, the client is guided into trance and is then immersed in a future context reviewing changes and describing their origin:

Clinician: And now it's been how long since our work together ended?
Client: About six months.
Clinician: And how have you been experiencing yourself?
Client: OK . . . I've been doing OK . . . feeling all right.
Clinician: What has happened that allows you to continue to feel better?

Client: I guess I was able to let go of him . . . I needed to but wasn't able to . . . but now I have.

Clinician: Whom are you talking about?

Client: My son . . . my son . . . I wanted him to stay with me . . . a while longer. He's still just a college student . . . but he needed his life to be his own.

Clinician: Has he moved out or is he living with you?

Client: He's moved out . . . gotten his own place. He loves it . . . but I still miss him. It's only been a couple of months.

Clinician: And you can continue to miss him . . . and you can even enjoy missing him . . . knowing that he likes his life . . . the life you gave him . . . that is his to enjoy . . . and you can look back over the changes . . . the decisions you've made . . . and you've learned something valuable, haven't you?

Client: I haven't lost him.

Clinician: That's right.

Client: And I know I have my life to live now . . . *my* friends, *my* career, *my* life.

Clinician: And how did you come to know this?

Client: I learned I can't hold on forever . . . and that my life is mine and his is his . . . and maybe it's something we talked about . . . or maybe it was your patients in the waiting room I noticed . . . I remember thinking . . . they want answers . . . and they probably already know what they should do . . . but don't have the guts . . . and that thought stuck with me . . . and I wanted to think I had the guts . . .

Clinician: And you did, didn't you?

Client: I guess I did . . . because he's on his own.

From the above exchange, it is apparent that the client was aware, at some level, that a change would be indicated in the area of her relationship with her son. Subsequent sessions involved providing feedback and experiences that could solidify the new pattern of responding to her son's independence with a new response of acceptance. This change was a significant one in the client's experience and was a useful base on which to build other meaningful changes as well.

D6   Metaphors Regarding Expectancy and Ambivalence

Most of the approaches described thus far have been direct in their style and structure. While approaches that directly engage the client in interaction and directly relate to the client's specific situation are widely applicable, it is likewise true that many clients (especially when in the midst of depression) feel unable to deal directly with what are experienced as overwhelming problems. In such instances, the pattern known as the "therapeutic metaphor" can be useful. Zeig (1980a) described the practical capabilities of metaphors in diagnosis, establishing rapport, making and illustrating a point, suggesting solutions, getting clients to recognize themselves, seeding ideas, increasing motivation, and decreasing resistance. A number of works have elaborated upon the applicability of metaphors and provided comprehensive guidelines for their construction and delivery (Gordon, 1978; Lankton & Lankton, 1983; Rosen, 1982).

Metaphors often involve the use of other people (past clients, family members, or others who exemplify a point well) with and from whom the client can identify and learn. Metaphors that simply describe other individuals with similar problems who have achieved positive results may indirectly suggest that recovery from depression is possible, and this may build motivation to participate in the treatment process. Such metaphors may not be accepted, however, if the client's frame of reference is one of "personal helplessness" (Seligman, 1983). In such a case, the client maintains the belief that while others may succeed, "I know *I* can't." When personal helplessness is evident, or even suspected, the use of metaphors describing others' successes can further compound the client's depression, and thus are contraindicated.

Metaphors to build expectancy in the earliest stages of treatment need to match as closely as possible the client's experience of helplessness and hopelessness, and any other significant aspects of his or her ongoing reality. In the following example, a metaphorical approach is used to validate the client's understanding of her own experience (depression and confusion about its origin) and to seed the idea that change is not only possible, but hopefully will be considered inevitable:

> I worked with another client once who was so unhappy with her life, and she didn't seem to know why. . . . On the surface, everything seemed all right in her life . . . she had a nice family, nice possessions, a nice life . . . but she knew that there was something deeper inside that needed attention . . . and she didn't consciously know just what it was . . . not yet . . . but she did believe that people could change . . . and feel so much better . . . even though she didn't know how . . . just yet . . . and she was so unsure at first . . . and she had every right to be . . . and her feelings were so uncomfortable to her . . . . It seems no one's experience of depression is more uncomfortable than one's own . . . and there have been many changes you've experienced over the course of your lifetime . . . some planned . . . some unplanned . . . and with each new phase of life

> unfolding before you . . . you have found ways to change with chang-
> ing times . . . and sometimes you forget that . . . but why not take
> time now to remember times of change . . . that were truly impor-
> tant in terms of who you are . . . and how enjoyable to discover that
> you have some wonderful resources within you . . . deeply within
> you . . . that you can use now . . . as you enter a new period of
> changes . . . that can provide a lot of good feelings . . . that can unfold
> a day at a time . . . the way changes seem to always do. . . .

In the above metaphor, reference is made to changes one undergoes as
a function of the natural unfolding of one's life over time. Metaphors that
give the client access in a nonthreatening way to the recognition that he
or she has previously made successful changes under difficult conditions can be useful in establishing positive expectancy.

Metaphors that address the ambivalence of the client may be used to
build motivation to take action, a fundamental ingredient in the therapy
of depressed individuals. Metaphors that highlight the positive outcomes of trying new approaches, and metaphors that highlight negative
outcomes of remaining indecisive or passive at a critical decision time
may be employed. It is important to appreciate that such metaphors are
intended to build motivation and expectancy and not further frustrate
a client, who knows he or she needs to take some positive action but feels
unable to. The following metaphor was one used successfully with a
client who was agonizing and progressively getting more depressed over
the decision of whether to leave home to go away to school, or to live at
home and attend a local college:

> I had a friend named Will who recently was in almost the identical
> situation as you . . . and he's realizing only now . . . how much he
> has learned about himself . . . and that feels really good to him. . . . Will
> was trying hard to decide which graduate school to attend . . . there
> was one program that was quite a traditional one . . . that empha-
> sized older and more conservative approaches . . . and it was
> conveniently near his home where he could live with his parents
> . . . who wanted to keep him safely at home . . . and he didn't really
> feel he could disappoint them and move out . . . and the other pro-
> gram was one that was newer and much less conservative and nar-
> row . . . and was in another city . . . and he thought he should be
> conservative . . . but he very much wanted to learn things beyond
> what was offered in the program close by . . . and he really couldn't
> decide which program to enroll in . . . and both programs had very
> positive possibilities . . . and both had firm deadlines for enrolling
> or else one's place was given to someone else . . . and he couldn't

decide . . . and when he was asked to state his intentions . . . he really couldn't decide . . . and when he asked the program director of the second, less conservative program in the other city for more time to think about his plans . . . he was told he was obviously not interested and that his spot would be given away . . . and he ended up in the more conservative program . . . and is living at home . . . and he feels very trapped there . . . and I think he has learned a lot about making decisions . . . when the opportunity to choose is there . . . and before decisions are made for him. . . .

In the above example, a number of different characteristics of depression are addressed indirectly: ambivalence; inappropriate responsibility for one's parents; inappropriate guilt; the loss of an opportunity by indecision and fear; the affirmation that one needs to know what is in one's best interest and act on that information; as well as other such patterns that can convey important messages in a memorable way because of the metaphor's parallel content to that of the client's concerns.

Metaphors may be used appropriately at any stage of the therapy and may be considered particularly valuable as tools for enhancing motivation and building positive expectations. The following is another example of a motivating metaphor, one that contains the messages that "one must work in order to succeed" and "one gets what one deserves."

And you've probably heard the old saying, "There's no such thing as a free lunch," . . . and you know enough to appreciate . . . that putting in . . . energy . . . and time . . . as necessary ingredients of success . . . allows you to let go . . . comfortably . . . of the nontaxing . . . effortless . . . frame of mind . . . that wants and expects something for nothing . . . and there's a particular story . . . that has become one of my favorites . . . and it's going to sound very specific at first . . . but as it takes on more general meaning with each time you hear it . . . it will be the kind of story . . . that functions in the same way . . . as other stories that you've heard a million times and yet enjoyed each time . . . in a different way . . . it's the story of a woodcutter . . . and another man . . . from many, many centuries ago . . . who came before a judge to settle their dispute . . . the judge asked the woodcutter to explain . . . his presence . . . and the woodcutter said slowly . . . and with quiet determination . . . "I have spent all day . . . working so hard . . . to earn my silver coins . . . and this man thinks he's entitled to half . . . and I refuse to give him half. . . . *I* got up before sunrise this morning . . . loaded up my donkey . . . walked miles to the forest . . . unloaded my donkey . . . began with my axe to make difficult stroke after difficult stroke to chop down trees. . . . It was *I* who carried the axe. . . . It was *I* who

cut the wood into small bundles ... it was *I* who bundled them ...
and loaded them onto the donkey ... *I* was the one who sweated in
the hot sun ... and *I* was the one who strained my back ... and *I*
deserve the pay" ... and the judge turned to the other man ... and
asked him what he did to deserve half the pay ... and the man
said ... "If it wasn't for me, the woodcutter's work would have
taken twice as long. ... I was the one who complained about how
heavy the axe was ... I was the one who cursed the trees when they
wouldn't fall in the right direction ... I was the one who screamed
at the mule when he wouldn't budge ... I was the one who complained
about how hot the sun was ... and without me ... the work would
have taken twice as long". ... The judge sent one of his courtsmen ... to
get a silver tray ... and he grabbed the bag of coins from the
woodcutter, who angrily tried to retrieve them ... unsuccessfully
... and then the judge ... took a coin from the bag ... and dropped
it loudly ... onto the silver tray ... and then another coin ... was
dropped ... loudly onto the tray ... and then another ... and
another ... and with each coin ... the woodcutter grew angrier
and angrier ... while the other man smiled greedily ... and when
the bag was half empty ... the woodcutter reached for it ... and the
judge blocked his effort ... and the other man smiled even more
greedily ... and the judge continued to drop coin after coin until
the entire bag was empty ... the woodcutter was furious ... thinking
the judge was going to take away his earnings ... the other man was
delighted ... and then with one quick motion ... the judge poured
all the coins back into the bag ... and threw the bag to the
woodcutter ... and turned to the other man and said ... *"You made
the sounds of the work ... and now you have heard the sounds of
the pay"* ... and little by little ... as you think about sounds of
work ... and the illusion of effort ... it might occur to you ... at a
very deep level ... that what one thinks one is doing ... can be very
different ... than the reward one does or doesn't get ... and I
wonder ... and you can wonder ... whether it's time ... to do work
... or whether it's time to make sounds of work ... and only you
will know ... just what that means to you ... you can ignore it ...
and pretend that I wasn't talking to you ... or you can understand
intuitively ... why the woodcutter ... deserved what he got ... take
your time in processing those thoughts ... and let part of yourself
move forward in time ... to tomorrow and the next day ... and all
the next days ... and discover for yourself ... where there's time to
work ... and where there's time to just make sounds. ...

SUMMARY

The strategies described in this chapter are largely hypnotically based, with an emphasis on building and guiding the associations of the client. While some of the strategies involve formal hypnosis, i.e., an overtly identified hypnosis procedure, the majority of them can be used without the presence of a formal hypnotic induction. It is possible to use one's skills as a communicator to introduce ideas meaningfully, present them at a manageable pace, and tailor them as well as possible to the personality and needs of the client.

Building expectancy as a means to engage the person in the treatment process as well as to increase the likelihood of a successful therapy is a beginning point for any psychotherapy. It seems difficult to overstate how vital to the therapy is this phase of building expectancy. The patterns presented in this chapter are those that have proven useful in the treatment of depressed individuals, making them potentially quite valuable since it is the absence of positive expectations that may hamper effective treatment or lead the client to drop out of treatment prematurely.

7

Facilitating Flexibility: Let Me Count the Ways

The capability of human beings to form generalizations on the basis of even a single experience is potentially both an asset and a liability. On one hand, developing a stereotypical pattern for dealing with the routine demands of life affords one the luxury of not having to think through a familiar experience each time, approaching it as if it were novel. If you had to think about how to open a door each time you came upon one, or how to tie your shoes each time you needed to, such simple tasks would require an inordinate amount of attention. On the other hand, once a generalized pattern for dealing with some dimension of life (not necessarily limited to simple tasks like opening doors or tying shoes) is established, it can evolve a momentum all its own in shaping the individual's experience.

Attempts to block or reroute the momentum of the pattern through formal therapy or informal attempts at change all too often end in a frustrating recurrence of the old established pattern. In a variety of forms, the recognition of the tendency to maintain patterns has generally been dealt with in the literature on "resistance." The typical consideration has generally been one emphasizing that resistance is almost inevitably a property of the individual client. Numerous reasons explaining its presence range from "The client does not really want (or isn't ready) to change" to "The client is actually benefiting from the pathology." Reformulations of the nature of resistance in the literature of strategic therapy propose a different view, emphasizing the interpersonal nature and consequences of resistance as well as offering strategies for its appropriate handling. (For a detailed consideration of this subject, see Lankton and Lankton, 1983, and Zeig, 1980a.)

In observing the patterns of the individual seeking psychotherapy for depression, it is readily apparent that these are hurtful in some way. Perhaps the pattern interferes with the ability to think rationally or clearly about some aspect of living (as suggested in the cognitive and learned helplessness models). Maybe the pattern interferes with the ability to form a healthy relationship with another (as suggested in the interpersonal models), or perhaps it generates behaviors that are hurtful or ineffective for the individual. Regardless of the pattern's consequences on specific dimensions of experience, the consequences are negative ones inadvertently maintaining the pattern. The need and motivation to change on the part of the client are clearly present. Yet, the dysfunctional pattern remains. Having a positive future orientation, or positive expectancy, is a start, as the previous chapter suggested.

The next step in the sequence is actually one that overruns its boundaries and infiltrates each of the other stages of psychotherapy. This step is identified as the facilitation of flexibility. Once the seeds of recognition that change is possible have been planted, the client is likely to experience a shift in perception, initiating a hope that there will be a way to effectively resolve the problems that led to the involvement in therapy in the first place. If positive expectancy is imparted early on as suggested here, the client is then in the position of being able to consider that there may be alternative ways of being. Certainly the client is likely to have considered that before, but viable solutions were either never discovered or they were dismissed as too demanding in some way, with the demand exceeding the perceived supply of ability to meet it. With the help of the clinician, the client can arrive at a state of willingness to entertain the possibility of developing meaningful alternatives. The client must be given the message that new ways of thinking, feeling, and responding, and thus new outcomes, are possible. In addition, the clinician is providing the simultaneous message that by developing new ways of responding to old situations, the ability to go beyond one's previous limitations is assured. Ideally, the clinician can model attitudes and behaviors that contain messages such as:

1. There are many "right" ways to accomplish this goal.

2. If what you are doing is not working, i.e., is not getting you what you want for yourself, then be willing to do something else, instead of doing more of the same.

3. Independent of what is familiar to you, what would be the best response (i.e., the one most likely to assist you in attaining the desired outcome) in that particular context that concerns you?

   4. Change is inevitable, and moving ahead means leaving some-
      thing behind.

   Each of these messages has the common theme of developing a different response to a life demand. From the earlier discussion, it is obvious
that it is precisely the inability to generate a different response that
characterizes the rigid and fixed nature of depressogenic patterns. These
"rigidities" can occur on any or all of the dimensions described in
Chapter 3. Rigidities in thinking, feeling, or behaving can be viewed as
the basis for pathology, a reflection of the individual's inability (or
limited ability) to change with changing times. As has been pointed out
by a number of sources (Erickson, Rossi, & Rossi, 1976; Haley, 1973;
Samko, 1986), mental disorders seem to most frequently develop when
individuals do not allow the inevitability of changes over time to naturally occur, instead attempting to maintain the stability of the status quo
even to their own detriment.
   What factors influence one's ability to evolve flexibility as an evolu-
tionary device, and, similarly, what fosters the development of rigidity as
a mechanism for managing one's life? These are simple questions to
ask, but are much too broad in scope and intricate in detail to ever defin-
itively answer. It is possible, however, to consider some of the more
significant factors.

VALUES, BELIEFS, AND RIGIDITY

   Perhaps the most powerful barrier to personal evolution is a deeply
rooted value system that holds stability and tradition in the highest
regard. A value that, in essence, fosters an earnest desire to maintain
stability in the face of change has embedded within it a number of
related values, such as the value of commitment to an ideal or a goal in
spite of changing circumstances, the value of maintaining tradition in
spite of progress, and the value of what has been over what can be. A
deeply held set of values and expectations about how things "should" be
on the basis of what had been previously learned has certainly been a
common characteristic of depressed individuals seen in the author's
clinical practice. The values held at a deep level are the basis for the
conscious attitudes and beliefs that shape the individual's perception of
the world, and dictate the range of possibilities open to that individual.
(For a more detailed discussion of the role of values in treatment, see
Yapko, 1985a.) Certain belief systems encourage diversity and flexibility
in thinking, while others foster rigidity. Many of the beliefs that have the
capability of predisposing one to depression are encompassed in the

cognitive distortion patterns described so well by Beck (1983). Believing one's feelings are an accurate reflection of experience, as one example of a cognitive distortion, is a belief that can foster considerable difficulty, since the subjectivity of feelings can actually have little to do with more objective reality. There are numerous belief systems that are similarly harmful in their potential to distort experience. Three such beliefs are: "Where there's a will, there's a way," "All things happen for a reason" and "There is one right way to live."

"Where There's a Will, There's a Way"

Together with the corollary belief that "if at first you don't succeed, try, try again," these are two beliefs that have an equal capacity to motivate or frustrate. Often, the client invests increasing amounts of him- or herself in a cause of some sort, believing that through determination and commitment, success will be possible. It is unfortunate that often such an expenditure of emotion and energy is not enough. Ultimately, the outcome must be one that is *possible* for the individual to attain. Often, it simply is not.

Consider the case of a psychotherapist who suffered the torment of having a son who was diagnosed as a chronic schizophrenic. As a clinician herself, she was acutely aware of current treatment alternatives and their relative efficacy. Her son's chronic condition required massive amounts of her time, energy, and money. She had to deal with the harsh realities of having a son who was unable to care for himself, who was continually running away from each of the many residences arranged for him, including her own home, and who was simply deteriorating. She was also dealing with the feelings of inadequacy that she, a psychotherapist, would even have a schizophrenic son, and that despite her personal attachment and professional acumen she was unable to make any significant difference in his condition. The result for her was depression. In her ongoing desperate attempts to make a difference, ideally effecting a cure for her son, this sensitive and insightful woman fell in the trap of believing there must be a way. Her patterns, though hurting her badly, were obviously well intentioned, and her commitment and determination were admirable. A schizophrenic son is a lot easier to deal with when he is somebody else's son, the reader must be reminded, for the reality resulting from all the diverse treatments attempted was the frustrating lack of progress.

Therapy with the mother was brief, intense, and useful. Focused exploration of the value statement regarding the presence of a way when there's a will led to some very powerful new understandings as well as some genuine shifts in response. In several sessions of her therapy which involved hypnosis, she was given suggestions and metaphors that emphasized letting people be who they are. She was also given directives to carry out that were designed to highlight the need to know when to let go. As she let go of the belief that she could unilaterally make a difference (i.e., "cure" her son), she also let go of the depression. The situation continued to sadden and frustrate her, but she was able to start focusing her talents for her own benefit instead of going down in flames with her son. She didn't care about him less or ignore him. She simply began to let go of the beliefs that were hurting her.

"All Things Happen for a Reason"

One of the more interesting characteristics of human beings is their need for things to make sense. When an event occurs, a search for the relationship between cause and effect begins. People may have no objective basis for formulating a theory and then reaching the conclusion of its satisfactory ability to explain something, but once deemed satisfactory, the search for truth generally stops. When there is no objective means to explain something (i.e., no probable, reliable, valid explanation), guesswork begins. Belief in guesswork is what is commonly known as "faith." If one believes in a fantastic vision, that all things occur for some purpose, known or unknown, then when something occurs the immediate response is to begin the search for "the reason." In many instances, the attributions for an event can be most negative and can trigger the experience of depression.

Consider the example of a client who suffered depression, anxiety, and fear following a brutal and unprovoked physical assault. A woman in her mid-30s, the client began treatment with the author shortly after the assault took place. She had just parked her car in a public parking garage on her way to a workout at her gym. Seemingly out of nowhere, a man let out a wild yell and came running at her, obviously in a psychotic rage. She was unable to defend herself against him and was badly physically beaten. In the hours and days immediately following, she was in pain from her considerable injuries, as well as an emotional wreck. She was unable to sleep, interpreting every sound in the house as an intruder waiting to attack, and other similar signs of post-traumatic stress.

After just a couple of sessions focusing on rapport building and the use of psychological approaches to pain management, the client's depressogenic belief that the attack occurred for a reason was challenged. She had perseverated on the idea that there was a reason, that there was a message for her in the attack. She speculated that perhaps she should have been home rather than at the gym, and perhaps it was a sign that she was not a good enough wife or mother. For her to try and find meaning in such a powerful experience is certainly natural, but it was also aggravating an already delicate situation. When her assailant's record was disclosed showing that he had had more than a score of psychiatric hospitalizations, with aggressive behavior a common denominator, it had not swayed her belief that she was the target for a reason. Therapy involved overloading this belief by requiring that she generate as many plausible explanations for the attack as she could. This she did and it was actually quite easy to detach her from any one particular explanation and communicate that *if* there is *a* reason, one will never really know what it is. As soon as the guilt and self-blame diminished, so did the depression, anxiety, and fear.

D7   Overloading Reasons

"Overloading Reasons" as a strategy requires that the client generate *at least* half a dozen interpretations or explanations of an experience. This forces the client to develop a more flexible system for looking at things and from a variety of perspectives. The ability to dissociate negative feelings from any one explanation or interpretation is made easier as a result.

"There is One Right Way to Live"

Perhaps the most rigid belief system, this particular one is the culprit underlying prejudice and war on a broader level, and intrapersonal and interpersonal difficulties (to say the least) on a smaller scale. The tremendous pressure exerted on each individual to conform to arbitrary standards established by others is inescapable. The message from one to another is, in essence, "Live as I do and as I expect you to, or risk disapproval at least, rejection at most." For one whose sense of self is sufficiently strong to withstand the pressure, it is less of a problem. But for one who is easily made guilty and who values acceptance over self-validation, depression is a common consequence. Bending one's self into pretzel proportions in order to fit another person's expectations is a reliable path to depression, for as soon as one's self-image rests in the hands of another, one ceases to be an individual, with all that the term implies.

Consider the case of a young man in his mid-20s who had been quite depressed for nearly a year prior to this author's seeing him. He was out of work, living off the generosity of friends, and complained that he was not motivated to work himself out of his predicament. At his mother's insistence, he had attended a seminary throughout his adolescent years, with the goal of eventually becoming a priest. In his very religious family headed by the widowed mother, the sense of obligation to meet mother's expectations was quite intense. At age 20, he found that he could no longer accept the idea of devoting his life to the priesthood, and he left the seminary. This did not come about easily. The emotional turbulence, the guilt, and the anxiety were considerable. In sorting out his situation, the bind he was in was apparent. He was not living "properly," having disappointed his mother as well as himself. He could not approve of his own actions when she was so disapproving, and for as long as he bought into the idea that the right way to live necessarily involved making his mother happy, he was trapped in a most depressing circumstance. Therapy involved the building of an awareness for individual differences and the recognition that there are *many* "right" ways to live.

D8 | Valid Lifestyles

Instructed to list "Valid Lifestyles," according to *his* criteria, this client was also required to list next to each what specific groups of people would undoubtedly disapprove of that lifestyle. This structured activity led to intense discussion of the need to self-validate a lifestyle of his own choosing. By recognizing that what is valid to one individual is not valid to the next, he found it easier to accept the responsibility of making choices in his own behalf and all the consequences that go with such a responsibility. (This directive is described in clinical context in Case 4 of Appendix B.)

Other Beliefs

There are many belief systems that can rigidly entrench someone in a dysfunctional pattern. The above three beliefs are discussed with case examples of their manifestations in order to clarify the relationship between rigid belief systems and depression. "I shouldn't have to ask for help," "All things are purposeful," "A commitment is a commitment and must be strictly adhered to no matter what," and many other such commonly held beliefs all have a capacity to painfully restrict the range of individual choices available.

Beliefs establish expectations. Once one expects something to occur in a particular way or expects someone to respond in a certain way, one faces the inevitability of disappointment. Since ideal responses from other people or from the universe are less than routine, disappointment and frustration are likely. So what's the "logical" way to prevent disappointment? Exert *lots* of pressure on the person or the situation in an effort to make the desired outcome occur. What's the problem? The person exerts lots of pressure to make something happen but the outcome is objectively controlled by factors beyond the range of his or her influence. This pattern is so common among depressives that it constitutes a major theme of this book. Flexibility develops when expectations are less prominent and the ability to manage the spontaneous direction of events is enhanced.

BELIEFS AND RESISTANCE TO THERAPY

As values and beliefs restrict one's range of choices according to the limits of what one can and cannot do, it is apparent how one may also develop a diminishing range of experiences upon which to draw. When one's resources are of a limited nature for whatever reason (e.g., physical or mental limitations, impoverished social environment, a history of trauma), the types and qualities of experiences appropriate for managing the demands of life are obviously less than optimal. Thus, the very thought, feeling, or behavior that would be the best (i.e., most adaptive) response for an individual to display in a given context is simply not a part of the person's repertoire. Somehow this simple point seems to elude practitioners treating depressed clients. Such clients are told to "seek alternatives," but they don't know how to. Such clients are told to "get in touch with their anger," but it is a feeling long devalued and is unavailable. More examples are really unnecessary to reiterate the point that *telling a client what to do does not enable him or her to do it.* If the client does not have the potentially beneficial response available as a direct result of experience found in his or her personal history, the clinician cannot expect the client to demonstrate such a response. Indeed, more frustration ensues as the client discovers he or she cannot do as directed, despite no overt obstacles. What is generally called "resistance" frequently occurs when the client does not have the experiential frame of reference from which to generate the more adaptive response asked for by the clinician. Expecting someone with a history of impulsiveness to respond to the directive to "take time and think before you act" is absurd. Thinking before acting is exactly the kind of experience such a person lacks.

This view of resistance suggests a different response in the clinician. Adopting the perspective that resistance may be a communication from the client about his or her limits of capability allows the clinician to accept such a communication as readily as any other. If an approach does not generate the desired response from the client, the clinician can break the goal into even smaller components for the client to experience.

The clinician must be careful to give assignments that fall within the client's ability to experience success. Failure to carry out or satisfactorily complete a task can increase the client's experience of depression.

A particularly common basis for what is perceived as resistance is, in fact, related to the pattern of "global thinking," first discussed in Chapter 4. To the depressed person, his or her problems often seem overwhelming because all the issues are dealt with collectively (globally) rather than individually. The astute clinician will recognize that the need to break problems into manageable components is a skill the client lacks, and will model and facilitate such patterns through the experience of the therapy. The emphasis is on *experience,* the kind that is a different and more flexible frame of reference from which to respond.

BUILDING A BASIS FOR EVOLVING FLEXIBILITY

In the previous discussion, personal values and the beliefs and expectations derived from them have been stressed as pivotal in determining the range of one's capabilities. When one's value system fosters a rigid, stereotypical way of responding to life's demands, the ability to problem solve effectively through the discovery of solutions beyond the usual boundaries of thought and perception is diminished. It has also been stressed that the building through experience of a new, more adaptive frame of reference is a strong basis for meaningful change.

In the case of the depressed individual, any impairments in problem-solving capabilities will surface in one way or another either as an apparent inability to adapt to the reality of an ongoing situation or to change with changing times. In the former situation, the individual will either seem "stuck," or will be seen fighting a battle that cannot be won, i.e., trying to exert control over something or someone beyond the person's sphere of influence. In the latter situation, the individual will be seen as ignoring or minimizing feedback suggesting adjustments, effectively isolating him- or herself until the situation has reached a danger point that precipitates the crisis that often is the starting point of therapy.

The goals in facilitating flexibility include: 1) encouraging a variety of ways to view a particular event; 2) teaching a variety of problem-solving capabilities, or at least how to take advantage of others' capabilities instead of getting and staying "stuck"; and 3) facilitating the individual's discovery of that critical point where one must let go of what has been and move forward with what can be. Furthermore, the person must have access to the ability to be active in his or her own behalf at that critical moment, taking the step forward. This goal in particular has the greatest capability of prevention of later depressive episodes. Obviously, the stress of everyday living that can trigger depressive episodes can never be fully prevented, but certainly one can develop the sensitivity to one's feelings and to situational cues in order to know when to steer clear of potentially harmful situations.

Basically, the issue here is one of "letting go." In order to take a step forward in one's own behalf, one must also be willing to leave something behind. They are indivisible complementary sides of the coin of change. Values about stability and commitment, fear of the unfamiliar, fear of success, fear of failure, secondary gain issues, and a host of other explanations have surfaced as reasons for why people, even those in pain, might drag their feet in moving on. Each explanation has potential value in considering what may be inhibiting a particular individual, but ultimately, regardless of reason, the challenge is moving forward.

When do people "let go"? Under what circumstances will people move forward despite the anxiety or fear regarding the potential outcome(s)?

For some, external pressures force their hand, so to speak, and there is no choice but to adapt (e.g., when your family moves during your childhood years). For others, moving forward is a fluid movement based on the recognition (consciously or unconsciously) that a better, more adaptive alternative has become available. For still others, having to move forward or to let go is fought in desperate hand-to-hand combat, and change is not likely to occur until the person has attained a state of acceptance that there are no other alternatives. If, for example, we consider again the "where there's a will" belief, the holder of that belief will hold on and on despite repeated failing attempts at some overt or covert goal (like trying to change somebody or trying to maintain a status quo in some arena).

The latter scenario is undoubtedly the most common one in the treatment of depressed individuals. The example of the depressed mother with a schizophrenic son described earlier in this chapter is one that can illustrate the point about accepting a lack of alternatives as a basis for letting go. When this client described in detail the many psychiatrists, psychologists, social workers, residential treatment facilities, and day treatment programs she had approached in an effort to get help for her son, it was obvious how invested she was in the "where there's a will, there's a way" belief system. There was no need to challenge it. Rather, the author simply asked how she would know when the problem's complexity exceeded the capacity of the mental health system to deal with it. This was a simple reframing. Furthermore, she was asked how she would know when she had expended enough effort and when it would be all right to acknowledge that it was time to adopt a different way of dealing with the situation besides maintaining the aura of debilitating desperation. Simple as this may sound here, she had never given much thought to these types of questions. She had not defined where the point was to let go, and thus could not recognize one even if it loomed right in front of her. She was simply encouraged to begin to define a point for herself where she would know on *all* dimensions within her that she had done what she could and could do no more. With that frame of mind established, a paradoxical prescription of consulting 100 of "these type" therapists and another 100 of "those type" therapists catalyzed an awareness of the too high price for doing so, and the transformation rapidly followed. She concluded that she had done what she could and that the demand exceeded her supply. Again, her caring for her son was not diminished; rather, it was tempered with a more realistic recognition of the upper limits of her capacities in dealing with him. Furthermore, the need to establish, recognize, and protect her *own* limits was modeled through the therapy.

Metaphors for Facilitating "Letting Go"

The ability of metaphors, or anecdotes, to impart perspective and build an identification has been well described in the literature (Lankton & Lankton, 1983; Rosen, 1982; Zeig, 1980a). At the early stage of treatment in which facilitating flexibility is considered a preliminary goal preceding interventions more specifically focused on the client's individual issues, metaphors may be used to build a momentum of acceptance of ideas and tactics relating to flexibility and the inevitability of change. Such metaphors may be structured in at least two ways: those involving universal transitions, and those involving transitions unique to that particular client taken from his or her own personal history.

D9   Universal Transitions

Metaphors that involve "Universal Transitions" essentially describe changes that have occurred in some arena that is of interest to the individual. Perhaps technological changes can be described in terms of forward progress made and the often unseen costs for doing so, or maybe historical or social changes will be more impactful; but one can use whatever is most likely to appeal to the client on the basis of the clinician's knowledge of him or her. For example, one such metaphor might include the following ideas:

> Now I don't know if you have ever really considered this before . . . but you can now . . . because there's something very important to

know . . . that every bit of progress has a payoff and a price . . . and yet staying the same has a price . . . *if that were even possible* . . . but the forward movement of changes in the world has made for some wonderful possibilities . . . things you take for granted that you don't consider the implications of . . . but if you consider technology, for example, you really can see that *change is a wonderful thing that opens up many new possibilities* . . . and the cost gets lost in the shuffle . . . and when you fly in an airplane . . . the ability to travel great distances quickly is possible . . . but the clouds smell of gasoline . . . and when you use the telephone, you can share information rapidly and conveniently . . . but you give up some privacy . . . and when you drive in your car, you can get where you want to go at times of your own choosing . . . but the roads get jammed and the expense can be considerable . . . and when a *change promises greater benefits* than the costs . . . like the *changes you'll be experiencing* that you can't even predict just yet . . . *you'll grow quite comfortable* with the knowledge that *moving forward in any area has a payoff* . . . and a price . . . and your suffering has been enough of a price . . . why not *enjoy the payoff?*

In the above metaphor, the client is indirectly encouraged to think about the fact that change is inevitable, and that when the focus is on the value of the payoff rather than on exaggerating the cost, change can be tolerable at least, enjoyable at most. (This directive is described in clinical context in Cases 1 and 3 in Appendix B.)

D10 Personal Transitions

Metaphors of "Personal Transitions" that involve describing transitions derived from the unique personal history of the client will certainly have a greater emotional significance to the client. In the course of the clinical interview, information can be gathered about specific changes the client has undergone, both successfully and otherwise. The clinician can evolve an awareness for circumstances in which the client has acknowledged change, how it came about (i.e., through active or reactive mechanisms), and how it was integrated. (This directive is described in clinical context in Cases 1 and 3 in Appendix B.) Such personal anecdotes can then be woven together in a metaphor that highlights the person's strengths as capabilities that may be appropriately used in currently desired changes. Such a metaphor might be structured as follows:

Perhaps you'll remember describing to me the moves your family made as you were growing up . . . how you frequently found yourself having to adjust to new people, new places . . . and it's certainly unsettling in every sense of the word to have to move . . . and it's certainly exciting to want to move . . . to consider what lies beyond what one already knows that can be wonderful to experience . . . and each time you moved . . . and discovered new friends . . . and new places to play . . . and new ways to enjoy yourself . . . you gained something important . . . and what a wonderful opportunity . . . to move and find out you can adjust . . . and grow . . . anywhere you are . . . because of your ability to move on . . . and add to what you already have as parts of you . . . that you sometimes forget are even there . . . like the parts that know how to explore . . . and the parts that know how to enjoy new experiences . . . that you've already relied on so many times in your lifetime. . . .

Dialoguing with the client at this point about specific experiences brought up by the metaphor allows the clinician to expand on particular learnings and extend them into current circumstances as resources to be used in the service of change. Such dialoguing can be most dramatic at times, at once amplifying strengths and weaknesses while providing opportunities for packing one's psychological bags and doing some traveling.

Letting Go: Extending Levels

Sometimes a viable tool in facilitating "letting go" is the use of symbolic tasks that make the point on a "safer" (i.e., not particularly emotionally charged) level of experience. Once made, the clinician can make use of suggestions that infer that the learnings acquired on one dimension can be extended to other dimensions of experience as well, setting up a chain reaction of sorts eventually impacting the necessary dimension(s).

D11   Buy It and Throw It Away

A strategy of "Buy It and Throw It Away" may be used with clients. This strategy involves giving the directive that the client is to go out and buy something inexpensive, hold on to it for a short while (as little as a few hours), and then destroy it and throw it away. To direct someone to acquire something with the intention of rapid abandonment provides an experience that illustrates certain important points, including: something can be of importance for a very limited period of time and can then be discarded, something need not last forever in order to have value, and one need not get too personally invested in something because, in essence, "nothing is forever."

D12   Pack Rat

Similarly structured and especially designed for the "Pack Rat" type, the client may be directed to get into the garage, basement, or attic for a limited period of time each day that is to be designated as a "holding on and letting go" time. Specifically, clients are directed to find objects from their accumulations that can be discarded (either donated or thrown away).

D13   Moving

This directive can be a powerful one, especially in conjunction with metaphors about the experience of "moving"—how one must look through all one's possessions as one packs, deciding which accumulated things are no longer meaningful as they once were and are now simply "junk," and which things continue to have meaning and are worth keeping. The metaphor's emphasis is on the changes in feeling over time of what is valuable and what one has outgrown. This can seed the idea that what matters to one is subject to changes in perception and experience, again emphasizing the inevitability and acceptance of change. The "all or nothing" thinking that is a common cognitive distortion of depressives is chipped away through experiences on one dimension that can be extended to other dimensions over time. (This directive is described in clinical context in Case 4 in Appendix B.)

Discovering Diversity

Tom Robbins, in his novel *Even Cowgirls Get the Blues* (1976), made a statement to the effect that perhaps success isn't all it's cracked up to be. Robbins pointed out that when one attempts something and succeeds, one assumes that one has found the "right" way to do it. Failure, he suggests, may ultimately be more instructive because of its inherent demand to keep exploring alternatives. Finding a path to diversity of thought is difficult for anyone to attain given the patterning of the mind, yet some individuals are clearly more creative and expansive in their thoughts than others. For the depressed person in particular, who is often prone to dichotomous thinking and other distorted cognitive patterns (Beck, 1983; Burns, 1980), the need to develop an awareness for the gray nature of the world, instead of a black and white version, is often basic to treatment.

D14   A Day at the Zoo

One multidimensional directive that is nonthreatening and enjoyable to follow involves having the client spend "A Day at the Zoo." Specifically, the client is instructed to go to the zoo armed with pen and paper to take detailed notes on the diverse ways in which animals have evolved physiological and behavioral mechanisms for adapting to the demands of their native environments. The brilliant strategies that nature has developed for maintaining balance can provide some fascinating examples of the way the universe truly operates. The animals are especially adapted to a particular habitat, and through ongoing evolution their adaptive mechanisms have the capacity to both help and hurt. For as long as the habitat remains constant, the animal can thrive. If the habitat undergoes significant changes, the animal's adaptive capabilities are put to the test. At this critical point the animal will literally either adapt or die. Talking about the many endangered species and how they became endangered offers a prime opportunity to communicate indirectly about the life-sustaining capabilities that refined adaptational mechanisms provide. There are strong parallels between what occurs in nature and the dilemmas that occur during the course of a human being's lifetime.

It is a little known fact that the plant collection at the San Diego Zoo is monetarily worth considerably more than the animal collection. Plants, too, have the ability to offer metaphorical communications about the potential hazards of rooting in a changing or unstable environment. One can expand upon the points about adaptation by pointing out in metaphor how humans have come to thrive on the planet because of their ability to adapt to diverse climates and conditions. The implicit message is that adaptation is critical to survival and that the capability to adapt is inherently human. Identifying this resource is a necessary step before accessing and using it. (This directive is described in clinical context in Cases 2 and 4 in Appendix B.)

D15   Polling Ploy

Another strategy for facilitating the discovery of diverse ways of thinking is the "Polling Ploy." In this strategy, the client is directed to "conduct a scientific investigation" in which others are asked, in a neutral manner, to describe their positions and rationales on issues of personal importance to the client. The client is directed to create a questionnaire or compose interview questions that provide a structure for such interactions, and to utilize the instrument with familiar or unfamiliar others, depending on which is likely to have greater impact. The inevitable discovery is that individuals can have virtually opposite opinions on an issue and yet each have a rationale or justification that is sound. Each rationale the client is exposed to offers the possibility of a "reframing," and further demonstrates that there are many "right" ways to think about an issue. Dichotomous thinking can thus be minimized, and a greater diversity and depth of thinking on an issue may be facilitated. (This directive is described in clinical context in Case 1 of Appendix B.)

D16 Viewpoints

If the client, for whatever reason, is not willing or able to conduct such a poll as described above, an alternative strategy is to have the client take a variety of social issues, order them in a hierarchy of emotional investment from personally apathetic to emotionally charged, and write out at length at least two (more, if possible) "Viewpoints" on that particular issue. Furthermore, the client is to generate at least half a dozen arguments in support of each of the different viewpoints. It may require research in one form or another in order to carry out this task effectively, but the client certainly has ample opportunity to discover adequate support for differing views on an issue, to derive confirmation of the validity of his or her own views, and to entertain perspectives previously overlooked or trivialized. The net effect is to begin to build greater acceptance for what is, rather than unrealistically and depressogenically striving for what cannot be.

One cognitively based rigidity common among depressives is what Beck (1983) has described as "negative interpretation." Events in the individual's life are interpreted according to a negative framework, so that in almost anything the client experiences, however neutral or positive, the conclusion is a negative one that serves as a fuel for depression. (This directive is described in clinical context in Case 1 of Appendix B.)

D17 A Variety of Interpretations

In order to build some flexibility into the individual's interpretive style, the client can be directed to generate "A Variety of Interpretations" for ongoing daily events, with a specified number of interpretations to be positive, neutral, and negative according to the clinician's directive. Generally, the author will require at least three positive and three neutral interpretations for every negative one. Initially, this strategy is best used with routine experiences that carry little or no emotional charge (i.e., why the grocery clerk short-changed him or her) for the individual. When the client has become practiced with quickly generating "A Variety of Interpretations" for an event, it becomes more difficult to rigidly lock into only the negative one. A variation of this strategy was previously discussed in the context of the belief that "all things happen for a reason."

Systems theorists have written extensively on the presence of rule-governed patterns that maintain the system. The "homeostasis" or stability of the system is a consequence that can only be derived from patterns of interaction that allow for and utilize continuous feedback and adjustment in a rule-bound manner. The rules may be clearly identifiable and known to all members of the system, called "overt rules." Or, the rules may be hidden, known only to some or only in degrees to others, called "covert rules." Some family therapists have described the process of therapy as making covert rules overt, making the processes of feedback and adjustment of the system more efficient. (This directive is described in clinical context in Case 4 of Appendix B.)

D18   Identify the Rules

In consideration of this aspect of rigidity, a directive for the client to "Identify the Rules," both overt and covert, of the systems and subsystems associated with his or her depression can be useful. Specifically, the client is encouraged to think in terms of what the rules are that dictate what is and is not possible in responding to personal issues (if the depression seems more of an intrapersonal experience) or in significant interpersonal relationships (if the interpersonal dynamics seem significant in the depression's etiology). The client is first encouraged to think about rules in other contexts, such as rules dictating interactions in his or her family of origin (e.g., "Never criticize mom's cooking," "Always be home on time") or rules governing interactions at work (e.g., "Always make the boss think the new ideas were his or her own"). (This directive is described in clinical context in Case 2 of Appendix B.)

D19   Rule Breaking

When the client has become adept at identifying rules governing interactions, the client can then move into the more impactful and experiential phase of *identifying and acting out* "Rule Breaking" (and therefore liberating) patterns. The client is encouraged to identify the rule, identify behaviors consistent with that rule, and identify behaviors inconsistent with that rule. If the client identifies the rule as "be agree-able," for example, he or she can describe diplomatic patterns in use and go on to describe confrontive or even aggressive patterns and contexts in which to appropriately use them. Directed to act them out, in small steps and in safe contexts in which to experiment, the client can be slowly shaped into a more expansive range of possible behaviors.

This pattern may be of special significance for clinicians. Psychother-apy as an art and science has evolved some fairly rigid rules about what is and what is not appropriate for a clinician to do. Obviously, some of these rules are absolutely vital to the well-being and progress of the client, yet others are virtually arbitrary rules established within a partic-ular school of therapy that are vestiges of the past. Rules that suggest a clinician must always be supportive of the client, must always attempt to put the client at ease, and so forth are not rules that allow for other potentially therapeutic possibilities. Clinicians who believe in the need to always provide support for clients, for example, will be likely to experience difficulty in using confrontation even when it is indicated. Certainly the provocative, rule-breaking, yet effective strategies of clini-cians like Milton Erickson provide strong suggestions for the growth that can occur when rules are identified and deliberately disrupted.

As a final dimension for consideration on the subject of flexibility, the mechanism(s) an individual uses to solve problems is obviously of primary importance. The client becomes "stuck" in some way when the problem's complexity (or emotional significance) exceeds the client's capacity to deal with it effectively. The person may be a wonderfully skilled problem solver in other areas, but experiences partial or total blockage in the face of the depressogenic circumstances. Likewise, it is also possible that the person is a notoriously poor problem solver, unable to break the global requirements into component steps, or per-haps unable to effectively gather information or tap information sources appropriately.

D20 A Flow of Steps

When the clinician encounters the client's inability to problem solve effectively, the opportunity to both solve a problem and teach a problem-solving skill arises. Beginning with a general goal, the appropriateness and meaningfulness of the goal can be defined. The clinician can then direct the client to carry out the task of breaking routine behaviors of a goal-oriented nature (e.g., taking a shower) into its component parts (turning on the water, stepping into the shower, getting wet, and so forth). For the global thinker so often seen in cases of depression, developing "A Flow of Steps" toward a goal is precisely what has been a barrier to success. I am often struck by how frequently a client will say "I just want to be happy." If I ask what that means, or what "happy" looks or feels like, or what would bring it about, the response is usually one of an impatient stare at me as if to say, "Are you brain damaged or what? Don't you know what happy is?" Of course I do, but that is not going to help that client whose goal is so global and has no sequence of steps identified yet that can bring about the goal. Directing the client to identify steps in routine activities builds a framework for thinking about goal-directedness and sequencing appropriate steps to catalyze accomplishment. Building a variety of flow charts of different kinds of problem solving strategies (some utilizing logic, some gut feelings, some professionals' opinions, etc.) for different kinds of problems lets the client discover that he or she does not always have to know the answer, just where to get the necessary information or assistance in order to be able to move forward.

SUMMARY

A variety of ideas and strategies for overcoming the rigid patterns that frequently underlie depression have been described throughout this chapter. The general goal of facilitating flexibility is one that continues on throughout the therapy, with the clinician continually imparting the message that change is possible when new patterns evolve to deal with the demands one faces. Perhaps the most important reason for focusing one phase of treatment on the goal of facilitating flexibility is for the momentum of creativity it builds. As one's creative abilities are tapped through exposure to new experiences such as those in the directives discussed in this chapter, shifts in perception and emotional states are inevitable.

There is an old saying that offers a final point here: "Give a man a fish and you've given him a meal. Teach him how to fish, and you've given him a livelihood."

8

In and Out
of Control

The issue of control has directly and indirectly been described at various times throughout the preceding chapters as a potentially major issue in the etiology of depression. In this author's experience it is *the* major issue to address, although it is unlikely to be the only issue of concern. This chapter presents a more focused look at the many dimensions of control as a primary factor in the depressed person's life.

THE NEED FOR CONTROL

It may seem trite, but it is nonetheless true that human beings require a sense of control over their experience. Outgrowths of this need are manifested in countless examples. For instance, the highly valued religious beliefs for which people live and die are clearly attempts to bring the mysteries of the unknown (e.g., afterlife, the origin of the universe) within their grasp, giving them the illusion of some control as long as they live "properly" and commit to the proper deity. The old saying "There are no atheists in foxholes" exemplifies the principle that those who believe their lives are out of their control look for someone or something to take control (through prayer and bargaining) and make the impending threat go away. Even fatal accidents can be reframed as evidence of "God's will," providing comfort that there is a "plan," that things are in control. The possibility that experience may simply be random is much too threatening for many. People tend to hold on most tenaciously to beliefs that create meaning and help them maintain the illusions of control.

The fact that every system, whether governmental or family, whether large or small, has a set of rules that dictate the quantity and quality of interactions is a clear indication of human beings' recognition of the need for control in their dealings. At the level of the individual, the forces shaping one's perceptions of control are in existence and are operating continuously from the moment of birth. The process of socialization, an interpersonal process, is solely responsible for the evolution of one's relationship (however functional or dysfunctional) to one's sense of power. If one considers the learning history of the individual, one can find literally dozens of examples from every single day of the person's life where messages were received and integrated concerning power. Did mom and dad respond every time the infant cried? Did mom and dad encourage open exploration of their child's world or stifle such exploration in an atmosphere of overprotection? Did mom or dad lay out the child's clothes to wear to school each day, or could the child choose what to wear for himself? Did mom and dad encourage pursuing individual interests or were recreational or extracurricular learnings prescribed? Were mom and dad arbitrary in their moods and reactions or was there a high degree of consistency in how the child could relate to them? Was there even a mom and dad together in the home?

Each of these questions, and thousands more just like them, generate responses that indicate either one's need to react to others or one's ability to act on one's own needs or preferences. Both styles can lead to a distorted sense of personal power when distorted conclusions are drawn from significant interactions with the key agents of one's socialization (parents, siblings, teachers, etc.).

The need for control is the framework for "personal power." Power is generally defined as the capacity to influence: When one attempts to influence *anything,* one is attempting to exert control. Thus, one cannot exist without the other. For human beings to want to assert power and establish control are hardly a pathological phenomenon. Wanting and having control are fundamental to survival on all levels and so must be considered a basic and vital dimension of one's humanness. For some, it is an overwhelmingly powerful need, while for others it is weak and diffuse. It is evident in varying degrees in all people, however, The problem arises when one's patterns or methodologies for attaining or using power are inefficient at least, or are outright destructive at most.

THE EVOLUTION OF FAULTY PATTERNS
FOR ESTABLISHING CONTROL

In describing control as a basic dimension of people shaped through the specifics of an individual's particular socialization history, it can be useful to consider how the individual may evolve patterns that may manifest in clinical depression. Various psychosocial models of depression offer specific insights on this issue. The cognitive model suggests faulty thinking patterns are learned, probably on the basis of receiving distorted feedback from others, as well as from learning faulty problem-solving strategies. Interpersonal approaches emphasize the effect of social modeling and dysfunctional interactional patterns on the development of faulty relationship skills. The "learned helplessness" model suggests that one is exposed to random and aversive experiences that lead to an overgeneralization of one's inability to respond effectively. The behavioral model suggests one is intentionally or unintentionally reinforced for depressive behavior and ineffective patterns of life management. The psychodynamic model suggests the use of defensive mechanisms to redirect inwardly one's anger and sense of loss.

Regardless of a clinician's preferred model for explaining the evolution of distorted perceptions regarding control, clearly distorted feedback from others, and incorrect generalizations or conclusions from experience are the key elements in depression. If one examines each of the models and their presuppositions, the way each reflects a distorted sense of control can become quite apparent. For example, the cognitive distortions identified by Beck (1973, 1983) and Burns (1980) can each directly or indirectly be tied into the issue of control. For instance, "all-or-nothing thinking" is a pattern of overcontrol. Consider a statement such as "I'll never fall in love again," hardly an uncommon theme these days. The extreme nature of the statement reflects a polarization of thought (a dichotomous style of thinking that is one of Beck's cognitive distortions) and is a statement indicating that the person feels out of control in managing intimate relationships. Instead of establishing a more realistic goal of being able to better identify suitable relationship partners and build better relationship skills, the individual takes a "one size fits all" approach and employs the overgeneralization (which is another one of Beck's cognitive distortions) that all members of the opposite sex cannot be trusted in the context of a loving relationship.

Given the need for control in all people to one degree or another, it is not at all surprising to discover that compulsive patterns are often related to depression. Compulsive patterns are by their very nature attempts to control anxiety, fear, doubt, and of course, depression, through establishing a repetitive and even ritualistic way of managing aspects of one's experience.

Consider some common patterns of the compulsive personality. Such individuals are characterized as being highly moralistic and judgmental, excessively preoccupied with rules and protocol, and emotionally distant. Why the preoccupation with rules and judgments? The tendency to feel out of control (and thus anxious, afraid, doubtful, and depressed) is very strong if every detail of every experience that life has to offer is not covered in the rulebook. The rigidity of such patterns is well described in the literature on personality disorders, and although the majority of depressed individuals are not personality disordered, the tendency toward compulsiveness is quite common. When a person requires or expects others to follow his or her rules, he or she is inevitably disappointed, angry, and hurt when they do not. When a person adheres to a rigid rule system for managing the unpredictable and often difficult things that are a part of life, the ability to adapt flexibly as times and rules change is underdeveloped. It is these types of rigidities, as well as others described in the remaining chapters, that can get and keep depressions going.

The above discussion of rules to guide one's choices is quite closely related to the discussion in Chapter 7 on values, particularly those values that impair one's ability to respond in the most useful of ways. Faulty learnings about control (i.e., learnings that inhibit one's ability to recognize the best response in a given context) are often unwittingly encouraged by various socialization agents. Religious teachings—a profound influence on people's values and perceptions—promote such learnings as "Judge not, lest ye be judged." To encourage people to be accepting and trusting of all others is to consider all people as acceptable and trustworthy. Given the number of robbers, murderers, rapists, con men, and other hurtful people, teaching people to be anything but selective and critical in their evaluations of others is a disservice. Even a humane teaching such as "The Golden Rule" is a nice principle, but may be unrealistic and potentially harmful. Being nice to someone does not necessarily mean he or she will be nice in return. The world is not so unfair as to require ongoing paranoia, but neither should we disarm people's critical faculties in assessing who is and who is not trustworthy.

The point of the above discussion is that the values and perspectives one evolves can lead to rigid patterns that ultimately prove destructive to the individual. The author is frequently astonished to find out how naively some clients have dealt with other people or with personal issues, using some flowery phrase as the rationale for their responses. When they discover that others are playing by different sets of rules, they end up in the kind of pain that leads them to seek therapy.

D21   Me Mapping

Given the involvement of early learnings about control, power, responsibility, and other issues central to depression, it can be a useful assignment to have the client identify his or her values that underlie the range of choices likely to be perceived by him or her. This exercise is called "Me Mapping." The client can be encouraged to form a list of specific personal and social issues, such as power, responsibility, prejudice, capital punishment, and abortion. The longer the list and the more specific it is about personal belief characteristics, the better. Alongside each issue can be made a continuum that has at either extreme the opposing viewpoints of that particular issue. For example, on the issue of "control," one could establish a continuum that has a "high need for control" at one pole and a "low need for control" at the other. The client is then directed to identify a point on each continuum that is indicative of the position of various "significant others" in his or her life. Thus, the client is required to think about the positions of each of the people that played a significant role in his or her development. The client can consciously discover how readily such positions can be identified or likewise may discover that their positions are unknown. Either outcome provides for interesting and useful discoveries.

In the next step, the client is asked to identify a specific spot on each continuum that represents his or her position on the issue. The client is able to validate his or her own positions and contrast them with those of significant others. Where values overlap and where they diverge can be a significant discovery. In the next step, the client can be asked to map out *specific* behaviors in which he would engage if he were to "live" that particular value. Last, the client can be asked to identify behaviors in which he would not engage if he were to hold that identified value. This exercise is most valuable for stimulating recognition of the need to know and operate consistently on the basis of one's personal values. The preventative opportunities to avoid situations where one might compromise oneself is an added benefit to this strategy.

The clinician has the opportunity at various points in the intervention to identify the values and beliefs of the client relative to control and power. Of particular interest are those values and beliefs that strip one of the recognition that one can meaningfully influence one's own responses to a situation. (This directive is described in clinical context in Cases 2 and 4 of Appendix B.)

AMBIGUITY REGARDING CONTROL

Given the vital nature of control as a sort of glue that holds one's life choices together, it may be readily apparent why distortions about control can have such a profound impact on the quality of one's life. Confusion about control takes one of two forms: either the individual tends to undercontrol situations or the person tends to overcontrol situations.

The individual who undercontrols situations is the person in the helpless "victim" mind set. When opportunities arise in which the individual could act in a specific way in order to favorably influence the outcome of a situation or escape a hazard, he or she does not act. The experiments of Martin Seligman (1973, 1974, 1983) in which subjects evolved a passive, helpless response to controllable circumstances represents this situation well. In those experiments, Seligman exposed subjects to aversive, uncontrollable stimuli. Regardless of any attempt made to escape the aversive stimulus, escape was not possible. Later, when escape or avoidance was possible, subjects made no attempt to escape, operating on the previously established, yet now false belief that no effort to escape could succeed. Seligman termed this phenomenon "learned helplessness."

The individual who overcontrols situations will attempt to exert control over situations that are, in fact, beyond the range of his or her influence. For such individuals, there is a blurring of the lines between hope and reality. The individual may know what he or she wants and will attempt to attain it, only to become increasingly stressed and depressed as the goal slips further and further away. By interpreting the inability to attain the goal as evidence of personal failure rather than as having attempted to reach a goal outside the sphere of one's influence, depression is a predictable consequence.

One of the diagnostic categories described in Chapter 4 is the "master-victim" category. Typically, the depressed person is prone to the victim mind set, but it is also true that many individuals who are quite masterful in their lives are prone to depression. When one is used to getting what one wants and is generally successful as a problem solver, the illusion (overgeneralization) can be created that all problems can be solved and that all goals are attainable. Many highly competent and well respected individuals become depressed on this basis. One example is the "high achiever" who accomplishes many respected and acclaimed tasks, yet who suffers depression as he or she gets caught in the trap of his or her own value: Worth equals achievement (i.e., "You're only as good as what you do, not just by being who you are"). This is why the high achiever can accomplish something quite significant but can feel good about it for only a short period of time, if at all. The emphasis is on "doing," not being valuable for simply "being." It is, at best, a conditional love acceptance, and while it may lead to a high level mastery over one's life, it also leads to the emptiness and pain of depression. One recent popular book, *The Imposter Phenomenon* (Clance, 1985), approached this subject from a different angle, identifying the high percentage of high achievers who cannot accept their own level of mastery, considering themselves skilled imposters, but imposters nonetheless. The consequences are self-doubt, anxiety, depression, and a feeling of not deserving the level of recognition and appreciation attained.

No one can be a victim or a master *everywhere,* and so it is important for the clinician to identify and utilize as learning opportunities those situations in which the person is unclear about what is and what is not controllable. The clinician can simultaneously assess how generalized (i.e., pervasive) the tendencies toward mastery or victimization are in the individual, an important factor in how direct or indirect treatment should be, and how long therapy is likely to take.

Using many of the diagnostic categories described in Chapter 4, the undercontrolling (victim) type of individual seems likely to display the following patterns: global, other-directed, open, enmeshed, people oriented, extrapunitive, ambiguous about personal values and personal worth, highly reactive, past oriented, and low in ability to compartmentalize.

The overcontrolling individual, i.e., one who attempts to control others or things beyond his or her sphere of influence, can be described as having these characteristics: excessive guilt, intrapunitive, concrete, internal locus of control, enmeshed, linear, and task oriented.

In the above patterns commonly found among depressed individuals, the establishment of and responsiveness to complementary parts (i.e., capabilities) is basic to the treatment.

PRESENTING PROBLEMS TYPICAL OF
AMBIGUITY REGARDING CONTROL

The above characterological descriptions of individuals ambiguous in one direction or another regarding control are general descriptions. Some case descriptions that are typical of individuals presenting problems of depression demonstrating distorted perceptions about control are presented in this section.

Undercontrol: Case 1

Jenny was a 36-year-old woman who worked at a university in a capacity that brought her into close contact with the students. Jenny sought therapy for depression, anxiety, and poor self-esteem, which she reported had been ongoing for more than five years. She tied it to her divorce, which came painfully slowly after she had worked very hard at trying to make her marriage work. Jenny described her inability to "let go" of people or things to which she was attached. She cited as evidence her holding onto a job she did not like and in which she felt unappreciated, her inability to think of her ex-husband as an "ex" husband, and her current conflicts about a romantic relationship with a foreign student who was studying under a temporary student's permit. He had full intentions of eventually returning to his native country to marry and had openly said so. Despite his openness about his intentions, Jenny was hopeful that he would change his mind and stay with her for evermore.

Jenny had open opportunities to find a new job and date others. Rather than masterfully control the two situations that were most painful to her, Jenny was letting things deteriorate further at work and was making more demands of a man who would no doubt reach his limit with her and eventually leave. Jenny's victim mind set was leaving her depressed and with no sense of ability to make choices in her own behalf. Her fantasies were that by staying in her current job and by escalating the pressure on her romantic interest, she would eventually be appreciated and loved. These are the fantasies of a victim hoping for a rescue.

Undercontrol: Case 2

Jim was a 26-year-old male who presented the symptoms of depression, excessive guilt, poor relationships with women, and poor self-esteem (this case was first described in Chapter 7, pp. 87–88). His demeanor alternated between angry descriptions of abusive experiences he had suffered and tearful and sad self-recriminations for his passive acceptance of such experiences.

Jim described being the only male growing up in a home in which he lived with his mother and two sisters. He reported that in an interaction occurring at a young age, he questioned his mother about sex. He reported that she physically handled him in order to teach him about his body and its responses. He felt very ashamed and guilty about this as time went on and was in conflict about the double bind he felt she placed him in. He saw her as acting seductively after that episode, often making sexual remarks and innuendos, and then telling him he had a dirty mind if he responded to her. Jim spent a number of years in the seminary preparing to be a priest and, much to his mother's dismay, abandoned it, for which he felt quite guilty. He came to therapy with the intention of releasing anger, and with the hope that he could build enough self-esteem to get into a healthy relationship with a woman. He had felt abused in the few relationships he had been in—either lied to, cheated on, or manipulated for money.

Clearly, Jim saw himself as a victim of his life's experience. He felt trapped as the only male at home, double-binded by his mother, abused by women and, in general, out of control of his life and feelings. To feel so victimized by others as to find it impossible to trust *anyone* and thus live a one-dimensional existence that precluded intimacy is a tragedy.

Jim did not feel any ability to control the way interactions went, nor did he have the ability to appreciate the implications of others' patterns of responsibility (and trustworthiness). He would "lose himself" to women in particular, responding globally and noncritically, and he was often taken advantage of as a result. As a victim, Jim's self-esteem was predictably poor. A basic understanding of others' motivations and styles for dealing with various life events was lacking, thus allowing him to be easily victimized.

Overcontrol: Case 1

Chris was a 45-year-old male who sought therapy for depression, uncontrollable angry outbursts, and an agitated confusion about his future. Chris had been working as a scientist for the government for more than 20 years and had earned the recognition of his superiors and colleagues as a skilled problem solver. Much of Chris's self-esteem was tied up in the fact that when all others failed on a project, he could stay with it and work it through, much to his supervisors' delight. Recently, he had been given a project of a very sensitive and intricate nature, and although understaffed and under a seemingly unrealistic deadline, Chris accepted the challenge. It triggered an overload. Chris became intensely frustrated, then angry, then depressed with the project itself and the employers who he felt burdened him with it. He withdrew, could not concentrate, and became very angry with the organization of his department to the point of making specific recommendations for restructuring in order to make things more efficient. No one responded, apparently assuming that he was just blowing off steam in frustration and that it would be best to "ignore it and it'll go away." Chris's further attempts to get support failed and, as they did, his sense of abandonment and feelings of depression became amplified.

Chris built his own reputation of being the "miracle man" problem solver, the John Wayne of technology. Chris's values of honoring a commitment and taking on responsibility to the utmost of his capabilities were certainly noble, but if one does not have an ability to temper those values with a recognition of one's limits of tolerance, the result is clear. Chris was attempting to control the outcome of a project over which he did not have sole control. Chris was attempting to control the system of which he was only a part, and he discovered painfully that the wheel did not run the car. Recognizing limits to his abilities and sphere of influence, learning to ease off of projects not in his direct control, and learning to heed such recognitions were vital to his learning that despite his skill and intelligence, he could not control it all as he would like to.

Overcontrol: Case 2

Warren was a 43-year-old man who sought therapy shortly following a suicide attempt involving an overdose of tranquilizers. Warren's attempt followed a major disappointment at work. Warren worked for more than 20 years as an engineer in a well-known company. He was of the belief that his many years there represented a slow and steadily progressing career, but one that was unfulfilling. He had long felt that the company was not responsive to his ambitions, creative input, and loyalty. He felt that if he kept up his "beyond the call of duty" performance, he would eventually be justly rewarded for his efforts. Recently, he had completed a graduate degree in counseling psychology, indulging his long-time interest in human behavior. He had hoped and expected that completion of the degree would earn him a promotion in another department in the company, and he had received an indication that this would probably occur. When the company then hired someone else to fill the spot from outside the company, Warren's disappointment was so agonizing to him that he attempted suicide. Seen several days later, he was still very tearful and depressed, and even went so far as to bitterly blame himself for being selfish in wanting to die when his family relied on him so much. It was obvious how overresponsible Warren was, believing that he could control others' reactions to him by being a good employee, a good father, a good husband, and so forth. To attempt to control an organization in the way Warren did was almost inevitably going to lead to depression. It was Warren's assumption that ambition would be rewarded, that creativity would be appreciated, and that loyalty would be admired. In interviewing Warren, it was startling to him to hear the author ask, "Where did you get these ideas? When did you ever see that company actually respond that way to someone?" He attempted to impose his values on the company and could not cope when they responded differently than he thought they should. If he had responded to their actual style, rather than his own assumptions, he would have seen that he could not control their appreciation of him and that his creative energy might better be directed elsewhere, where it might be rewarded.

PATTERNS OF TREATMENT

Given the relationship between depression and a distorted view of what is and is not controllable, the overriding goal is to work with the client to develop a more refined awareness for first identifying when one is distorted in one's perceptions and then what to actively do to gain better perspective.

D22   **How Much Control?**

A starting point for facilitating recognition of the quality and the extent of the individual's distorted sense of control is with a structured exercise, "How Much Control?" The client is encouraged to make a list of routine interactions and events experienced in the course of daily living (e.g., discussing a social or political issue with friends, accepting or refusing a social engagement, talking with the boss about events at work, disciplining the kids). If possible, a goal is identified for each interaction or event. The client is then asked to rate on a scale of 1-10 how little or "How Much Control" he or she thinks he or she has to influence the outcome. Furthermore, the client is asked to define as well as possible *how* he or she knows what degree of control is present relative to that event. The clinician can note how easy or difficult it is for the client to recognize goals and controlling mechanisms, as well as how weak or strong the client's sense of control is in a variety of commonly encountered situations. (This directive is described in clinical context in Case 2 of Appendix B.)

Strategies for Dealing with Undercontrolling Clients

For those clients who present as being victimized by situations in which there are useful options available to actively utilize, the general goal is to build a recognition that one is *not* trapped by circumstance and that acting in one's own behalf is both feasible and desirable. In those situations where circumstances cannot be changed, the goal may be to alter one's reaction to those circumstances. Either goal implies an ability to gain a degree of mastery over one's experience. The "learned helplessness" model suggests a gradual behavioral shaping strategy in dealing with depressed individuals who show evidence of a victim mind set. Task assignments and hypnotic sessions can be utilized to motivate and facilitate the discovery of choices.

D23   **A Reasonable Chance of Success**

A session using hypnosis to build a mind set of expending energy in one's behalf because of "A Reasonable Chance of Success" might be utilized, employing direct suggestions as well as metaphors. A client in trance might be given such suggestions as:

> I knew a woman who, not unlike you, had grown up in an environment that was quite unpredictable . . . the weather was unpredict-

able . . . her dad's moods were unpredictable . . . her friends were unpredictable . . . and she learned to wait and see what would happen around her . . . before bothering to find out what was inside her, her feelings, her needs, her goals . . . and she was always wanting to go places, but felt she couldn't because she had to wait and see . . . and she was wanting to talk to her dad about her life, but felt she couldn't because she had to wait and see . . . and she wanted to do new things with her friends, but felt she couldn't because she had to wait and see . . . and by waiting and seeing, she missed lots of opportunities to *go ahead and do things* in her own best interest . . . and what would others have done if she had gone ahead? . . . I wonder if they could have adapted to her actions in a way similar to her adjusting to theirs . . . and you may want to consider what you want for yourself . . . and how valuable your needs are . . . and what you can do to meet them . . . starting with a willingness to explore the possibilities . . . that you can experience more and better things . . . which you can enjoy discovering . . . a day at a time. . . .

D24 Learned Helplessness

Using a description of the laboratory experiments by Seligman that led to his "Learned Helplessness" model (1973, 1974, 1975, 1983) in which test animals were exposed to aversive uncontrollable events can be a useful therapeutic metaphor to deliver to the client in trance:

And there's an experiment I'd like to tell you about that you may learn a lot from . . . and I wonder just how many different possibilities will occur to you about your own experience changing as you consider some laboratory dogs that were divided into two groups . . . one group of dogs was harnessed, dangling in mid-air, unable to be mobile . . . the others were unharnessed, free to run. . . . The harnessed dogs were given painful shocks, but could not escape them . . . the others were also given shock, but could run away . . . a sensible reaction to pain . . . and when the harnessed dogs were unharnessed and were again shocked, though they could now escape, they did not even try to . . . their previous experience led them to conclude they could do nothing . . . even though they really could do something . . . because now isn't then . . . and what was true then may no longer be true now . . . and you won't even know until you try . . . and I wonder whether you realize that depression clouds one's ability to discover the harness is gone . . . and there's more for you to do than you've realized . . . and you can discover your ability to develop effective ways to manage your life . . . a day at a time. . . .

While metaphors such as the above can be useful to help build receptivity to the idea of developing control, designing tasks that can be successfully accomplished can help build a positive momentum of change. Hopefully, such tasks will eventually help establish a generalization in the client's mind that he or she can not only set goals but also actively progress toward their accomplishment. As the undercontrolling client begins to learn that it is possible to be actively goal oriented, he or she also discovers that such an approach provides a sense of relief as well as self-image-enhancing feelings of mastery. The clinician can offer a great deal of support and opportunities for the client to internalize such awarenesses, continually driving home the recognition that some aspects of life previously considered uncontrollable are, in fact, controllable. As the boundaries of the client's awareness expand, great care must be taken to continually facilitate the ability to discriminate between those situations that are and those that are not subject to meaningful influence by the client.

D25 | Prescribing Depression

A paradoxical strategy that has been described in the literature (Haley, 1973; Watzlawick, 1978; Zeig, 1980b) is "Prescribing Depression." The clinician directs the client to establish a scheduled "depression time" that can allow him or her to accept the suggestion to "fully appreciate its purposeful nature." In symptom prescription strategies, the client is asked to deliberately carry out a pattern that has previously been occurring spontaneously. In directing the client to create such an experience, the clinician is thus altering the usual pattern, lifting the depression out of an intrapersonal context into an interpersonal one between clinician and client. Second, the client discovers that instead of being a victim of depression, he or she can exert some degree of control over where and when episodes occur. Third, carrying out the prescription alters the person's perceptions and feelings about depression, for trying to bring depression on deliberately makes it feel much less overwhelming, establishing a new association to old feelings.

D26 | Prescribing Patterns of Depression

The clinician can likewise use symptom prescription strategies for other, more specific dimensions of the person's depressogenic patterns. "Prescribing Patterns of Depression" involves directing the client to "be negative," "be whiney," "be passive," and so forth. Exaggerated compliance can be useful in rapidly mobilizing the client's resistances to having such experiences.

D27   An Ordeal for Relief

In a variation of general symptom prescription strategies, an ordeal may be included in the directives (Haley, 1984). In formulating "An Ordeal for Relief," the clinician is constructing a scenario in which the client is to display the symptomatic pattern in a way that will make it very inconvenient for the client to act it out. Prescribing the symptom of "be depressed" can be beneficial in and of itself. Combine that directive with the directive to "be depressed" from 2:30 A.M. to 3:45 A.M. while standing in the corner of the garage and shining shoes can generate a lot of resistance to such an experience. In essence, if framed properly, the client can then resist being depressed, and implicitly, therefore, assume some control over the experience instead of remaining its hopeless victim.

D28   Exaggerated Helplessness

Prescribing "Exaggerated Helplessness" in particular can help mobilize the recognition in the client that he or she is not helpless at all. For example, the client can be directed to stop and ask others for directions to go places already known to him or her. Having to wait to hear someone's directions when a person already knows where to go can build a strong feeling of recognition that "I know where to go, I don't need someone else's directions." This feeling is one involving power and autonomy and can be a useful resource to be able to refer back to later in the therapy.

D29   Ask Others

The client can be directed to "Ask Others" how to do something he or she already knows how to do. Amplifying the feeling of confidence in a person's knowledge of his or her skills can be a useful resource to utilize as therapy progresses.

D30   Wait Passively

Another strategy aimed at the undercontrolling client's sense of helplessness involves having the client "Wait Passively" for things to be done for him or her. For example, one woman who was quite passive in her responses was directed to wait until others opened doors for her, even her doors at home (although she lived alone!). She was instructed to wait two minutes for someone to open the door, and if no one did, she could then open it for herself. Her reactions to waiting out two minute periods became progressively stronger, and after only a few days was aware of being extremely annoyed with the task. She developed a strong awareness of ways in which she had been passive to a fault and was now evolving an association of irritation with passivity. This awareness became an excellent resource for later sessions that emphasized taking greater control over her experience. Ultimately, the frustration of waiting for others became a catalyst for finding independent solutions.

A most common basis for what seems to be undercontrol, or helplessness, in a client's responses is the experience of ambivalence. The author has come to view ambivalence as an identifiable consequence of not controlling the controllable. Is the client genuinely ambivalent, i.e., equally torn in two directions as suggested by the "approach-avoidance" framework of understanding? The author's experience has been that it is much more common for the client to consciously or unconsciously know what is desired, but feel that he or she does not have the power or the right to have it. Often, the client who is absorbed in the turmoil of ambivalence about a decision needing to be made seeks input from the therapist with the overt or covert hope that the therapist will provide a better justification for doing what he or she wants than could have been arrived at independently. For example, one man sought therapy regarding a dilemma concerning his marriage. He described his marriage as "dead in the water," and had been romantically involved for a number of years with another woman he very much cared for and wanted to be with. His belief in the sanctity of marriage and the family made it an overwhelming problem for him to even consider leaving his wife of 22 years and their two children, ages 17 and 19. Basically, the depression arising from his ambivalence was viewed as a consequence of knowing what he wanted to do but feeling that he was lacking the "proper" justification for doing so. What is a "good enough" reason for divorce?

D31   Encouraging the Worse Alternative

Milton Erickson's strategy of "Encouraging the Worse Alternative" (Haley, 1973) is excellent for facilitating movement in an otherwise seemingly motionless client's decision-making process. By being encouraged to pursue the alternative that is *least* desirable to the client, he or she is polarized into discovering the negative feelings associated with that alternative, and simultaneously "discovers" what the preferred alternative is. In the above example, the client refused to participate in couples' therapy. As an individual in treatment, he was directed in exaggerated fashion to try and rekindle love and attraction for his wife, pursue relationship counseling, and "put his shoulder to the grindstone" and find a basis for continuing. The more the man was told to forego his desire to be with the woman he loved in favor of staying in a marriage that truly seemed beyond any hope of restoration, he became adamant that there was no way to go on living a charade and that a divorce must be obtained. Obviously, in order to use this strategy, the clinician must be quite sure the person really *does* know what he or she wants despite apparent ambivalence. Otherwise, the danger exists of pushing someone in a direction he or she follows on blind faith in the clinician, only to end up somewhere worse. Furthermore, unless the clinician senses the client will resist the push in the direction of the worse alternative, this strategy can be quite hazardous and is contraindicated.

D32   He Who Hesitates Is Lost

An indirect strategy for facilitating decision making and escape from ambivalence involves the use of metaphors that illustrate the truism, "He Who Hesitates Is Lost." The metaphor is used as a vehicle to encourage making an internal decision to act before external circumstances interfere. The following is an example of such a metaphor:

> A friend of mine recently went through an experience that really was most instructive . . . on a number of levels. . . . He had wanted to get a new job . . . one that paid more and afforded him greater prestige . . . and in a moment of willingness to help himself get what he wants . . . he applied for a job. . . one that involved moving to another city. . . . He wanted it very badly . . . but was uncertain about moving to make things happen . . . and it was soon after that he was called and offered the job . . . and he asked for a week to think the offer over . . . and they politely agreed he could take a week to decide . . . and a week of going back and forth in his feelings went by . . . and when they called him a week later . . . he asked if he could have three more days in order to decide . . . and they politely agreed he could have three more days in order to decide . . . and when they called him three days later, he asked if he could have another day to decide . . . and they politely agreed he could have another day to decide . . . and when they called him the next morning and asked for his answer, he asked if he could tell them later that day . . . and they impolitely told him they gave the job to someone else apparently more enthusiastic about the opportunity . . . and he was quite upset because he wanted that job, but he made himself afraid . . . thinking of too many things to do at once . . . instead of

knowing he could move and work and live one day at a time . . . and
there comes a time to take action . . . before the chance slips away. . . .

Any strategy that turns the depressing paralysis of ambivalence in a
positive direction will also facilitate the recognition of one's ability to
make decisions in one's own behalf. In the above metaphor, the man
loses an opportunity because of paralysis, not incompetence. The message is one that also addresses a global thought pattern, i.e., overwhelming
oneself with *all* of what is involved. The client may thus learn that
instead of focusing on the frightening aspects of what there is to lose by
moving on, he or she can look at what will be lost by staying put.

In this section there have been various strategies described as a means
for facilitating the awareness on the part of the client that action in his or
her own behalf is fundamental to recovery. For the client who tends to be
a passive victim and ends up in depressing circumstances as a result, a
goal of treatment is to build a recognition in the client that his or her
mind set is itself the creator of the illusion of helplessness. The message
is, rather than assuming action will be useless, to at least look for some
objective evidence that this is or is not so. These issues will be described
further in the next chapter.

Strategies for Dealing with Overcontrolling Clients

The other side of the "ambiguity regarding control" coin is the tendency observed in many depressed individuals to attempt to control
outcomes (e.g., reactions in others, events) that are not recognized as
objectively being beyond the sphere of their influence. In many instances,
depression is a reaction to discovering the uncontrollable nature of
something significant to the person. When an individual is heavily
invested emotionally in realizing a particular outcome, his or her judgment can get cloudy about what it takes to define the goal as realistic and
then accomplish it. The person who magnifies his or her abilities to
control events is in for a major letdown when it is discovered that
variables outside of one's control can ruin everything.

The degree of emotional investment in specific outcomes concerning
such important issues is obviously necessary, yet it can be tempered
with a greater awareness of what one is assuming about the persons or
situations and other variables that can affect the outcome. Once such
variables are identified in a methodical way, each can be considered
from the standpoint of which are and which are not within the person's
direct control. In such cases, the focus is clearly an internal one on one's
own goals, rather than an external one which might promote the awareness

of whether circumstances warrant such expectations. For example, if a woman is so internally absorbed with her professional goals that she does not observe the company's disinterest in such goals, she will much more likely be hurt when the discrepancy is inevitably discovered.

D33   Peter Pan

The goal in identifying this pattern of overcontrol is to facilitate maintaining any attitude of mastery over circumstances that is already present, while simultaneously building a self-preserving system of not investing oneself too heavily in situations one cannot control. Initially, the client must be oriented to the idea of easing up on the tendency to push heavily for certain goals when those goals are not in direct control. Then the client can be oriented to the necessity to better learn to identify assumptions and variables influencing results. A relatively safe and gentle way to orient the client to such learnings is through the use of metaphors, of which the following is an example:

> Sometimes there's a thin line between fantasy and reality . . . and what seems absurd to one person can be very real to another . . . and there's an old story I'm sure you've heard many times over the years . . . but probably not at a time you really needed to hear it . . . the way it can teach you something valuable about yourself right now . . . and you can certainly pretend that it's just a story . . . but you can know at a much deeper level that there's a point for you to consider . . . that can really make a difference . . . and it's the story of a boy who refused to grow up . . . as if one can choose whether one grows up or not . . . and Peter Pan's desire to stay the same forever and live in Neverland with the lost boys can teach one a lot . . . about feelings . . . about the unknown . . . about freedom . . . about responsibility . . . and no one can stay the same forever . . . time passes . . . and people grow . . . and people change . . . and how frustrated one could get if one truly wanted the hands of time to stand still . . . which is beyond anyone's control . . . and Peter Pan's efforts to never grow up . . . and retain the qualities of youth . . . are efforts that can only end in despair . . . and one really ought to consider one's goals carefully . . . and what is fantasy . . . and what is reality . . . and how good it feels to know you can do a lot about what's real . . . and you don't have to do anything about what's not . . . and how can one know what's real . . . and what's not . . . and there's a lot to learn about such things . . . and one can even learn from a story as simple . . . and as complicated as Peter Pan's. . . .

Behavioral prescriptions can allow the client to experience the limits of their belief systems, building a receptivity to the potentials of alternative ways of doing things. The depressed individual's thought that "I should be able to control this" when it refers to something the clinician perceives as objectively uncontrollable is the clue suggesting the appropriateness of the following directives. Initially, the clinician might choose to discuss rationally the issue of control and where the client's perceptions appear to be distorted. Use of behavioral directives can facilitate integration of the learnings at a deeper level while building new associations in the context of "real life."

D34   Control the Uncontrollable

The directive to attempt to "Control the Uncontrollable" is a straightforward prescription. The client is first asked to list a number of things that he or she recognizes as definitely being outside the realm of his or her control. Typical items on such a list might be the weather, the outcome of a sporting event, the passing of time, and so forth. The client is then directed to devote a period of time each day (or during the therapy session) to attempting to control those things. The client is encouraged to use whatever means he or she can to bring about a specific outcome. These might include various tactics like desperate pleas, tantrums, or those strategies the person has been using all along to try and make things go his or her way. The client is instructed to act "as if" such tactics could make attaining the goal possible. This kind of role play exercise has had the effect in many individuals of bringing deep feelings of resentment, frustration, and anger to the surface, where they could be dealt with in the therapy. For others, it has afforded them a humorous look at the futility of trying to control situations when there is clear evidence that control is not possible, and the obvious need to first determine the viability of such controlling tactics. (This directive is described in clinical context in Cases 2 and 4 of Appendix B.)

D35   Skilled Manipulators

Often, the expectation or goal that the client has and strives to accomplish is not conscious, and he or she is not aware of using manipulative tactics of any kind in order to make something happen. When attempts to manipulate others is a prominent theme in the client's behavioral and relational patterns, the client may be directed to carefully observe and identify the techniques of those "Skilled Manipulators" who attempt to influence the thoughts, feelings, and behaviors of others. For example, the client may be asked to watch television advertising carefully, identifying strategies, such as sexual innuendo, used to promote product sales. Once such tactics are identified, the clinician can direct the client to identify similar ways he or she uses to get what is wanted. In a variation of this strategy, this author has directed clients to watch television evangelists very closely and identify their manipulative tactics. The typical, forcefully stated presuppositions by each regarding the "right" way to live and the "right" way to believe are often embedded in statements manipulating the fear and guilt of the listeners. Given the large number of individuals influenced in this way, they are obviously methods that work. By actively and critically viewing the evangelists' use of negative manipulation tactics, the client may externalize (i.e., see as if outside oneself) his or her similar patterns and thus dissociate from them. (This directive is described in clinical context in Case 4 of Appendix B.)

D36   Crusade

To make the point even more overt, the clinician can direct the client to choose an issue to which he or she is quite indifferent and to become actively involved in a "Crusade" for or against that issue. In essence, the client is being asked to take a position and on the basis of that stand attempt to convince others to take a similar stand. Since the "crusade issue" is not of personal importance to the client, he or she need not be emotionally invested in the outcomes of his or her attempts to influence others. The client thus has a safe context in which to learn the diverse reactions to an idea or cause and how difficult it truly is to get support from some people for *anything.* When the client learns this in a relatively neutral context, it is easy for the clinician to use this experience as a basis for the client's learning that when one attempts to control others' feelings or actions, one is inevitably in over one's head. One can ask the client "How difficult would it have been for you to handle the responses you received if you genuinely cared about the issue?" in order to drive home the point that one is especially vulnerable when one cares about an issue and when one looks for support in what may be the wrong places. (This directive is described in clinical context in Case 4 of Appendix B.)

SUMMARY

The various strategies presented throughout this chapter are each capable of promoting an experiential learning that can build a new understanding of a client's under- or overreliance on issues of control. When the client is able to challenge his or her own automatic assumptions about whether something is or is not controllable, a more careful positioning can take place such that the client can actively move in and take charge or can back away and retreat from the situation at hand. Sometimes, however, the response to the now self-generated question "Can I directly control the outcome I want in this situation?" will be "I don't know." When it is self-evident to the client that the outcome is or is not controllable, it becomes easier to make a decision about one's plans. When the controllability is uncertain, the client must know how to problem solve: how to identify what the demands of the situation are, what solutions can be self-generated (if any), and most important, who else can act as a competent source of information in order to develop more and better solutions.

9

Where the Chips Fall

Each of the various models of depression that suggest a specific course of therapy for depressed individuals has a focal point that can be identified as either predominantly or exclusively intrapersonal or interpersonal. The multiple dimensions of experience that are inevitably a part of any problematic pattern (described in Chapter 3) make it clear that some of the problem's dimensions will be experienced to the greatest extent on intrapersonal levels, while others will be experienced to the greatest extent on interpersonal levels. In this chapter, many of the patterns commonly found in depressed individuals that are manifested in the destructive ways they deal with themselves will be discussed. As a general framework for considering these depressogenic intrapersonal dimensions of experience, the depressed client's patterns can be thought of as rigid and dysfunctional ways of managing control-related issues. The need to address the values associated with such patterns, as well as the main issue of control, has been discussed previously.

It bears repeating that the issue of locus of control is one that is central to the structure of the human personality. Thus, distortions or ambiguities related to the issue of control will inevitably cause distortions or ambiguities about other vitally important dimensions of experience.

How the individual recognizes and utilizes the various dimensions of him- or herself is critical to the person's level of functioning. Such dimensions include his or her personal values, personal power, sense of responsibility for experience, expectations, and personal needs and motivations. If an individual does not manage these variables well, each can have a most negative impact on the person's sense of well-being.

122

These variables have been discussed in a general way at different points in previous chapters but will be placed in the context of intervening strategies in this chapter. The general goals continue to be 1) identifying which specific pattern(s) on which specific dimension(s) of experience seems to have the greatest depressogenic impact, and 2) providing structured experiences for the client that disrupt those patterns while simultaneously facilitating the possibility of acquiring a new, more functional pattern.

Another variable that is significant in the genesis and maintenance of depression is a distorted sense of personal responsibility. This pattern is discussed at length in this chapter.

DISTORTIONS RELATED TO ISSUES OF PERSONAL RESPONSIBILITY

The distorted sense of personal responsibility that is common among depressed individuals can take many different forms. In general, the distortion involves a tendency — ranging from mild to extreme — to assume either too little or too much responsibility for ongoing experience.

A person's sense of responsibility is a derivative of a person's sense of control. If one believes one is in control of a situation, one consciously or unconsciously senses the ability to control the situation's outcome. Implicitly, one assigns to oneself the responsibility for attaining that outcome. Likewise, if one does not believe one has any control over a situation, one does not assume responsibility for its outcome.

In the case of the depressed individual, a distorted sense of personal responsibility is manifested in large part by how the individual deals with the credit or the blame for much of his or her experience. Is the individual an extrapunitive "blamer," who puts the burden of responsibility for whatever happens to him or her on others, as though merely a passive victim of others' choices? Is the individual an intrapunitive guiltmonger who blames him- or herself for things that happen that could not have been managed any better by anybody else? How an individual deals with blame and responsibility directly influences his or her sense of guilt, patterns of relating to others, sense of competence, and self-esteem.

People naturally make attributions of responsibility for their subjective experiences, tracing the event's origin as soon as the question arises, "Why did this happen?" The need to understand and explain is a well-known trait of human beings, and the many virtually arbitrary beliefs that people hold about the origins of things like the universe and human personality are attempts at forming credible attributions. Identifying whether a causative factor for an experience is internal or external is a basic tendency; thus, when the search is done with a restricted field of vision, the consequences can be quite negative, as is the case with depressed individuals.

Attributions of responsibility and blame for one's circumstances are key issues needing to be addressed in psychotherapy with the depressed client. A variety of strategies described below may be used to clarify recognitions of what one is and is not responsible for, and thus where the credit or blame goes for the events of one's life. Thus, excessive or inappropriate guilt can be reduced or eliminated, patterns of relating to self and others can be improved, and depression can subside.

STRATEGIES FOR DEALING WITH PATTERNS
OF UNDERRESPONSIBILITY

One of the ways a distorted sense of responsibility manifests itself is in the client's lack of assertions of his or her feelings or wants. The depressed client who consistently views him- or herself as a victim of others' insensitivity complains that others do not consider his or her feelings. When this is the case, the client is clearly underresponsible relative to the events taking place in the relationship. The client is simply not a full member of the relationship. Typically, the person's self-esteem is so poor that he or she is afraid to express feelings, make realistic demands, set limits, or even disagree with another person out of fear that the other person may get angry or abandon him or her. Self-negation is the main pattern in what has been appropriately described by Satir (1972) as the "placater" personality style. The client operating in this mode is likely to be frustrated and angry much of the time because the passive, placating role demands silent subservience. Such anger cannot be expressed directly, however, for to "bite the hand that feeds you" is recognized as unwise. Therapy in such instances, at least in part, involves building the recognition that in order for the relationship to be a healthy one, each person's feelings must be recognized as equally valid. The self-negation of the underresponsible individual precludes him or her from attaining such a recognition independently.

Self-Negation

When the client invalidates his or her own feelings or wants, there is no longer a legitimate basis for asserting them. Such a client will minimize the importance of his or her feelings, or negate his or her worth with self-critical statements like "I have no right to feel this way." It is actually quite an absurd statement, because it completely misses the point: The person already *does* feel that way! Questioning the right to feel that way sends one off on a tangent that delays or prevents dealing with the actual feeling. The client does not have a sense of adequate justification for his or her feelings, and in the search for such a justification he or she grows more depressed.

D37 Self-Justification Shuffle

In such cases, the clinician can direct the client to justify everything that he or she does. The author calls this the "Self-Justification Shuffle." The prescription is given that the client give at least three rationales for all the activities he or she carries out. Thus, the client is required to offer three reasons for why he or she is wearing those particular clothes today, why he or she drives to work on that particular route, why he or she chose those particular foods for lunch, and so on. The expenditure of mental energy to try and justify what one does soon becomes burdensome for most. Most important, what the client discovers is that each of the justifications is essentially a rationalization for doing what one wants to and for feeling what one feels. As the client discovers that all the justifications are after-the-fact explanations for doing or feeling as one wishes, it becomes the basis for a more self-determined recognition that "the fact that I feel this way is justification enough to do as I wish." To make such a statement does not imply callousness toward others (as if a "placater" could become callous anyway) but it does imply a self-determination and self-acceptance that can only enhance the depressed individual's self-esteem.

D38 Invalidating One's Own Feelings

In another strategy, the client may be directed to assert feelings, but to preface each with an apology. The client, in essence, is told to say, "I'm sorry, but I feel (good, bad, angry, happy, etc.) with what you're doing." Inserting a self-negating apology, or excuse ("Perhaps I have no right to feel this way") before a statement of one's feelings can highlight to the client the absurdity of "Invalidating One's Own Feelings" when they are so significant in determining the quality of one's experience. The goal is to catalyze the recognition that one is entitled to one's own feelings, and the finesse of high quality living involves whether and how one chooses to express them.

One aspect of the self-negation process involves one's own motives and actions. The tendency in the depressed client is to interpret his or her motives and actions in a most negative and pathological way, thus acting as an inescapable and harsh self-critic that is continually chipping away at his or her self-esteem. The pattern is usually unconscious so that the individual does not recognize the internal harassment—he or she simply experiences the consequences of bad feelings.

D39   Pathological Interpretations

A symptom prescription strategy may be used to amplify awareness of such a pattern and build a resistance to engaging in it. The prescription requires having the client generate three "Pathological Interpretations" for all of his or her actions, particularly neutral ones such as choosing a particular food from a restaurant menu. When the client is pushed to do what he or she has been doing spontaneously for a long time, the pattern is no longer "personal property," but is a response to the clinician. This paves the way for the eventual dissociation of the pattern from ongoing experience.

D40   Healthy Interpretations

Reversing the strategy is a good follow-up idea. After the client has become adept at generating pathological interpretations, the client can be directed to now generate positive and "Healthy Interpretations" for his or her feelings and actions. Typically, this is experienced as a much more difficult task to carry out. The client's history of negative interpretations has often distorted his or her perceptions to the point where identifying positive interpretations falls beyond the range of vision. There is a learning curve that occurs, however, and while the first positive interpretations come slowly, an acceleration soon follows and the client can become more practiced at seeing a positive basis for his or her feelings and actions.

As a follow-up strategy that blends the previous two, the clinician can employ directive 17. Described in Chapter 7, this directive has the client generate three positive and three negative interpretations for his or her actions and feelings. By this point in time, generating a "Variety of Interpretations" has become well practiced, and what the client discovers is that the process of attributing motives and explaining actions is often arbitrary and unprovable. When the client can generate equally plausible explanations for a circumstance that is positive or negative, the client discovers firsthand how arbitrary his or her past history of focusing only on negative interpretations has been. Furthermore, the client learns experientially that the after-the-fact explanations are just that—after the fact. The bottom line is that the person made the decision to act on the basis of what seemed to be the best choice at the time.

☐ D41 ☐ The Best Choices

The preceding point is one that addresses the issues of self-negation and blame, and it is a statement in which I genuinely believe: The client *is* making "The Best Choices" he or she has at a given moment, based on the person's range of personal resources and degree of access to those resources (Bandler & Grinder, 1979; Lankton & Lankton, 1983). The reframing occurs when an "error" becomes "the best choice available." When the client can accept the inevitability of making choices that eventually prove to not be the best, for whatever reason, self-acceptance is made easier.

Perfectionism

The inability to accept the inevitability of making less-than-perfect choices from time to time is another aspect of self-negation that is rooted in distortions regarding responsibility and control. If the individual believes that he or she should always be able to generate the ideal response or outcome in a given situation, the belief becomes a basis for negating feelings that might interfere or rejecting dimensions of oneself that can become hazardous to the person's mental health. To strive for perfection is certainly a wonderful goal, but one must do so with a clear sense of where the boundaries are separating reality from idealism. Specifically, what is "perfection"? Is it possible to attain? What does it look like? What are the criteria defining it? Is its attainment in one's direct control?

Often, the individual strives for perfection as a means to avoid criticism or as a means to avoid disappointing significant others. In the former situation, the distortion in responsibility is evident when one is afraid of making a mistake and being visibly responsible for it. In the latter situation, the individual is attempting to control others by attempting to make them react with the most favorable reactions possible.

☐ D42 ☐ Unrealistic Perfectionistic Goals

Therapeutic metaphors may be constructed on the theme of an individual with "Unrealistic Perfectionistic Goals" who is feeling depressed about the inability to accomplish them (not realizing they are unrealistic), and then experiencing a change in perspective about them that leads to a healthier way of life. This theme is illustrated in the following metaphor:

> And I can tell you about a woman I know who was growing more and more depressed over time . . . who was really feeling badly about herself and her life . . . because she was feeling so alone and lonely . . . she had been married . . . and she described her marriage as satisfactory, but not exciting . . . so she left her husband of eight years . . . to find a man more exciting to her . . . a more perfect man . . . and that was about five years ago . . . and she created a checklist of characteristics she would require of her next husband . . . and her image of what the perfect man would look like, be like, and act like was very clear to her . . . and she went out on lots of dates . . . met lots of men . . . went to lots of social events . . . and ended up more and more frustrated and depressed with each passing day . . . she was losing hope of finding the perfect man . . . she wanted him to be perfect . . . and was perfectly willing to wait for the perfect man . . . even though she grew more and more depressed simply waiting . . . and one day she was complaining to a friend of hers about the less than perfect men she'd been meeting, and her friend listened patiently for a while, but she grew more and more annoyed at her friend's complaints and she finally blew up . . . and angrily denounced her checklist . . . and her intolerance for less than perfection . . . and her unrealistic goal of trying to find perfection when no such thing exists in human form . . . and how she'd been so selfishly absorbed in her own images of perfection that she'd missed the opportunity to really love and be loved by someone who was different than her ideal image . . . not better, not worse, just different . . . and all of a sudden it seemed to dawn on this woman that her checklist was quite unnecessary . . . that a caring, loving human being can take a lot of different forms . . . and her friend's angry outburst shook her up a little, but she settled back down into a much more accepting and realistic frame of mind . . . and I don't think it's a coincidence that she met a man she fell in love with not long after that interaction . . . and she's quite happily married these days . . . and she describes her husband as "perfectly imperfect . . ." and she's quite happy about that. . . .

The above metaphor matches the general dissatisfaction that precedes an unrealistic need for perfection, the futility and depressing aspects of doggedly striving for perfection, and the need to be open to other ways of approaching issues that can facilitate resolution. In this case, a confrontive friend pushed the solution into the woman's awareness helping her discover that forms other than one's subjective ideals can be equally up to the task at hand. Bending rigid expectations of perfection to encourage greater acceptance is one very important dimension of facilitating flexibility in one's life. (This directive is described in clinical context in Case 1 of Appendix B.)

D43   Never to Offend the Spirits

Another metaphor that reframes perfectionism as less than desirable was contributed by one of the author's associates, David L. Higgins, M.A. The metaphor describes how "Never to Offend the Spirits."

> Long ago, a particular group of Indians were very skilled in making elaborate pottery and weaving beautiful rugs and fabrics that had many purposes . . . motivated, it seems, to join with . . . and reflect . . . the beauty and grace of their world . . . some pieces were decorated with symbols of lore that had been passed down from generation to generation, others with indications of what was seen in nature . . . always created and detailed with care and appreciation for the process . . . inspiration expanding from within . . . gentle blending of the individual and his or her surroundings . . . colors brilliant and subdued . . . pure and basic . . . always extracted from the earth under their feet or from the world within their sight . . . undulating textures and linear shapes unfolding in controlled spontaneity . . . as each thread was passed from side to side . . . or with each subtle movement of their hands along the clay . . . new shapes evolving from old shapes . . . through gentle manipulation of raw materials . . . raw materials from so many sources . . . resources quite familiar . . . perhaps an image held for what would evolve, but always surprises along the way . . . the unexpected . . . the useful and appreciated . . . And you might be interested in knowing that in that world *only the spirits could be perfect* . . . and the spirits would be very offended should any mortal achieve perfection in any way . . . even accidentally . . . and so each rug . . . each piece of fabric . . . each piece of pottery . . . was given an odd line or an odd mark or an odd color . . . a *deliberate* departure . . . from the perfection of the evolving pattern . . . a purposeful mistake . . . carefully placed there by the artisan . . . in order to avoid offending the spirits . . . and there is one very important thing that I would like you to do . . . just for you . . . until we meet again . . . be perfectly certain . . . to never offend the spirits. . . .

D44   Be Perfect

In another strategy for dealing with perfectionism, the client may be given the paradoxical prescription to "Be Perfect" on every dimension of his or her life. The client can be directed to do all things perfectly, with no imperfections allowable anywhere. Thus, the client is directed to shower perfectly, dress perfectly, maintain perfect posture, breathe perfectly, eat and drink perfectly, and so on. Perfection is demanded of things that literally *cannot* be done perfectly. What objective criteria are there to define "perfect showering," for example? Prescribing that the client carry out such mundane tasks within an atmosphere of perfectionism can mobilize his or her feelings of being trapped in an impossible situation — one that parallels perfectly the self-made trap of requiring perfectionism of him- or herself in an area equally as arbitrary as showering. Used positively, the frustration and resentment of the client can be the perfect catalyst for his or her redefining "perfection" in a more realistic and self-directed manner. A most important reason for redefining perfection and adequacy is that very often the client's original concept of perfection is not even his or her own. Rather, it is the individual's interpretation and reaction to the expectations of someone who is powerful (i.e., some significant other) in his or her life. (This directive is described in clinical context in Case 1 of Appendix B.)

☐ D45 ☐ Make Deliberate Mistakes

Another behavioral prescription might involve having the client deliberately plan and execute a specified number of mistakes each day. This particular directive was described by Watzlawick (1978, pp. 136-137) and is structurally a paradoxical assignment. The client is told that he or she must make a certain number of mistakes each day, each deliberately planned and carried out. Making wrong turn-offs on the freeway, arriving at the wrong time to a meeting, wearing his or her underwear backwards, and other such harmless erroneous tasks may be offered as examples of areas in which to "Make Deliberate Mistakes." A double-bind effect is created when the clinician further requires that the mistakes be made "perfectly." If the client complies and makes mistakes, he or she has made mistakes. If the client makes the mistake of not making mistakes, he or she has made a mistake. Since the mistakes are made in compliance with the clinician's directives, the client needs not feel responsible for them. This gives the client the opportunity to discover through direct experience that making mistakes does not lead to the end of civilization or cause any of the other dire consequences that may have been so greatly feared. Movement in the direction of acceptance of one's own humanness, i.e., the inevitability of making mistakes, may then be possible. In the intrapunitive style of many depressed clients, the self-punishment that accompanies mistakes is far worse than anybody else's reactions and is tied up in guilt and self-esteem issues. This strategy can help facilitate greater self-acceptance and allow mistakes to be things to be learned from instead of things to be chastised for. (This directive is described in clinical context in Case 1 of Appendix B.)

D46   Redefine Perfectionism

A reframing strategy may also be useful in addressing the issues of perfectionism and poor self-esteem. Perfectionism has been held as an ideal in the mind of the client, a highly desirable goal that had been held uncritically. When reframing is applied in order to "Redefine Perfectionism" as negative, it can reduce the intensity of the drive for perfectionism. Bandler and Grinder (1979, pp. 171-172) described a similar process in the example of Carl Whitaker working with a man who regretfully admits that "I'm not the perfect husband." Whitaker's response was "Thank God! I'm so relieved! I've had three perfect husbands already this week and they are so dull." "Perfect" is reframed as "dull" in this example. Reframing "perfect" as undesirable in some way can catalyze redefining the nature of perfection and move the client in the direction of not just tolerating his or her humanness and inherent flaws, but actually appreciating them.

Reframing through metaphor is possible when the goal is to have perfectionism reconsidered. In one case first described in an article on the subject of anorexia nervosa (Yapko, 1986), this approach was used with an anorectic male in college working toward a career in medicine. He was told about another client of mine, an attractive young married woman who reported that she was unable to experience orgasm with her husband. As a result, she felt frustration with herself, her husband, and the marriage. In part, the metaphor was told as follows:

> In describing their marriage, she commented on how he was "the perfect man," how he never has a hair out of place, dresses impeccably, always says and does everything with robotlike efficiency, including his lovemaking . . . and she told me that sometimes when he gets undressed to come to bed she half expects to see a big "S" for "Superman" on his chest . . . and she resented his perfect way of doing things . . . and she told me she was "dying for him to make a mistake and be human" so she could feel for him. . . . (Yapko, 1986, p. 229)

In describing the seemingly unrelated experience of a woman with sexual problems to a man with anorexia, the reframing of perfectionism as undesirable is suggested, as well as the need to be sensitive to and aware of the relationship to one's partner. This indirectly encourages the client to "get out of yourself" for a while in order to learn more about the needs of others and how to deal with them constructively as part of the personal growth process.

By learning more about the needs of others and the realities of others' lives, the client can come to know in a more balanced way that no life is perfect and that "imperfect" can be reframed as lovable and worthy. (This directive is described in clinical context in Case 2 of Appendix B.)

Blame

At the outset of this chapter was a discussion concerning the relationship between patterns of blame and patterns of responsibility. In the case of the underresponsible individual in particular, the tendency is for the person to act as a "blamer" (Satir, 1972). The blamer is one who is quick to attribute fault to any or all others in proximity to whatever happened. Basically, whatever occurs with which the individual senses something wrong is a product of others' shortcomings (e.g., their ignorance, insensitivity, lack of planning, and so forth). It should be quite evident how strongly a "victim" mentality is operating in such people, given their perspective that they must suffer the consequences of others' lack of ability. To be in a position of being able to blame others presupposes a lack of perceived responsibility, thus their inclusion in this section on patterns of underresponsibility.

D47   Blame Others

A symptom prescription strategy may be used to facilitate an awareness of the tendency to blame others or circumstances to an unrealistic and unfair degree, alienating others while maintaining a depressogenic victim mind set. The client may be told to "Blame Others"—constantly. Rather than risking whatever social life the individual might have, the client is directed to "blame out loud" for specified (and inconvenient) periods of time when others are not around. To have a "blaming time," the client is encouraged to "criticize everything and everyone for not doing things in just the right way, which is *your* way." While he or she drives on the freeway, the client may blame others for being so stupid as to own a different type and color automobile, blame the city for allowing buildings to be built, blame nature for putting trees or hills in particular places, and so forth. Whatever hostile or blaming demeanor the client may have had becomes a caricature after he or she follows this directive for any length of time. Furthermore, there is a powerful new association built around the issue of blame, namely, that it can quickly get quite absurd if one is so one-dimensional in one's ascribing blame. (This directive is described in clinical context in Case 3 of Appendix B.)

D48   Encouraging the Blame

In an in-session role play strategy that brings the previous strategy into the realm of direct interaction with the clinician, the prescription of blaming excessively can also be useful. In an example of this pattern, a 57-year-old, seriously depressed woman who had recently suffered the loss of her husband of 35 years presented herself to the author for treatment. Since his death, she had not left her home, terrified to emerge as an independent adult. She had been married to the "perfect husband who took care of me completely." She had never had to fill her own car with gas, had never had to make a bank deposit, never had to do many of the errands most people do routinely. Her overresponsible husband's death left her totally unable to manage her own life independently—he had, in effect, killed her with kindness.

In an early stage of treatment, the client was encouraged to express her resentment about his death to him directly, as if he were in the chair opposite her, and to bitterly blame him for dying. Quite emotionally, she did so. Somewhere in the midst of her hurling blame at him, it dawned on her that "it probably wasn't his idea to die. . . ." "Encouraging the Blame" allowed her to stop the blaming and begin working on her acquiring the skills necessary to live life competently. (This directive is described in clinical context in Case 3 of Appendix B.)

D49   Denying Oneself

In a strategy attempting to catalyze the acceptance of responsibility for one's actions, called "Denying Oneself," the client can be asked to construct a list of personal accomplishments or personal experiences, however good or bad. The client is then directed to deny having anything to do with any of them. For example, the client can deny that he or she had parents, deny that he or she was born, deny that he or she was ever a child, and so forth. Hardly a "heavy" strategy, this may give a chance to the client to see him- or herself quite differently than from the usual perspective.

D50   All Excuses

In a variation of the above strategy, the client can be instructed to carry out assigned behaviors erroneously, and then immediately offer any and "All Excuses" for the outcome of those behaviors. The image is a caricature of irresponsibility, similar to the kind of exchange that occurs in the old comedy act of the Smothers Brothers. Mid-song, Tom Smothers would make a silly error in the music or lyrics, and brother Dick would stop the song to gently harass him. Tom offers rambling excuses, including "Well, the lighting was bad, and I have a hangnail, and lunch wasn't very good, and besides . . . mom always liked you best!" The lightheartedness of such an interaction can still bring to the fore the blaming style and its one-dimensional limitations. (This directive is described in a clinical context in Case 3 of Appendix B.)

Withdrawal

One of the most common symptoms that someone manifests when he or she is caught up in depression is the withdrawal from contact with others. The tendency to isolate is a social withdrawal, and the unfortunate effect is to inadvertently compound the depression. The depressed individual stops going places, stops doing things, stops seeing friends, stops answering the door or the phone, and little by little ends up alone with the same depressing thoughts and feelings spinning around and around inside. With little or no new input coming in as a result of the isolation, it places the entire burden of recovery on the client. Realistically, the burden is always on the client; however, the clinician and other interpersonal contacts can certainly act as effective catalysts in the recovery process. Facilitating more and better contact with others is a main focus of Chapter 11, so suffice it to say here that there are some directives that may be used to encourage being active and involved in living as opposed to being passive and withdrawn in mid-depression.

D51   Do Enjoyable Things

Recreational approaches that encourage the depressed client to "Do Enjoyable Things" are behavioral prescriptions that can lead the client to discover some important insights into the way he or she is managing his or her time and stress levels. In one such recreational therapy approach, the client is directed to make a list of as many things as he or she can think of that are fun — enjoyable things to do. Ideally, the list may contain 20 or 30 items, such as hiking, swimming, listening to music, reading a book, and so on. The client can then code each item according to which things can be done spontaneously, which require planning, which can be done alone, and which with others. The client may also be asked to indicate when was the last time he or she engaged in that activity. Clients typically discover that they have not done the things they enjoy doing in a long time. Such a realization highlights the point that "if you don't do things that you enjoy doing, how can you expect to feel good?" The underresponsible client who withdraws and passively responds to life's opportunities maintains a helpless position. Recreational activities mobilize positive energy, demand involvement, reduce the effects of stress, and give a person mastery over his or her own time. Furthermore, when an individual is depressed and experiencing anhedonia and apathy, having a concrete list of things to do can prevent the "what's there to do?" question that otherwise seems inevitable. The client discovers a self-controlled and reliable way to "get outside of oneself" (out of the typical depressive internal focus), a shift that is a common denominator of many of the commonsense remedies for depression (e.g., "Go volunteer at a hospital," "Go take a class," "Go develop a new hobby," and all the similar "get moving" messages). (This directive is described in clinical context in Case 1 of Appendix B.)

D52   Physical Exercise

With the recognizable benefits of activity in general, the benefits are even greater when the activity is of a physical nature. Particularly effective with those clients who have not previously been very attentive to the physiological dimensions of experience, and as a useful reframing of the body for those who have had vague somatic complaints, "Physical Exercise" can be a valuable means for enhancing self-image and catalyzing recovery from depression. Directives to join a nearby health club or to establish an exercise program suited to one's own preferences encourage the client to become active, to redefine the relationship to his or her body, and to become physically stronger as a metaphor for building internal strengths. The many physical and psychological benefits of exercise have been well documented, and to encourage the depressed client to pursue such healthful patterns may be considered a routine part of treatment. It is harder to feel badly emotionally when one is feeling good physically, just as the reverse is true. People in pain, for example, usually have a pretty hard time being cheerful.

D53   Symbolic Exertion

Disguised exercise and "Symbolic Exertion" might be another means for accomplishing a similar goal. Milton Erickson frequently had those he worked with climb nearby Squaw Peak in Phoenix. A moderately difficult hike, the winding paths that create the illusion that one is almost at the top only to discover another curve to navigate with a little farther to go than one had thought are aspects of the climb that really hold one's interest. Erickson would describe the directive to hike Squaw Peak as a metaphor for the problem and the therapy: climbing (fighting) the uphill battle of day-to-day existence, followed by an opportunity to "get on top of things" and "see the world from a different perspective." Borrowing on Erickson's strategy, occasionally the author will direct a client to take a hike on a particular trail in the mountains just east of San Diego. The trail is easy-to-moderate, if one is in reasonably good health, and its name captures most people's imagination: the Azalea Glen Springs Trail. A person might imagine beautiful flowers, open meadows, and springs overflowing with water all around him or her on such a trail. A person might imagine such things, but in fact the flowers and meadows are very scarce, and the only springs around are underground, marked by a sign over a pipe that dribbles a little water now and then. For clients who tend to exaggerate experiences, this trail is a perfect metaphor for delivering the message, "Respond to the reality, not your exaggerated expectations." This type of message, in addition to the physical demands and involvement of going on such a hike, can mobilize some very useful thoughts and feelings to be used well later in the therapy.

STRATEGIES FOR DEALING WITH PATTERNS OF OVERRESPONSIBILITY

In the case of the overresponsible individual, the person has created the dysfunctional illusion of personal responsibility for many or all of the things that go on around him or her. Dealing with such highly responsible individuals is in many ways easier than dealing with those who have no real sense of responsibility for themselves. Simply put, it is easier to tone down a sense of responsibility than it is to create one. An overresponsible individual is generally quick to assume the blame for things that go wrong, is prone to take others' feelings into account to an extraordinary and often self-destructive degree, and is likely to become entangled in messes that he or she should not be a part of.

If an individual is socialized to believe that what he or she does is central to what others subsequently do, that person comes to believe that he or she is a trigger for events. Certainly this can happen in a family environment in which children are given too much power in the family's interactions. It is often startling to interview parents who make the most serious of personal choices (such as moving or remarrying) solely on the basis of the children's input. In any event, such distorted interactions can lead the person to believe that he or she is the underlying factor in decisions or events that, in fact, were *not* or should not have been a function of that person's choices.

It is unfortunate that overresponsibility is often promoted in individuals through their participation in various personal growth and so-called "higher consciousness" groups. Some of these groups promote the philosophy that "whatever goes on around you is a reflection of you; you have created and will create all of your circumstances." Such groups would have all participants internalize the belief that "you are directly or indirectly responsible for all that happens in your life." Many people become overresponsible as they assume responsibility for things they are not and cannot be responsible for. The result is largely inappropriate self-blame and an ambiguity about concepts and realities of responsibility (Hockenstein, 1986).

Differentiating between what one is and is not responsible for can be as difficult a skill to evolve as is identifying clearly the controllability factor. Consider the mental health profession in general. Given the advanced training in principles of human behavior and (theoretically) the greater degree of psychotherapists' insight through having ample opportunities to learn from clients and colleagues what does and does not work in living life, why are "mental health" professionals so unhealthy? Mental health professionals are notoriously poor at avoiding overresponsibility (i.e., overinvolvement) in their relationships with their clients. The results include a high rate of depression, suicide, and substance abuse within the profession (Laliotis & Grayson, 1985). Therapists who lend their clients money, give them a place to stay, see them at odd times and places, and are "up" when clients are up and who are "down" when clients are down are giving clear signs of overresponsibility. The reason? Such people care, and caring without an established upper limit of involvement can draw more and more of one's energy. The emotional investment clouds the lines of judgment as to the limits of responsibility. It is easy to understand how difficult resolving issues of overresponsibility can be for the average client when even mental health professionals are unclear about it. (It would seem to be a useful addition to clinical training programs to include a lecture or three on "how to stay sane in an insane profession.") Therapy with overresponsible individuals involves setting up the client to discover experientially the limits of his or her responsibility.

Just as underresponsibility surfaces in the victim dimension of interpersonal relationships, overresponsibility also surfaces most dramatically in the context of relationships with others. This will be discussed at length in Chapter 11. In the remainder of this section, the focus will be on the relationship between a pattern of overresponsibility and other dimensions of intrapersonal experience.

Guilt, Self-Blame

Resolving the ambiguity about what one is and is not responsible for is a vital part of the overall treatment of depression. One of the major diagnostic criteria for depression involves this very dimension of experience, namely the symptom of excessive or inappropriate guilt. Does guilt not presuppose responsibility? In other words, would one feel guilty if one did not also feel responsible? It is apparent from working with many under- and overresponsible individuals that when the lines blur as to how responsibilities are distributed in a relationship (with others or oneself), depression is soon to follow.

Consider the case of a 26-year-old woman who sought therapy for depression. Chris was still living at home with two very demanding parents while she was attending graduate school. She had never before attempted to move away from home, and even casual references to moving away to take a job or establish an independent home were responded to by her parents with either anger or stony silence. Chris knew what she wanted to do and what she would eventually need to do in order to help herself, but could not yet do so because of paralyzing guilt. She wanted to move out of her parents' home and live independently, but she was afraid that "it will kill my parents." Why does she assume responsibility for her parents' discouraging a sense of autonomy in her?

D54   Responsible to a Fault

In Chris's case, a series of metaphors were used in the context of hypnosis sessions with the goal of promoting an awareness of the inappropriateness of taking responsibility for her parents' reactions. The theme of the metaphors involved someone or something being conscientious and "Responsible to a Fault," such that others were or would have been rendered powerless by virtue of their passive position. This theme is evident in the following example of such a metaphor:

> The world of nature is enjoyed by almost everyone . . . people like the beauty and the diversity of animals, for example . . . but people do not realize that animals of all shapes, sizes, colors, and temperaments have to face certain realities . . . just as people do . . . animal families are not unlike human families in some ways . . . the establishment of a territory in which to live that is all one's own . . . the

bonding of a family . . . the anticipation and finally the arrival of an offspring or two . . . the proud parents . . . the protective parents . . . and love takes a lot of different forms in the animal kingdom. . . . Consider the bears as an example of the wisdom of animals . . . a mother and her cubs are inseparable in their earliest weeks and months of life . . . if you really want to anger a bear . . . get near her cubs . . . she protects them fiercely . . . as she teaches them how to hunt for food . . . how to survive in the wilderness . . . how to live . . . and how to grow . . . and the cubs have time to play and be young . . . but they also know the seriousness of what they must learn . . . in order to be on their own eventually . . . and then one day, the mother will chase her cubs up a tree . . . and then abandon them . . . she leaves them on their own . . . to live for themselves . . . to grow and change and learn as their lives go on . . . and a huge part of her responsibility . . . is to reach a point of no longer having to be responsible for others . . . their lives are their own to live . . . and she knows she can't live it for them no matter how much she cares for them . . . and it may seem cold and callous on the surface . . . especially when one sees the desperate search of the cubs for their mother . . . but she has a greater wisdom . . . a broader perspective . . . and an intuitive sense that each life is valuable in what it allows its bearer to do . . . and what seems cruel on one level . . . is actually the greatest gift of all on another, more important one . . . and I know of no recorded instances of an insecure mother bear preventing her cubs from becoming independent. . . .

If the client has issues surrounding abandonment, is feeling uncared for by others, or is assuming too much responsibility for others' feelings, the above metaphor can be useful, as can others with a similar theme.

Guilt and self-blame are closely related. Whereas the underresponsible individual tends to be a blamer (extrapunitive), the overresponsible individual tends to be martyrish and intrapunitive. The intensity of the self-blaming can be so great that it becomes the focal point of the person's mental energy, precluding awareness of other interpretations or perspectives. Guilt can be an incredibly profound agent of paralysis in an individual's life, and disrupting the overresponsible person's tendency to wallow in it is a key goal of treatment.

D55   Disconnecting the Guilt Button

A strategy for depersonalizing the issue of responsibility involves directing the client to clip out those articles in the newspaper that describe some disaster somewhere. Articles describing natural disasters like earthquakes, droughts, or floods will do especially well, as will articles describing other such catastrophes as plane crashes, train derailments, oil spills, and so forth. The client is then directed to explain aloud (to herself or someone else, perhaps the clinician) how he or she was responsible for those events happening. The explanation should have as much credibility as the person can muster in an effort to be convincing, and when the client can do this, he or she may be more than a little surprised at how easily guilt is evoked. The ability to experience guilt in the absence of an event one is even remotely attached to is often a powerful interrupter of the person's sense of responsibility. The individual learns experientially that there is, in essence, a "guilt button" that works all too efficiently, even when there is a clear recognition that no guilt should be present. Previously, in life events, the client may have been unable to recognize the guilt's inappropriateness because he or she always found a way to be connected to the problematic situation. With no connection, not even a remote one, the inappropriate guilt is more easily dissociated, and thus "Disconnecting the Guilt Button" is made easier.

D56   Guilt for All Ages

To remove the personalization for responsibility to an even greater extent, one can direct the client to claim responsibility for events that occurred prior to the individual even being born! The author calls this strategy "Guilt for All Ages." For example, with one inappropriately self-blaming member of a couple seeking treatment, the author directed the overresponsible wife to make a list of 10 significant negative historical events that had occurred prior to her birth. Events such as Lincoln's assassination, the fall of the Roman Empire, the crucifixion of Jesus, and the bombing of Hiroshima were usable items on her list. She was told to attempt to convince her generally underresponsible husband that she was to blame for these events, and to do so in as convincing a manner as she possibly could. She was able to play the role very well and offered some very moving admissions of guilt. For her, the effect was dramatic. So easily could the woman assume blame for things that occurred in her life that she actually shocked herself with how guilty she could feel about events that occurred long before her birth! Such experiential learning made it much easier for the woman to accept that not all guilt is justified and that she could learn to take active steps to more carefully scrutinize events in order to better determine what manner and degree of responsibility, if any, she might have had.

Self-Sacrifice, Punishment

The observant clinician might find that there is a manipulative quality to the patterns of self-blame that some people demonstrate. Self-blame can have a self-sacrificing, martyrlike quality to it and contain the implied message that "I'll be the scapegoat here so that you don't have to bear the burden of guilt . . . and how will you acknowledge me for doing so?" It is as if there is an unspoken agreement between the two people in some relationships that one will be the responsible one and the other the irresponsible one.

D57 On a Crucifix

When a martyrish, manipulative quality seems apparent in the over-responsible individual, the clinician who is familiar with sculpting body positions à la Satir (1972) can consider arranging the client in a particular bodily position during an interaction with a significant other, or in a role play with the clinician of such an interaction. Specifically, the client can be positioned standing against a wall, arms perpendicular, head hung down, as if "On a Crucifix." The client is instructed to bemoan his or her plight with some variation of "After all I've done for you, how can you do this to me?" When relevant personal examples are used in this unusual strategy, the client's sense of entitlement and martyrdom can come to the fore, affording him or her a lighter glimpse of a serious pattern.

D58 A Need for Self-Punishment

Where there is guilt, "A Need for Self-Punishment" may be likely to follow. Haley (1984) described a general framework that he called "ordeal therapy." In essence, a clinician using ordeal strategies will make it more inconvenient for the client to maintain a symptom than to abandon it. Haley described a depressed man who was told to either find a job within a week or shave off his highly prized mustache. The expectation was that it would be less costly on a personal level for this man to find work than it would be to shave. Any blame that might have been hurled at him for his prior lack of drive to find work was an issue that was bypassed completely when the ordeal succeeded.

D59 Guilt Hour

Directing clients to perform tasks that are more arduous than letting go of their symptoms can be a viable therapeutic strategy. In a blend of an ordeal and a symptom prescription, the client may be directed to engage in a more concentrated version of a pattern he or she routinely does. Furthermore, the client can be directed to do so at a very inconvenient time and in a very inconvenient place. For example, the assignment of a structured "Guilt Hour" to be experienced on a daily basis can be given with the explanation that "such a structured time will be more efficient than the random, haphazard episodes of guilt you've been experiencing." The client may be asked what the least comfortable place in his or her home is, and that can be the "guilt spot." A corner in the garage or attic, a spot in the yard, or some other inconvenient place will do. Having to awaken in the middle of the night, or extra early in the morning, is bad enough. To have to go stand somewhere and confess endless guilt for all the evils in the world can become very absurd very quickly. Building resistances to feeling guilty is the goal of such a strategy, and with some individuals, such resistance is tapped and catalyzed quite readily.

Perfectionism

Earlier in this chapter there was a discussion of perfectionism from the standpoint of underresponsibility, i.e., where perfectionistic tendencies exist to maintain a position in which one can avoid blame or failure. In this section, we can consider perfectionism in some people from an opposite perspective: as a tendency of overresponsibility. To feel that one must be perfect and never disappoint others' expectations traps one into a life of forever filling obligations — a *very* responsible position.

In essence, the individual feels obligated to "make others happy" (or proud, or satisfied, or whatever). To "make" anyone *anything* presupposes a power to do so, and the lengthy discussion about the inability to control other people or their reactions presented in the last chapter might leap to mind. The strategies from that chapter designed to clarify one's inability to control others are often appropriate to use with such individuals.

D60   Minute-by-Minute

Typically, underlying the perfectionism is a combination of a strong need to control and an elaborate set of expectations. The rigidity of one's expectations can be amplified and then disrupted by assigning the client the task of mapping out the upcoming week's schedule for him- or herself down to every minute. The client makes a "Minute-by-Minute" schedule of everywhere he or she will be and everything he or she will be doing for the week, and is then instructed to follow the schedule as planned. The task is an impossible one, of course, since no matter how hard one attempts to maintain "perfect" control over one's time, one encounters spontaneous events that make such a detailed schedule ridiculous to even try and follow. Traffic jams, phone calls, lines to wait in, and so forth, all disrupt the best of plans. The client again learns the limits of his or her control and learns that perfectionism and overcontrol are unrealistic paths to attain desired recognition. Feelings of obligation can also become a focus for resistance in such a strategy, while selectivity for fulfilling some worthy obligation is encouraged. The net effect is to learn to be willing to risk disappointing others when it means taking better care of one's own needs, allowing one to take on less burdensome and impossible tasks like "making others happy."

The other strategies for disrupting patterns of perfectionism presented earlier in this chapter are also useful in dealing with the overresponsible individual, but require a different framing (i.e., rationale given to the client) for their utilization. The implicit suggestion before was "Assume some responsibility since you have been deficient in doing so." The implicit suggestion now is "Lessen your sense of responsibility since you are taking on more than is your fair share." (This directive is described in clinical context in Case 4 of Appendix B.)

Personal Purpose

One aspect of overresponsibility that has profound implications for the process of psychotherapy is that of human beings' need for a sense of personal purpose or meaning. For many individuals, in having an inflated sense of responsibility for someone or something, the "meaning" of their lives is defined. Such individuals do not usually take kindly to a clinician's advice to "lighten up" in that area. When so much of oneself is invested in a particular area of personal responsibility, easing up on the overkill of overresponsibility is not all that easy nor is it all that desirable to the individual. The role of purpose in one's life has been well described in the literature of psychology, and perhaps it is the works of Viktor Frankl and Rollo May that define and address the issues best. Frankl's *Man's Search for Meaning* (1963) is a book the author frequently recommends to others as a moving account of how powerful can be a will to survive rooted in a sense of purpose. The "existential crisis" is much more than a theoretical construct when one encounters individuals suffering depression because of the obvious absence of any sense of purpose in life.

Consider the case of Adam, a 48-year-old man who suffered a psychotic depression with marked anxiety at the age of 36. He had been working as a stockbroker for quite a few years, suffering the enormous stresses of dealing with huge sums of money and fearful and demanding clients concerned about their financial well-being, all the while struggling to support a family that he hoped could enjoy the fruits of his labors. The stress became too much and Adam collapsed under its pressure. He was hospitalized, placed on medications for anxiety and depression, but did not receive any psychotherapy. His dysfunctions rigidified, and although he was intermittently able to maintain low demand employment for short periods of time, 12 years later he was still battling deep depression. Now it centered on the issues of a lack of worth because of his inability to work consistently and provide directly for his family as he once had. He could not adjust to being unemployed day after day, year after year, nor could he function well enough to go to work in the kind of job he could be proud of. With no sense of purpose, Adam's deep depression occasionally surfaced in ruminations about suicide, and less occasionally, dramatic but ineffective suicide attempts.

D61   Promoting Purpose

"Promoting Purpose" as a general strategy involves orienting the client to the need to have a greater purpose in life than is now experienced. Often, depressed clients are aware of their depression but are not aware of the lack of sense of personal purpose beneath it. A couple of case examples can illustrate this directive in a clinical context.

Milton Erickson described (in Zeig, 1980a, pp. 285-287) the case of a 52-year-old woman who had been living in a socially withdrawn state of deep depression for quite a long time. The woman's only involvement was a passive one with her church. On a visit to her home, Erickson noticed that the woman had three African violet plants in full bloom, a plant he recognized as quite delicate. Erickson gave her the "medical order" to purchase more plants, as well as gift flower pots, potting pots, and potting soil. She was to break off a leaf from each plant and plant them in order to grow more African violets. Once she had many such plants, she was directed to send one plant to every member of the church who had an occasion to receive one, such as births, christenings, engagements, and weddings. Erickson commented that "anybody that takes care of 200 African violets is too busy to be depressed" (Zeig, 1980a, p. 286). From the directives Erickson gave, the woman developed a sense of purpose, as well as a vehicle of social contact. This is a good example of a multidimensional intervention.

In another case illustrative of the use of directives related to a sense of purpose, Erickson described (in Zeig, 1980a, pp. 287-288) a woman who had been suffering depression over her apparent inability to carry a pregnancy due to her severe arthritis. Contrary to the other physicians involved with her case, Erickson advised her to go ahead and get pregnant, which she did. Her arthritis improved, her depression lifted, and she carried the baby full-term and delivered a baby girl she named Cynthia. At age six months, Cynthia died of crib death. The woman again became severely depressed, with thoughts of suicide. Erickson unexpectedly chastised her for her willingness to destroy delightful memories, and then directed her to plant a eucalyptus sapling that she was to name Cynthia. She was given the future orientation suggestion to "look forward to the day when you can sit in the shade of Cynthia" (Zeig, 1980a, p. 283). At a one-year follow-up, Erickson visited the woman at her home and found that she had followed the directive about the eucalyptus and had also planted extensive flower beds. She was also much improved physically and was emotionally well. Erickson commented that "Every flower she grew reminded her of Cynthia, as did the eucalyptus tree that I named Cynthia" (p. 288). With the woman's sense of purpose tied in to pregnancy and child rearing, she was devastated when her sense of purpose was gone. Erickson's directives gave her the chance to find another outlet for her important caretaking interests.

Cases such as those above highlight the relationship between involvement in living and one's mental health. It is an ongoing process to discover the meaning or purpose of one's life, and only a clinician sensitive to such issues can be truly effective in facilitating clients' discoveries in this very important area. Directives to "get involved" in activities in which a client's skills and values are effectively channeled in a positive direction can be a useful starting place in cases where one's sense of purpose is ambiguous. For some, the internal void is simply too massive to fill, but for others the directives to "get out of yourself" will have rapid curative effects. (This directive is described in clinical context in Cases 1 and 3 of Appendix B.)

SUMMARY

The relationship between one's distorted sense of responsibility and one's experiences of guilt, victimization, power struggles, and poor self-esteem is clear. More than a problematic symptom in a depressed individual, the way one deals with issues of responsibility is a core element of one's personality. Those individuals who are not currently suffering depression, but who are unclear about "where the chips fall" in their lives, are at risk for episodes of depression later. Patterns of living can amplify or diminish one's experience of daily stress, and the need to be as clear as can be reasonably expected about where one needs to assume greater responsibility and where one needs to assume less responsibility is a key to minimizing episodes of depression. The clinician who senses an ambiguity about issues of responsibility in *any* client can contribute significantly in the effort to prevent some episodes of depression and reduce the destructive effects of others.

10

A Part and Apart

Regardless of one's preferred theoretical framework for organizing one's thoughts about the nature of humans, it is readily apparent that subjective experience is a consequence of the interaction of multiple dimensions of experience. Many schools of psychotherapy tend to focus on one dimension of experience to either the total exclusion or limited consideration of other dimensions of experience. To focus on one dimension of experience implies that other dimensions of experience are not in focus (or are less in focus), thus creating a discontinuity of awareness between the two (or more) focal points. The "figure-ground" perceptual process is one way of describing the phenomenon; "selective attention" is another. Perhaps the most useful way to consider the ability to take a global experience and break it into identifiable component parts that can then be selectively altered (either amplified or diminished in their prominence) is to think in terms of "dissociation."

Many clinicians are aware of dissociation only in the context of psychopathology, where dissociation may be the central feature of a disorder, such as in "multiple personality disorder." However, the ability to experience dimensions of oneself that under "normal" conditions are operating interdependently on an independent basis is a key mechanism that operates in all human beings. Dissociation as an inherent capability of all people is a mechanism that allows experience to be compartmentalized, i.e., divided into discrete and more manageable components. Without such a mechanism, experiences would run together in ongoing confusion, and an individual would have no ability to stop doing (thinking or feeling) one thing in order to begin another. Thus, the mechanism

147

of dissociation is in itself neutral in terms of value. It has equal capacity to enhance or diminish experience, depending on the way(s) in which it is applied and the outcome it generates.

With this guiding concept about the nature of dissociation, it is possible to begin to think of people as comprised of many different dimensions, or parts. How, where, and to what degree the various parts are connected determines the overall configuration of the individual personality. In the "normal" personality, the awareness of self as one part (which is actually composed of many parts) is well connected to the awareness of the external world as another part of one's experience. When the awareness of one dimension of self is split off from awareness of other parts of self, the resulting dissociation and concomitant amnesia together comprise the major elements of the abnormal condition known as multiple personality disorder. Awareness is split, or dissociated, and one part may not have awareness of other parts. This is an example of dissociation as a catalyst for a pathological condition. For an example of dissociation as a positive mechanism of coping, one might consider the "out of the body" type of experience commonly described by those who have suffered some sort of violent trauma. Such dissociation from a painful reality is a positive coping mechanism in such instances.

When the dissociation of parts of self is not so extreme as in the multiple personality, dimensions of the person may still be unconscious but they simply do not interfere with the person's ongoing stream of consciousness. In such instances, the person may recognize dysfunctional parts of him- or herself, but not know how or why they came about. By focusing on the dysfunctional part, labeling it as "bad," "crazy," or some similarly negative term, the part evolves its own identity and is thus effectively dissociated from the rest of ongoing experience through the way one relates to it. The negative part may be repressed, denied, projected, catered to, or reacted to in any one of countless other such ways.

What is the net effect of labeling dimensions of oneself in a negative manner? Diminished self-esteem at least, self-loathing at most. The individual feels helpless to get rid of the "bad" part, and may expend unbelievable amounts of psychic or physical energy in efforts to "gain control" of the part. Often, this is not done on a conscious level. In fact, the person may not even be aware of the repression of the unacceptable part of him- or herself, only consciously experiencing the negative consequence of doing so, namely the symptoms derived from that negative part's existence.

Consider the case of David, a middle-aged husband literally dragged into therapy by his wife, Ellen, who saw him as very depressed and who was frustrated over his apparent inability to be affectionate towards her.

Ellen felt she could ease his depression if they could be closer. Other than occasional intercourse in a mechanical manner, Ellen stated that he did not hold her, hug her, kiss her, speak tenderly to her, or otherwise engage in any sort of soft intimate contact with her. David replied that he was uncomfortable with displays of affection and that Ellen "should know" that he loves her and "knowing that should be enough for her." One way of conceptualizing this problem in David and Ellen's relationship is to think of David as not having comfortable access to his tender feelings and their expression. The assumption is that David has the capability of being affectionate with Ellen ("the person has the necessary resources for meaningful change"), but the resource of "tenderness" is dissociated from his awareness and from the ongoing involvement of the relationship. The ability to help David find that dissociated resource within himself and to develop and extend it into his relationship with Ellen can become a goal of treatment. The use of hypnosis in particular to access, organize, and mobilize resources is especially useful in such endeavors. The desirable resource is present in the client but is dissociated, and therapy involves building an association, or a "trigger," for the resource to become a part of experience in the desired context. The use of directives to build new associations is another way of intervening to make previously dissociated resources available in particular contexts where it would be desirable to have them.

In the case of David and Ellen, it is quite possible that David's discomfort with tenderness is an interpersonal statement of his feelings for Ellen, despite his protests that no such negative feelings exist. It is also quite possible that David is genuinely uncomfortable with displays of affection, as his behavior and words suggest. In the latter case, one might conclude that David is repressing affectionate parts of himself because he has, for whatever reason, deemed them undesirable. If David views such displays as "unmanly" or as evidence of being "too vulnerable" or "too emotional," then what he is doing is actually a sensible thing that is consistent with his framework for living. What happens, however, when David is able to undergo a change of perspective ("reframing"), where a display of affection is transformed from "unmanly" to "a sign of the *strength* that it takes to know and express his feelings"? David may not have been conscious of his labeling "tender" as "unmanly," yet he has been aware of Ellen's dissatisfaction with him for reasons that confused him. If David were the underresponsible type of individual, no doubt he would accuse Ellen of being "too demanding." If he were the overresponsible type, no doubt he would blame himself for being an inadequate, emotionally sterile man in great need of psychological help.

The above example of David and Ellen illustrates a most important point for working effectively with depressed individuals: *For many depressed individuals, the depression is a direct or indirect consequence of the attempt to deny, purge, or repress parts of oneself labeled as "bad," which are, in fact, integral to healthy functioning.* Such a dissociation of vital parts inevitably creates an imbalance in the person's experience, and depression is often the result.

The oldest and moldiest cliché phrase in all of clinical work is "You need to get in touch with your feelings about this." This statement is a direct one, presupposing a dissociation from one's feelings. If the feelings (or thoughts or behaviors) are too threatening or are devalued as a result of one's learning from experience, then dissociation is a most useful insulating mechanism. Dissociating the dimension of experience on which the threat exists is an adaptive maneuver, yet when depression is the consequence, it is obviously not a very functional maneuver (notice the distinction between "adaptive" and "functional"). Once the necessary resource is effectively dissociated, unless the right environmental (i.e., situational) cues establish a reassociation to the part, it is most unlikely that such a reassociation will occur. This, in essence, is the job of the clinician—to access, organize, mobilize, and otherwise make available to the individual the healthiest possible use(s) of the part(s) of him- or herself that has been dysfunctionally dissociated. The general goal is to identify parts of him- or herself that the client has consciously or unconsciously rejected and redefine them as useful. Implicit is a recognition of the need to rebalance the person's system so that each part of the person has the ability to express itself appropriately in context.

Here is another example to consolidate the point about the relationship between dissociating parts of oneself and the experience of depression. Consider the case of Karen, a 39-year-old woman presenting as moderately depressed. Married and the mother of two children, Karen was generally quite passive, but prone to occasional explosive outbursts of "uncontrollable rage" in which she threw things and said things she would later feel terribly guilty about. She had seen a number of other clinicians prior to the author's seeing her, but their treatments of antidepressant medications and ventilation of anger with batacas (foam rubber bats used to beat defenseless chairs or pillows) did not have any significant therapeutic effect.

Karen's personal history included an upbringing in which she was expected to be "the perfect little girl." Raised in a strict religious home, Karen was expected "to be seen, but not heard." The consequences for being heard (when she dared to try and be) were entirely negative. Consequently, she evolved a demeanor that was quiet and overly placating much of the time, primarily in an effort to keep her unpredictable and explosive father in check. At no time during Karen's development did she feel she could express anger or feelings of dissatisfaction with her life, and she developed more and more mechanisms over time to "turn the other cheek" when situations became uncomfortable. She got married at a young age to a quiet, nonthreatening man, and in her relationship strived to maintain peace at all costs. Karen's viewpoint regarding the unacceptability of anger eventually catalyzed a dissociation of anger and diminished her ability to respond appropriately to related feelings like frustration and irritation.

Karen's attempt to rid herself of angry feelings was obviously a futile endeavor. How can so basic a feeling as anger be excised from one's emotional makeup? For Karen, it was repressed as best she could manage, but inevitably anger would build with each cumulative frustration, and then instead of having a functional mechanism through which to express anger, it would come out explosively and with no appropriate parameters. Thus, encouraging her to use foam rubber bats to release anger *could not* have worked. Karen was not in touch with anger, generally speaking. Talking to someone about being angry when he or she is not connected to the feeling is often an exercise in futility. The greater goal before encouraging ventilation of anger is to build an association that permits recognition of its very existence in various forms and degrees. When anger is so repressed that its existence is denied, as it was with Karen, a vehicle like "aggression training" is unlikely to build an acceptable association to the ventilation of anger. Often, the reason anger is repressed in the first place is because the individual feels that if he or she *does* get angry, it will be an uncontrollable rage, or at least it *seems* uncontrollable to the individual. When one is so sensitive to a feeling like anger, even a little can seem like a lot. In Karen's case, an acceptance of the inherent validity of angry feelings needed to be developed before anger could be recognized within herself. Once accepted as valid and then recognized as occurring within her, patterns of appropriate expression could be established. For as long as angry feelings were devalued and dissociated, however, no progress could have been made in facilitating Karen's acceptance of such a basic part of herself.

Issues around feelings of anger are a common dynamic in depressed clients. The classic "anger-turned-inwards" model of depression is one that conceptualizes depression as a result of unexpressed anger that is inadvertently turned on oneself. Therapy derived from that model encourages the ventilation of anger, even provoking it through deliberate actions intended to so infuriate the withdrawn person that he or she externalizes the anger and directs it at the clinician. Unfortunately, the mental health profession has been a bit confused about anger in particular, at times branding it a basic emotion needing full expression ("Get in touch with and express your anger") and at other times branding it a "useless" emotion. It should be apparent that *when anger or any other feeling is treated differentially (i.e., separated and labeled), the individual's ability to effectively utilize that dimension of him- or herself in an integrated way may be impaired.* Getting a client in touch with "the anger" is an effective dissociational strategy, and when it works, it is likely to *amplify* the person's awareness of anger in him- or herself. Conventional wisdom has been that getting the person in touch with his or her anger and supporting its expression will decrease the level of anger in the individual. The author's experience has often been to the contrary—that getting people in touch with anger just makes them angry. This is particularly true when the anger is an ongoing experience derived from ongoing frustration, such as when the person is a poor problem solver or a poor learner and as a result is unable to get what he or she wants or feels entitled to.

Consider the implications of dissociating parts of oneself one considers "bad." How many different dimensions of human experience can be considered "bad"? *Any* dimension of experience can be labeled "bad" by somebody somewhere, thus an infinite number of dissociations can occur in humans. The evidence for this is readily apparent in the range of emotional disorders that human beings can demonstrate. A young woman labels hungry feelings "bad," dissociates such feelings, and manifests anorexia nervosa as a result. A man labels sexual feelings "bad," dissociates such feelings, and manifests an erectile dysfunction as a result. A woman labels feelings of desiring a career instead of a family "bad," dissociates such feelings, and manifests passive-aggressiveness in her relationship with her children. The ability to uncover dissociated dimensions of experience in emotional disorders is usually easy to do. Building the reassociation of ways to utilize those dimensions of experience is quite a bit more difficult. The point remains, however, that it is the dissociated parts of oneself that often have not been dealt with well. Disorders of one type or another, especially depression, are a predictable consequence.

Dissociation plays a pivotal role in many of the diagnostic patterns described in Chapter 4 relative to depression. Obviously, the depressed individual's dissociative capabilities play a role in exaggerated involvement in a past temporal orientation over others, in identifying parameters influencing an external locus of control, in establishing too rigid or too diffuse personal boundaries, and in establishing a global thinking style. Furthermore, one might consider one of Beck's basic descriptive characteristics of depressed individuals — the tendency toward negative interpretation of events. Given the entire spectrum of possible interpretations of an event, how is it that the negative portion of the spectrum is noticed and amplified while the positive portion of the spectrum remains apparently invisible? To notice and respond to only one portion of the spectrum is to effectively dissociate the other portion. Similarly, the eternal optimist, who sees only the positive, is also dissociating experience, but the consequence certainly feels better.

It may be apparent by now that dissociation as a process has an equal capacity to help or hurt. In the case of the depressed individual, the depression that arises from a sense of inability to purge, deny, or control parts of oneself is a frequent dynamic. Even when this is not the direct cause of the depression, the elements of dissociation that maintain negativity in the face of positive possibilities are apparent and must be addressed in treatment in some way. The goal in working with concepts and patterns of dissociation relative to depressed individuals is to first highlight and then achieve "integration" or "reassociation" of dysfunctionally dissociated aspects of experience. This point is simply another way to describe the major premise throughout this book that therapy involves pattern interruption and pattern building. The therapeutic goal is to establish new and better responses to the demands one faces. The remainder of this chapter considers strategies for making use of dissociative and integrative capabilities of clients.

DIRECTIVES RELATING TO DISSOCIATION

In having a conceptual framework that allows for the recognition that dissociation is a neutral process which has an equal capacity to hurt or help an individual, it can be more readily understood how dissociation can be viewed as an integral part of the process of therapy and personal transformation. Those therapists who are unfamiliar with the concepts and techniques of clinical hypnosis as a model of communication and influence (see my earlier book, *Trancework: An Introduction to Clinical Hypnosis,* published by Irvington Publishers, 1984a, for a detailed explanation) may not fully appreciate the inevitability of dissociated states (called "trance") in the process of personal growth. It is true, however, that all change involves a setting aside of one's usual framework (i.e., habitual patterns) for responding in order to respond differently. Thus, whether one induces formal, overtly identified trance states as a hypnotist might, or whether one uses other therapeutic techniques to guide the learnings and experience of the client (i.e., "informal hypnosis"), dissociation from one's previous patterns while building new ones is a basic part of the process.

The use of therapeutic metaphors to facilitate dissociation can be most beneficial in working with depressed individuals. The client is rigidly entrenched in a hurtful pattern of one type or another, has labeled significant dimensions of him- or herself as pathological, has felt hopeless and helpless regarding the ability to control or purge those hurtful dimensions of self, and is emotionally in a precarious position. Metaphors may be used to build an identification for the client of the negative dissociation inherent in trying to excise parts of oneself, particularly when the part is a strong one that may even be basic to the person's personality. The stronger the part, the more effort it takes to respond to it, the more intense the depression is likely to be as a result. The metaphor can then involve the teaching that it is possible to move from dissociation to integration. In a way, the very use of metaphor as an approach models this teaching. In using a metaphor, the clinician is talking about some other person in some other situation, directly or indirectly related to the client's problem. By talking about someone else in some other context, there is a degree of removal from the immediacy of the therapy. As the client learns from the metaphor, the distance is closed and the message becomes immediate, thus a transition from a dissociated teaching to an integrated learning.

As stated earlier in this chapter, often people are not aware that they have dissociated a part of themselves. Even if they did know, it would be seen as a necessary and justifiable thing to do given how "bad" that part is. Metaphors to identify the futile nature of trying to "get rid of" parts of oneself and instead identify the more realistic goal of learning to relate to those parts more beneficially can be a meaningful way to build the mind set necessary for later attempts at integrations of new responses.

D62 Different Parts

Before one can begin to actively use "parts" of an individual in different therapeutic combinations, it can be useful for the clinician to orient the client to the nature of the work and to his or her inherent capability to do the work meaningfully. Building the recognition of "parts" of oneself as a preliminary step to using them effectively may be facilitated through the use of metaphors that involve breaking global experiences into their component parts. Consider the following metaphor as an example of one that can orient the client to the ability to acknowledge and respond to "Different Parts" of him- or herself:

> And I can tell you about a young boy I saw not long ago . . . who had been a model fourth grader . . . good grades, hard-working little fellow . . . and toward the end of the school year he underwent a transformation . . . he stopped doing his schoolwork . . . he stopped being nice to other children . . . he grew sullen and withdrawn . . . and nobody knew why . . . and then I saw him . . . and found out things of great importance to him . . . that he loved his teacher so much that he wanted her to be his teacher again . . . and he was trying to fail in school in order to stay with that teacher . . . and sometimes what seems odd on the surface, or even crazy, may make sense at a deeper level . . . but it became apparent that a part of him wanted to stay firmly put another year . . . but I also discovered a part of him that would be proud to be a big fifth grader . . . and I found a part of him that was quite curious about what fifth grade would be like . . . and I found another part of him that was excited about it being near the end of the school year . . . looking forward to a summer away from school . . . when there's lots of time to think and change one's mind . . . and another part that was sad at saying good-bye to friends for the summer . . . and there were *lots* of parts to this boy . . . and I wonder which part of him you would have talked to if *you* wanted him to know that lots of changes are part of growing . . . the curious part? . . . all I know is . . . when I talked about different parts of growing up . . . he listened very closely . . . and he's doing very well in fifth grade, you'll feel better knowing. . . .

In the above metaphor, the idea is seeded that seemingly strange behavior can be purposeful, that change involves letting go, that there are different parts of self, and that the quality of one's experience is determined to a significant degree by which part(s) one focuses upon. The metaphor implies that one can focus on whichever part of oneself is best able to catalyze successful adjustment. The language of "parts" has now been introduced to the client, as has the concept of being able to selectively amplify or diminish parts of his or her experience in order to achieve a higher purpose. (This directive is described in clinical context in Cases 1 and 2 of Appendix B.)

D63   You Have It, So Use It!

Another metaphorical strategy relates to the history of how one might develop a desire to "get rid of" parts of oneself and then encourages the higher learning that the greater goal is learning to better *use* such parts of oneself. The message is "You Have It, So Use It!" The following is an example of such a metaphor:

> And there's a man I worked with once who was most distressed . . .
> feeling suicidal . . . feeling terrible . . . and he really didn't think
> things could get any worse . . . or any better . . . and he would have
> terrible anxiety attacks . . . and waves of guilt that would come over
> him . . . in certain situations . . . like when he was driving and would
> see an attractive woman on the street . . . he'd suffer so much
> anxiety that he'd pull off the road and sometimes it would take
> hours to become calm enough to resume driving because he "knew"
> he shouldn't ever have sexual thoughts . . . or aggressive thoughts . . .
> and his thoughts and feelings seemed so out of control to him . . .
> and he was terribly depressed about it . . . and had been for a long
> time . . . and he knew how it came about . . . for when he was a very
> young boy, a nun at the parochial school he attended wanted to teach
> him a lesson . . . about being pure of mind, body, and spirit . . . and
> she forcibly held his hand over a candle, burning him badly . . . while
> telling him that this pain was nothing in comparison to the eternal
> burning all over one's body one would suffer in hell . . . and warned
> him that God knows his thoughts and deeds . . . and he better be
> careful . . . and for years and years he was a very good, conscien-
> tious, fearful boy . . . and he became a good, conscientious, fearful
> young man . . . and he managed to control his feelings as best he
> could . . . but as he got older, his sexual feelings and his aggressive
> feelings naturally became stronger . . . and harder to ignore . . . and
> each pretty girl he saw triggered anxiety and guilt . . . and each rude
> act of others toward him triggered anxiety and guilt . . . and he tried
> to purge himself of such feelings . . . and grew more depressed with
> each day's inability to do so . . . and I wonder what made him think
> that he could purge sexual feelings . . . or aggressive feelings . . . as
> if that were humanly possible . . . and I showed him what is known
> about brain anatomy and physiology . . . where the brain's sexual
> and aggressive centers are located . . . how such basic dimensions
> of self are "wired in" so to speak . . . and to fight one's own nature is
> a lot less useful a goal than is to learn how to express such natural
> feelings in a healthy way . . . and he really came to know that . . . at
> even the deepest levels in himself . . . and he came to know he
> would have all kinds of thoughts and feelings . . . some basic . . . some
> quite sophisticated . . . and he could learn to manage all of them . . . in
> a way that really feels good . . . and what a relief to him. . . .

The above metaphor illustrates the futility of trying to purge dimensions of human nature, the depression that can result, the shifting of

perspectives with new experiences and information, and the potential resolution of the problem.

The inability to accept and effectively utilize parts of oneself is no doubt a part of many people's depressions. Often, the person does not have any recognition of the purposeful or useful nature of the part(s) labeled as "bad," but is acutely aware of the negative consequences of what the part is intending to do. Along these lines is suggested the use of the strategy involving reframing "depression as a warning signal" that a change of some sort is becoming necessary. (This directive is described in clinical context in Case 4 of Appendix B.)

D64   Bad Can Be Good

The clinician can use the following directive intending to facilitate the client's discovery that what seems like a "bad" part is actually *not* bad, rather is purposeful and even useful in some contexts. The client learns "Bad Can Be Good," as perspective shifts. The client is instructed to first list the various parts of him- or herself that seem relevant to the issues at hand. Second, the client is to label the parts as "good" or "bad" according to his or her usual framework for doing so. Third, the clinician and client can together discuss which parts labeled "bad" are the targets for patterns of behavior in which the client actively engages in an effort to reject or "get rid of" those parts. Fourth, the client is then asked to identify the possible positive value of those particular parts. What do they allow the person to do? What strengths and what values do those parts represent? As a fifth and final step, the client can be asked to identify a context in which that "bad" part is actually useful, and how it is useful there.

The multidimensional effect of the above strategy is to communicate the relative value of all parts of self, to point out the context-determined nature of the value of parts, to promote self-acceptance, and to validate the person as worthwhile despite his or her depression and self-rejection.

D65   Letting Go and Reclaiming Parts of Oneself

Another strategy for facilitating the experiential learning that what one perceives as "bad" parts of oneself may actually be quite useful is one the author calls "Letting Go and Reclaiming Parts of Oneself." The client is instructed to make a list of at least 10 items that best represent him- or herself in response to the question, "Who are you?" The client may list social roles, physical, social, or intellectual characteristics, belief systems, or whatever. The client is encouraged to include a balanced representation of characteristics, i.e., things liked and disliked about him- or herself. Next, the client is asked to rank the items from least to most important and memorize the ranking. The client is then asked to close his or her eyes and "use some imagination." The process then proceeds as follows:

> Imagine that you can let go of the tenth item on your list . . . that you let go of it and it's no longer a part of you. . . . That's right . . . let it go . . . and now I want you to notice the effects of having let it go . . . how are you different? . . . What has changed? . . . What can you now do that you couldn't do before? . . . What can't you do that you could before? . . . Do you like yourself more or less without it? . . . How do people react to you without it? . . . How does it affect your behavior, feelings, and thoughts? . . . and take a moment to experience yourself without that part of you there anymore . . . and now let go of number nine on your list. . . .

The client is then guided through the experience of sequentially "letting go" of each part, including number one. The client is encouraged to experience the changes derived from giving up parts of him- or herself until the last one is "gone." The second phase involves "reclaiming" parts, as follows:

> . . . and now you can reclaim item one, taking it back and making it a part of you again . . . and notice how it feels to do so . . . with it back, how are you different? . . . What can you now do that you couldn't before? . . . What can't you do that you could without it? . . . and notice all the ways that part serves you . . . in ways you never even realized before . . . and now go ahead and reclaim the second item on your list. . . .

The client has the experience of "being without parts of him- or herself" for a while, and very often such distance allows for the discovery that parts he or she had not appreciated are actually quite purposeful. Typically, clients report experiencing relief in being able to get back their parts, even the ones they thought they did not have any use for!

D66   Six Step Reframing

The "Six Step Reframing" strategy described by Bandler and Grinder (1979, p. 160) is one that involves dissociation and is mindful of the purposeful nature of seemingly purposeless parts of the self. In this strategy, the general goal is to identify the intention of the hurtful part and to generate positive ways to meet the intention in order to interrupt the "old" dysfunctional pattern while building a "new" functional one. This strategy is outlined below:

(1) Identify the pattern (X) to be changed.
(2) Establish communication with the part responsible for the pattern.
   (a) "Will the part of me that runs pattern X communicate with me in consciousness?"
   (b) Establish the "yes-no" meaning of the signal.
(3) Distinguish between the behavior, pattern X, and the intention of the part that is responsible for the behavior.
   (a) "Would you be willing to let me know in consciousness what you are trying to do for me by pattern X?"
   (b) If you get a "yes" response, ask the part to go ahead and communicate its intention.
   (c) Is that intention acceptable to consciousness?
(4) Create new alternative behaviors to satisfy the intention. At the unconscious level the part that runs pattern X communicates its intention to the creative part, and selects from the alternatives that the creative part generates. Each time it selects an alternative it gives the "yes" signal.
(5) Ask the part "Are you willing to take responsibility for generating the three new alternatives in the appropriate context?"
(6) Ecological check. "Is there any other part of me that objects to the three new alternatives?" If there is a "yes" response, recycle to step (2) above. (Bandler & Grinder, 1979, p. 160)

The above reframing strategy provides a greater range of choices to the client as he or she responds to everyday demands. As an intervention strategy, it deals effectively with the issues of secondary gain and the establishment of a new level of balance following the integration of the changes. Furthermore, by establishing a more direct contact with the part of the person responsible for the problematic pattern(s), there is a greater respect for the integrity of the individual who is able to choose a better response rather than have one imposed upon him or her.

D67 The Parts Model

In a related strategy, which psychotherapist Paul Carter calls "The Parts Model" (Carter, 1983), he also emphasizes the purposeful nature of seemingly destructive parts and strives to reach a better balance of their intentions and their outcomes. The Parts Model is a variation of the six step reframing in its stronger development of oppositional parts so that fuller expression of all parts is made possible. This model also conceptualizes depression and many other disorders as a consequence of an inability to accept and effectively utilize parts of oneself. The recognition is that when basic feelings like anger or a desire for closeness with others are rejected as "bad" for whatever reason, the person stagnates from the lack of ability to develop that part into a useful one. Consequently, the person's energy is drawn in the direction of working to keep that part the same, creating a dysfunctional imbalance that can be rectified through the following strategy:

Step I: *Intention:* What is a wish or goal of yours?
   a) Name a goal in positive terms (Your Desired "Part").
   b) Specify the feelings, images, sounds and tastes that are consistent with and associated to the goal or wish.

Step II: *Opposition:* Is there any opposition to your goal?
   a) Specify any conflicting experience into a sensory image that you can see, feel, and hear.
   b) Name the part (Your Opposing "Part").

Step III: *Transformation:* What is the intention of your opposition?
   a) Ask the opposing part what it wants, what is its goal?
   b) Specify its wish in terms of a complete experience, i.e., feelings, pictures, sounds and tastes.

Step IV: *Choice:* What other ways can you satisfy your opposing part?
   a) Access to creative state.
   b) Generate as many choices as you can to satisfy the intention of the opposing part.

Step V: *Integrity:* Which of these ways will be O.K. with *all* of your parts?
   a) Check the choices with the opposing part to find out if they truly and completely take care of its wish.
   b) Check to find out that no other part opposes the choices.
   c) If some part opposes a choice, you may discard the choice, or shift to Step II and take care of this new opposition.

Step VI: *Integration:* How can this occur in the future?
   a) Imagine a future time in which you have achieved your initial goal.
   b) Review the steps you took to get there, i.e., training, study, exercise.
   c) Imagine some difficulty and opposition; then experience using your new choices.
   d) Build a new self-image that includes all your parts in balanced harmony. (Carter, 1983, pp. 5-6)

The above steps allow for a greater degree of contact with parts of oneself, while also facilitating an enhanced self-image that integrates those parts. The ability to identify parts that can be thought of as occurring in complements is an especially useful idea that has been developed and described in a number of schools of therapy, but especially in the Gestalt approaches.

D68 Amplifying Polarities

The strategy of "Amplifying Polarities" of an individual involves dissociating and amplifying (i.e., increasing or enhancing its ability to communicate its purpose or needs) parts of a person that seem to be in conflict. Thus, when an individual is ambivalent about some issue, as is often the case with depressed individuals, each part of the person can be "given a voice" in matters, so to speak. Parts that have been suppressed that can now express themselves can do a great deal in facilitating recovery when the client comes to know and own those parts. The ensuing dialogue between parts in conflict may be the first time that the client has ever dared to make direct contact with parts of him- or herself deemed unacceptable. As often occurs in the context of larger society when two prejudiced and mutually suspicious individuals meet, the prejudice and fear dwindle away when the other is no longer unknown. Working with an individual's polarities has been a consistent theme of Gestalt approaches (Perls, 1969; Polster & Polster, 1973).

D69 Develop the Underdeveloped Parts

In a behavioral strategy that parallels the previous one, the clinician and client can identify the valued parts and devalued parts of the person, easily done according to which parts have been most developed (the valued ones, obviously). The underdeveloped, complementary parts are thus identified simultaneously. The clinician then directs the client to engage in those activities that will "Develop the Underdeveloped Parts" in order to attain a more functional internal balance. For example, consider the case of Chris first described in Chapter 8. As a scientist by profession, Chris's emphasis is on rationality and logic. Chris had been working to excess on a very difficult project for which he was understaffed and overburdened. It was a project that *he* chose to take on because of its significance and because of the rave reviews he knew he would get if he could "pull off the impossible." Well, he could not pull it off and essentially went down in flames in the endeavor, ending up severely depressed. The parts of him that valued the "significance" and "difficulty" of a project as the requisites for becoming involved in one were already quite well developed. The complements to those parts, "insignificant" and "easy," were not used at all as criteria in deciding on a project. Thus, when Chris was disengaged from the original, hurtful project and was needing to choose another one on which to work, he was directed to choose one that would be short-term, easy, and insignificant. To deliberately choose an insignificant project to work on amused Chris greatly and helped establish a framework for directives to follow that included developing a "recreational" part, a "humorous" part, a "carefree" part, and other such complements to his usually intense demeanor.

D70 Going Fishing

Finding the complements of those parts the person tends to habitually rely on is certainly a preliminary goal to developing them. A metaphorical "Going Fishing" strategy may be used to elicit an awareness of underdeveloped parts of oneself that are appropriate to develop. The clinician might utilize general suggestions of discovering previously unknown things about oneself when exploring. The client may best experience this strategy when in a formally induced trance state. The projection of meaning by the client into the general ("process") suggestions in such a metaphor guarantee a personalizing of the experience while creating the possibility of a meaningful discovery of internal resources to be utilized in therapy.

> And sometimes people come into therapy already knowing there is something important to be learned . . . something that can really be an important discovery . . . a personal discovery . . . that provides a lot of good feelings . . . strong, positive feelings . . . the kind one gets when one goes exploring in some place not totally familiar . . . and maybe you can remember . . . from an earlier time . . . the experience of going exploring . . . I can remember the lake, the cliffs, the ravines I used to live near and explore as a child . . . and perhaps you can remember some place like that that you explored . . . and the satisfaction of finding wonderful things you didn't know were there . . . things that made a difference in the way you feel . . . and exploring inside is at least as fascinating as exploring outside . . . the parts of you that you know so well . . . the ones you notice and use everyday . . . the social parts . . . the feeling parts . . . and there are other parts, too . . . and they're parts your conscious mind doesn't know as much about . . . but your unconscious mind does . . . and if you think of a particular situation in which your conscious mind was confused, or uncertain . . . you might become aware now of a whole different part of you that might have responded to that situa-

tion . . . a part that you can comfortably call by a name that best represents it, and what do you call this part? . . . (client verbalizes the part's name) . . . and "X" is a part of you, isn't it? . . . and it's a part you tend to ignore, isn't it? . . . and one can think of other situations in which "X" would be a wonderful part to respond with . . . and can you describe a couple such situations and how "X" will respond then? . . .

The client is encouraged to explore him- or herself to acknowledge some parts as conscious and familiar and others as (dissociated) unconscious and less familiar, and to identify different personal parts that can respond to a situation other than the habitual ones. The interaction between the clinician and client can allow numerous exchanges to take place about the nature of and diversity of personal parts.

D71 Bridge Techniques

A couple of techniques also appropriate for "going fishing" for dissociated parts are the "Bridge Techniques." One is the "affect bridge" technique of Watkins (1971), which involves having the person bridge a current feeling in a current context with the same feeling in a past context ("Notice the feeling . . . intensify it . . . and drift back to the earliest experience you can recall in which you have the same feeling"). The other technique is the "somatic bridge" technique of Araoz (1985), which involves utilizing an awareness of one's body to facilitate an awareness of any repressed feelings ("Notice the feelings in your body right now . . . and let them grow stronger . . . and let the awareness of your body allow you to discover something of importance to yourself . . ."). Both techniques allow the client to discover resources in a respectful, nonimposing manner. Letting the feelings, whether emotional or physical, become the focus of attention for a while can let a rich array of images and memories drift to the surface for use in therapy.

The above techniques can be accomplished with or without formal induction of hypnosis. There are a variety of hypnotically based techniques that have proven to be extremely beneficial to depressed clients, many of which involve age regression. Age regression as a basic trance phenomenon (Yapko, 1984a) involves the intense utilization of memory, and since it is readily apparent that learned patterns provide the framework for many individuals' depression, age regression can be utilized effectively with some clients. One must be especially judicious in the use of regression with depressed clients, however, for the "past temporal orientation" typical of such clients can lead the clinician to inadvertently reinforce a dysfunctional pattern. Regression is generally contraindicated when a positive future orientation has not yet been established.

D72   Positive Resources from the Past

Age regression strategies may involve the accessing of "Positive Resources from the Past" to incorporate into current and future contexts. Such a process first involves hypnotically dissociating specific parts of the individual that have been evident in his or her personal history from time to time. Then those parts are shifted into life situations the client faces where they would serve the individual well. Clients, in essence, have the chance through the hypnosis session to rehearse the use of their own positive capabilities in the situations where they most need them. Finding such positive capabilities in one's own history can provide an added boost to one's self-esteem.

D73   Revivification

Age regression may further involve guiding the client experientially through "Revivification," a category of hypnotic techniques for "reliving" past episodes as if occurring presently (described in Yapko, 1984a). Episodes to revivify with the greatest potential for catalyzing positive changes are those in which negative generalizations or cognitive distortions (Beck et al., 1979) were made. In general, the purpose of the method is to alter the way the significant experience is internally represented by the individual, that is, how the memory was incorporated and whatever conclusions may have been drawn from it. The memory is "reworked" in order to reach new, more adaptive conclusions. The "reworking" may come about from any or all of the following: uncovering repressed, pent-up emotions, shifting the client's focus from one dimension of the memory to another, helping the client access and mobilize those resources that might be effectively used in the revivified experience (giving the person the chance to control what was originally an uncontrollable event, for example); and using techniques of cognitive restructuring (Beck, 1983; Beck et al., 1979), which can be further enhanced by the presence of the trance state in the client. Once the memory has been reworked or reframed in this type of "critical incident process" where significant events are reexperienced and therapeutically resolved, the new positive feelings and thoughts related to the memory and to the related dimensions of self-image can be "brought back" and integrated with current patterns of functioning.

D74 | Changing Personal History

Another dynamic process involving age regression that is effective and versatile is the technique of "Changing Personal History" (Grinder & Bandler, 1981) involving some patterns similar to those of the "critical incident process" just described. Changing personal history involves guiding the hypnotized client back to earliest memory and providing a structured set of meaningful life experiences that unfold over time to live and learn from. The kinds of experiences to be structured for the individual are those that can provide positive generalizations about one's self and one's life.

The client is encouraged to experience the suggested scenarios and to use all the dimensions of each scenario to their fullest, most positive extent (Lankton & Lankton, 1983; Yapko, 1984a). Through a disorientation for time passage, the client can have months or years of experience in a single trance session. Thus, the person can have moving experiences of having the parent who was lost in youth, having significant interactions with others who enhance a strong, positive self-esteem, and so forth.

In order to fully allow for the positive learnings to generalize from the trance experiences to the rest of the individual's life, multiple sessions of changing personal history may be used in conjunction with ample utilization of posthypnotic suggestions. One might suggest that "these positive memories can be the framework from which current and future choices can be made, for all people use their past learnings to guide their choices." Such a truism allows the suggestion to be more easily incorporated. Amnesia may be selectively utilized to repress specific details of the instilled memories, while allowing the positive generalizations derived from them to assume an active role in guiding the person's ongoing experience (Erickson & Rossi, 1979).

D75 | A Voice in Matters

Dissociative patterns of hypnosis are part of the above processes, but a more pure form of dissociation may be effective in addressing dimensions of depression. For example, in the case of one depressed client, suggestions were offered to acknowledge her split feelings and split awareness regarding her situation. It was suggested that she acknowledge a part of her that is characterized as "negative" and simultaneously acknowledge a part of her that is characterized as "positive." Each part could be thought of as occupying its own place within her, each with its own unique set of characteristics.

Suggestions were given to concretize these parts, giving them each a place within her on the basis of how accessible she wanted that part to be, regardless of past patterns. Positively motivated, she chose to have her dominant side be positive and her nondominant side be negative. She was encouraged to internally dissociate one side from the other and listen to (i.e., auditorily hallucinate) each side's interpretation of events before reacting.

Suggestions were given about the ability to selectively choose positive or negative interpretations based on what would be most adaptive for the situation and what would be most subjectively pleasing. Experiences were provided hypnotically to deepen the awareness for the positive side's potential influence. Positive interpretations of experience had never had "A Voice in Matters" before, and as the client became able to respond to her positive side appropriately, her experience of depression lifted. This pattern is structurally similar to the distorted focus on the exclusively negative aspects of experience typical of depression, but the focus is now shifted to positive dimensions of experience to create a more balanced approach to life (since no one's life is good or bad *all* the time).

D76 Externalizing Significant Parts

Another general strategy involves the mechanism of "Externalizing Significant Parts" of the client that are normally kept within. This can be done in a number of ways. One such strategy is "aggression training" or "provocative therapy" (Farrelly & Brandsma, 1978), in which a client who suppresses feelings of anger is deliberately antagonized in order to get the person to externally express angry feelings. Other feelings may be externalized simply through their expression to the clinician, particularly those feelings the person is most ashamed of or embarrassed by (Spiegel, 1986).

D77 The Parts Party

Another such "externalization" strategy is the technique Satir developed that she calls "The Parts Party." In this group therapy technique, the client chooses from six to 12 fictional or real characters who represent significant traits to the client. These individuals are either very strongly liked or disliked by the client. Their likable or unlikable traits are identified by the client, and positive and negative characters are then evenly matched up. Each member of the group is given a character to play as the symbol of those traits, and then a "party" for all characters is held. The characters all interact "in role," exaggerating their characters' relevant trait(s). The client gets to see and experience different parts acted out, seeing them in a new way relevant to him- or herself which can help uncover their positive functions. At the end of the party, the client is encircled by all the parts and formally accepts each of the parts and the different capabilities each represented (in Carter, 1983).

D78 On Paper

Examples of another type of "externalizing" strategy are the various record-keeping and written exercises used in a number of different schools of psychotherapy. For instance, in the highly effective cognitive therapy approach, the client may be given a variety of written exercises (e.g., daily thought records and cognitive distortion recognition exercises) that take one's thoughts out of the realm of the internal and subjective and put them "On Paper" where they can be more objectively scrutinized. By externalizing one's thoughts—itself a pattern interruption technique—and by giving one the tools to recognize *and correct* one's own distorted thoughts, the helplessness pattern is also interrupted. Burns (1980) described many such written strategies that help dissociate the client from his or her usual thought patterns, while using *repeated practice* of "clear" thinking as a means *for integrating* the important learnings.

D79 Symptom Substitution

In some cases, the clinician might choose to use a strategy that is aimed simply at symptom relief. In circumstances where the depression is secondary to serious physical illness (e.g., cancer) and the prognosis is negative, or in circumstances where the depressed individual is somehow unavailable for or unlikely to benefit from more intensive treatment, "Symptom Substitution" as a deliberate strategy may be employed. Often the depressed individual somatizes the symptoms of depression; somatic complaints are more concrete, have more clearly identifiable parameters, and are generally inter- and intrapersonally more acceptable (Suinn, 1984).

Symptom substitution as a strategy may involve the controlled transformation of the emotional pain of depression into an acceptable physical pain, i.e., one that is mild, tolerable, and not disabling. Such a strategy of symptom substitution was described by Erickson (1954a). One might consider that somatic complaints where depression is the underlying feature are spontaneous and uncontrolled manifestations of this same process. The key to using this strategy lies in the controlled nature of choosing the site of symptom substitution, thus providing recognition at some level of an ability to control the symptom.

SUMMARY

In conceptualizing dissociation as a process that is equally capable of helping or hurting, it may be easier to identify where and how dissociation operates as a catalyst of positive changes in the therapy process. Noticing the dissociation that is integral to many therapy models (perhaps Gestalt and Transactional Analysis are the two most common examples) may help clinicians develop a greater deliberateness over which "parts" of a person can be positively accessed and which are better left alone (because of their imbalanced nature). For example, amplifying past hurts by focusing the individual on traumatic memories when the depressed person is already too past-oriented is likely to be antitherapeutic, yet is a common approach of clinicians. The idea of identifying, developing, and integrating complementary parts or repressed parts for the purpose of achieving a better sense of balance remains a dominant goal in the treatment of depression. Every therapy works with parts of an individual, but the most effective therapy occurs when the "right" parts (i.e., the ones central to the person's depression) are brought into a more useful configuration, where they can be utilized as effective personal resources for responding to life's ongoing demands.

11

Never and
Always Alone

The directives described in the previous chapters are able to bring the depressed client into contact with his or her depressogenic values, beliefs, and behaviors. Much of the therapeutic work can be done internally by the client as one self-limiting pattern is interrupted and replaced by another pattern that is more adaptive. Focusing exclusively on the internal world of the client, however, is inevitably an incomplete intervention, since the individual does not live entirely within him- or herself. Rather, the individual lives in a world that includes other people — *lots* of other people. One of the primary dimensions of experience described in Chapter 3 is the relational one, emphasizing the interpersonal aspects of an individual's life. The relational dimension encompasses the larger social system of which one is a part, and includes all of the people one interacts with, however occasional or distant in quality the relationship. Of course, the more significant relationships receive greater emphasis in intervening on this dimension, with special attention paid to the individual's relationship patterns relative to a spouse, children, parents, close friends, colleagues, employers, and others who are important in his or her life.

It seems impossible to overstate the role other people play in shaping a person's perspectives about the world he or she lives in. Society is a universal way of life, and each society intensely socializes its members in order for them to acquire the knowledge that will be necessary for them to participate meaningfully in that society. One learns what one can and cannot do, what can be expressed and what must be kept to oneself. Perhaps most important, one learns what is expected in each of the many social roles one plays.

Social psychology has accumulated a substantial amount of information on social roles and normative behavior in a variety of contexts. It is unfortunate that the many different branches of psychology seem to have little or no contact with each other, for the perspectives of each can contribute greatly to a better and more unified understanding of the various forces shaping an individual's life. In any event, social psychology's emphasis on interpersonal dimensions of experience can allow clinicians greater insight into ways to intervene in an established social system that will allow for positive changes in its members. Specifically, one must keep in mind that whatever occurs at the individual level of experience will have consequences elsewhere in the system, including interpersonal consequences. Thus, the other members of the client's system play a huge role in directly and indirectly reinforcing and extinguishing his or her patterns of subjective experience.

Consider, for example, the remarks of Adam (first described in Chapter 9), who had been a stockbroker before suffering severe depression. An intelligent and sensitive man, Adam attributed much of the paranoia that he experienced around others as a response to a value judgment from them that he was unemployed and, therefore, useless. Due to his incapacitating bouts with depression, Adam's wife and older children gradually became responsible for handling family matters. Out of the fear that they would aggravate his already delicate condition, Adam's family began to exclude him completely from the stresses of decision making, and inadvertently from a sense of connectedness with them. Adam called himself "the benevolent gargoyle" of the house—a curious expression of his sense of isolation and uselessness.

The pattern has been well described in the behavioral literature regarding depression. The depressed individual becomes too negative and too draining to be around, exhausting the attempts of others who genuinely want to help, until, in their own frustration, they leave. The depressed individual now has additional fuel for the depression fire, feeling both incompetent and unlovable. In another problematic relational aspect, the help that others provide during episodes of depression can inadvertently reward the person for being depressed. This occurs as a result of displays of attention, affection, and other behaviors that the depressed individual may find reinforcing.

Clearly, some interactional patterns are more functional and meaningful than others, and how the client patterns his or her relationships can cause or maintain episodes of depression. (This, of course, is the central theme of the interpersonal model of depression.) Relationship systems, once established, usually maintain stability. In order to do so, interactions tend to become ritualized. An expectation evolves, sometimes intensely, about how one is to be, and the pressure on an individual to live up to that expectation can be enormous. If the expectations are so firmly entrenched as to seemingly be beyond question, the conscious mind's critical nature is bypassed, and quite unconsciously the individual responds to the imposed guidelines. Finding out who imposed the guidelines is not always easy. Sometimes it is clear that the expectations *were* overtly established by someone significant; other times the individual discovers that he or she *assumed* something about others and imposed what have become hurtful standards on him- or herself. Regardless of the origin of the expectations, the individual's social system becomes a finely balanced one that does not easily allow for a shift in patterns. As pointed out earlier, a shift in one member inevitably causes a need to shift in the others in order to adjust themselves accordingly. Having to shift one's patterns is often hard anyway, yet may be experienced as especially hard when the individual did not even initiate the changes but is simply reacting to another. The sluggish response to the demand to change by family members appears to be "resistance" to change and may even seem like direct or indirect attempts to sabotage the client's efforts.

Dealing with the interpersonal consequences of one's life patterns is an ongoing part of living. In working with depressed individuals in particular, the interpersonal effects are quite marked, as Table 5 in Chapter 3 suggests.

If we consider some of the most common and disturbing patterns evident in relationships, we can think of power struggles (i.e., grappling overtly or covertly for control of the relationship), coercive and/or selfish manipulation, excessive dependency, too diffuse or too rigid boundaries between parties, overt or covert patterns of rejection or ridicule, and verbal or physical abuse in any of a number of other forms. The clinician who is sensitive to the relationship patterns in the depressed client's life is likely to find any or all of these negative patterns and will need to intervene in some way. In considering the use of directives for the treatment of depressed individuals, it may be helpful to consider the main issues of "control" and "responsibility" (discussed at length in previous chapters) in terms of the interpersonal implications. In order for the client to achieve as complete a recovery as possible, these issues must be sufficiently clear to be handled properly on *all* dimensions.

INTERPERSONAL MANIFESTATIONS OF AMBIGUITY REGARDING CONTROL

People want what they want when they want it. When what they want is from other people in general or from another in particular, the attempts to control others begin. It is hardly pathological to want things from other people — the needs for affection, approval, support, and other such interpersonal comforts are both universal and appropriate. The relevant issues involve the extent of one's needs and the tactics one employs in attempting to have those needs met. The person's self-esteem may be inappropriately connected to the feelings or actions of another, with depression arising when the other person does not do as desired. Consider the following examples.

In one woman in treatment, the presenting problem of an acute depression was clearly tied to her son's decision to attend graduate school in biochemistry instead of medical school, as she had hoped. She complained bitterly about his disrespect for her wishes, and the terrible disappointment she was having to cope with as a result of his decision. She described the many ways she had attempted to groom him for a career in medicine from the time he was a little boy, and how she felt betrayed by his going against her well-known wishes. Clearly, this woman was attempting to control the life of her son, and it is fortunate that he was well individuated and competent enough to make such important decisions for himself. Her tactics of attempting to induce guilt in him with her suffering did not overtly impact him, which further highlighted (to her) her inability to control him. Therapy involved developing accep-tance of her son's ability to decide what his own life should be about, building the recognition that competence was a manifestation of the ability to make decisions carefully and bear the consequences arising from those decisions. Therapy began with a simple but effective reframing: "How wonderful a mother you must have been in raising him to turn out so clear about who he is and what he wants." She had not yet seen it in that way, and this guiding perspective made the rest of the therapy work considerably easier.

In another case example, a woman went away for a weekend with a man with whom she had had an "on again-off again" relationship. The weekend was one that was meant to satisfy her need for closeness with someone. In general, she was quite dependent on others for a sense of self, and despite the lack of a true bond between herself and the man, she felt that she would at least have the enjoyment of being with him. Her covert agenda, however, was to attempt to deepen the man's sense of commitment toward her, assuming that if the weekend went well, the relationship could stabilize in an "on" position. Well, the weekend *did* go well. Upon her return, she described it as a passionate as well as a playful weekend. Her joy soon turned to despair and depression (again) when days went by without the man calling her. She assumed he would call and maintain (the illusion of) closeness with her and she was devastated when he did not. When she finally confronted him about his insensitivity, he coolly reminded her of what he had told her beforehand—that he was not interested in an ongoing and committed relationship. Therapy involved helping her to redefine her assumptions and expectations about others, and to more effectively respond to the reality of others rather than to the idealistic wish of how they "should" be. The man had been honest with her from the start, but what hurt her was finding out she could not control him through her manipulative tactics of seduction. Even her tears and depression did not sway him. Her internal focus on her own wishes effectively precluded an external focus and view of the reality of the situation—all too common a pattern among depressed individuals.

The internal emotional havoc related to depression that arises from trying to control uncontrollable events is derived from the amplification of anger, guilt, emotional distance, disappointment, and other feelings that may be acted out in a relationship with another person. The first example of the depressed mother is a typical example of intense anger and disappointment being focused on her son, who, if he had been a less secure young man, might have felt guilty about his mother's reactions and then complied with her wishes. In the second example above involving the seductress, her hopes and wishes were focused on another individual. When the individual did not conform, the anger and disappointment with the man's lack of commitment and intent to satisfy her wishes became intense. If he had felt responsible for her well-being or for her wishes being fulfilled, he may have become enmeshed in what surely would have been a destructive relationship.

"Instrumental depression" is a term coined by the author to describe those episodes of depression where the manipulative value of the depression is a key feature of its onset. In such cases, the depression is a tactic for getting compliance from others with little or no regard for the emotional price (in guilt, fear, or hurt) that those who comply must pay. This "get me what I want at any cost" pattern violates a most basic rule of healthy and positive relationships—accepting that everyone must make their own best choices for themselves. Presupposing that one is better able to judge what is good for someone than that individual is able to do for him- or herself is a pattern highly likely to lead to power struggles one cannot win.

Another aspect of instrumental depression involves the recognition that depression may be directly rewarded, in that experiencing depression leads to a positive consequence. In what may seem like a facetious example, consider the observation that at almost any party there is one person (usually a man) who seems down and withdrawn. It seems that there is always a compassionate lady at such parties, who accepts the burden of helping out this troubled man. Almost invariably, this is the guy who does not leave the party unattended. Depression can have its rewards. . . .

Another way of considering how ambiguity about "control" issues on an interpersonal dimension can lead to depression relates to social roles, as briefly discussed earlier. The role a person is in dictates to a large extent the expectations of others. For example, if one is in the role of teacher, then one is expected to lecture, to demonstrate, to discuss, to answer questions, and so forth. One might recognize that often depression is a consequence of having expectations of others that are unrealistic in some way and are inconsistent with the way the other person defines his or her own requirements. If one applies pressure on another to conform to the standards one associates with a particular role, then one inevitably creates a power struggle that becomes more and more emotionally charged over time. Thus, the letdown is even greater when the struggle is lost. Even what seems like a win is a loss, since the other individual simply complies: there is not true internalization of the expectations; there is only capitulation, a condition usually quite unsatisfying to the victor.

Consider this example. A husband and wife sought therapy for resolution of an ongoing heated disagreement that was causing them both to be depressed and irritable. The woman began by saying, "I'm 33 years old, and we have two sons ages nine and 11. I quit work to raise them and now they are basically raised—they're in school all day and don't need me so much. I very much want to go back to work." The husband's swift response was "No wife of mine is going to work—I'll leave her first!" Her exasperated response was one of pleading with me to "Fix him!" In getting the husband to state his objections to her going back to work, he offered lame reasons such as, "What if one of the kids get sick and the school nurse calls and nobody's home?" In dealing with the irrationality of his objections, layer after layer of nonsensical objections were stripped away until his bottom line fear was exposed, that if his wife returned to work, she would meet some combination of Paul Newman and Robert Redford, fall in love, and ride off into the sunset with him.

Considering this situation from the perspective of control issues, roles, and expectations, one can see that the husband had a very clear but rigid set of expectations about appropriate behaviors for a "wife" and "mother." Wife apparently meant "obedient woman," and "mother" apparently meant "immediate help available" to this man. Anything that threatened his expectations, such as his wife's tendency to want something more out of life for herself, created anger, frustration, and depression in him when the issues remained unresolved over extended periods of time. His insecurity manifested itself as an attempt to control his wife's whereabouts and interests, reinforcing the general principle discussed earlier that the more insecure one is, the more one attempts to control others.

This type of controlling pattern surfaces in countless interactions of diverse types. Trying to get someone to stop drinking, stop flirting, stop spending, start having orgasms, or to be nice, considerate, ambitious, or *whatever* is energy-draining and carries a low probability for success. Many of the strategies that are described in this chapter are intended to drive home the point that one cannot control others, and that the sooner one learns and accepts that, the sooner one will end the spiral involving anger, frustration, and depression. Attempting to manipulate others to get one's needs met is an inevitable part of human relationships. This is not the issue here. The issue is that people too often entrust others to meet needs that the other person *simply is not capable* of meeting. Either the person is not capable because he or she does not value that particular pattern and thus sees no need to expend energy needlessly, or is so inexperienced with the desired pattern that he or she is unable to demonstrate it capably. Consider the following example.

An attorney in his mid-40s sought therapy for depression. Despite his having a good marriage, nice children, a beautiful home, and a successful law practice, he had an extremely low self-esteem and felt he was only mediocre in meeting his life's demands. He described how he had "never" felt confident about himself. When a clinician hears that someone has "never" been able to do or feel something in particular, it's a cue to get some family history. In his case, he described a very cold, critical, withholding father who always left him feeling inadequate, despite his best efforts. He was "a good little boy," but his dad did not acknowledge this in him. He got good grades, he was never in trouble, he helped out around the house, and yet he never received the love, recognition, and positive feedback from his father that he desperately wanted. What one grows up with, one tends to take for granted. What one grows up without, one tends to desperately strive to attain (Massey, 1979; Yapko 1985a). In this client's case, the struggle to win his dad's approval became an obsession, consciously but more so unconsciously guiding many of his life's decisions. Graduating valedictorian of his high school class did not earn dad's approval, nor did graduating magna cum laude in college. Becoming a lawyer like his dad did not win any special recognitions either, and when he graduated and came to join his father's law practice, dad decided to retire and *sold* his son the legal practice. After he had taken over, the son's first change was to computerize the office, upgrading the capabilities. In bringing his father in to proudly show the technological advance, he was crushed when his father said, "I never needed a computer to run my practice. What's the matter with you that you can't do it on your own?"

In listening to this competent, sensitive man describe disappointment after disappointment, rejection after rejection, it was obvious how he had internalized all of his father's critical responses as evidence of his inadequacy. It had never occurred to him to question his father's nature, a pattern of being noncritical found in children of all ages. It's hard to play offense when one feels one has to play defense in order to survive. The author abruptly asked the man to name three things his dad approved of. He literally squirmed in his chair for 15 minutes before he burst into tears, unable to name anything. It was then very easy to make the point that the problem was not his inadequacy, rather that he used a primary feedback source that was very distorted— entirely negative. He had, in essence, been asking for something his father did not seem to have— approval. To entrust someone to give approval (or compassion, love, responsibility, communicativeness, or any other quality) presupposes he or she has it to give! What a costly and destructive assumption when it turns out not to be the case. Depressed individuals (with their internal focus on distorted assumptions) may assume others are deliberately holding back what they want and get depressed as a consequence. The clinician must question the assumption and literally ask, "You're assuming this person can give approval who isn't giving it to you. How do you know he or she even has it to give?"

Dealing with the unrealistic expectations that other people have the capacity to give or do anything is a fundamental part of intervening on the interpersonal dimension. It is necessary to develop the awareness that people have limitations, and that what may seem like withholding may not be withholding at all, but rather a sign of an absence of a particular quality or capability. When another person seems like he or she is withholding, the depressed person personalizes it and views it as objective evidence of his or her own inadequacy. When the person is able to assess more objectively others' capabilities, he or she is no longer having to personalize others' shortcomings. By attempting to control others' reactions (e.g., how much they approve) through one's actions, personal power is given away, and one is then at the mercy of others and their reactions. Thus, one's self-esteem is out of one's own hands and is fated to go up and down with the varied reactions inevitably received to just about anything one does. A well-developed sense of one's individuation is the only means for maintaining control over one's self-esteem (Yapko, in press). Controlling others' reactions is simply not a consistent possibility.

The primarily internal focus of depression occurs often at the expense of refined external awareness. Translated on the interpersonal dimension, it seems that depressed clients are generally not very good at assessing others objectively. The clinician can provide insight to ways to better assess others' capabilities, teaching the person to be more selective in who is entrusted to meet his or her needs.

DIRECTIVES FOR RESOLVING CONTROL ISSUES ON THE INTERPERSONAL DIMENSION

The assumption in this section is that the clinician will be making use of social contexts for these directives, i.e., they will be carried out through interactions with others.

D80   Redefining Roles

One pattern the clinician might want to interrupt relates to any negative consequences derived from the client's narrow definition of a social role that he or she occupies. If the client is depressed partially because his or her role is painfully restrictive in some way, the clinician can use a directive the author calls "Redefining Roles," which forces a reevaluation of the role(s) a client plays. The client is directed, for example, to define the role in question (mother, father, employer, employee, etc.) in extremely explicit terms of what someone successful in the role would *do*. The client is then directed to define just as explicitly what someone successful in the role would *never* do. This may be done in verbal or written form. The values that dictate the "shoulds" of the client's role definitions will no doubt become apparent to the clinician and can be discussed openly. Finally, the client is directed to go out and *do* some of the harmless things that may seem incongruous with the role in order to discover that it is not the role that is rigid in nature, but the client's interpretation of the role's demands. The client should be rehearsed for dealing with the feedback (e.g., confusion or criticism) from others for having behaved differently than usual.

D81   Bending the Role

As a follow-up to the above strategy, metaphors may be delivered to the client that deal with the central theme of personal progress and relief being derived from bending the parameters of a specific role. Such "Bending the Role" metaphors are abundantly available in the form of countless examples of social change arising from people having the courage to rebel against expectations of how they should behave. Racism, sexism, ageism, and other prejudices are rooted in people placing other people in categories or roles and directly demanding that they stay there. Progress is a by-product of *not* conforming. The following metaphor is an example of this pattern:

> And I have a client I'm working with who I can tell you about . . . because she's learning something that you might find very important . . . and very freeing . . . and she's only 15 . . . but her problem is a lot older than that . . . and she lives at home with her mother and stepfather . . . and she's a very bright girl . . . very ambitious and very energetic . . . and very sensitive to others' feelings . . . especially about her . . . and her stepfather is an old-fashioned man . . . who believes a woman's place is only in the home . . . where she should be a good wife . . . raise children . . . clean the house . . . do laundry . . . and all the things he thinks of as a woman's work . . . in his narrow definition of a woman's role . . . but his stepdaughter is bright . . . and curious . . . and wants a career . . . and when she brings home top grades from school . . . he really doesn't notice . . . when she shares how her debate competition went . . . he really doesn't notice . . . and when she gives him papers she has written to read . . . he really doesn't have the time . . . but he loves it when she bakes brownies for him . . . and he loves it when she gives him a back rub . . . and he loves it when she does "girl" things . . . and she feels so uncomfortable around him quite often . . . because she wants to do things that don't fit his expectations . . . and I wonder how you feel about her situation . . . and whether you feel she should be a good little girl for her stepfather . . . or whether she should pursue her own goals . . . even if they are different than what a good little girl would do . . . and you may be relieved to know that she is making the decisions for herself . . . and that she is wonderfully aware . . . that the only expectations she needs to live up to . . . are her own . . . and what a relief. . . .

The above metaphor illustrates the ways that roles and expectations can limit a person, can conflict with others, and how the greatest freedom comes from doing as one sees fit in managing one's life, despite the expectations of others. This metaphor simultaneously addresses the issue of approval seeking from others at one's own expense.

D82   Monarch for a Day

One way to break the pattern of expectations about how others are to behave is to externalize the expectations, which can be done with a strategy like "Monarch for a Day." For each of the parties in the relationship, the directive may be given that one assume the role of "king or queen for a day," while the other(s) is "slave for the day." What starts out as a humorous task assignment can quickly become serious when the "king's" commands are eventually defied. The "king" learns at the least that he cannot control the will of the "slave," and the "slave" learns that no matter how much one placates someone, it is simply never enough. This emphasizes the need to be more selective in placating others' needs or expectations. The roles should later be reversed, so that each member has learned from both roles. The balance between doing for self or for others is much easier to attain when someone has experienced both extreme ends of the continuum.

D83   Pretty Please Permission Seeking

Given the strong need for approval (external validation) that exists when someone's self-image is weak, the clinician must have a strategy for disrupting that pattern and facilitating self-validation. One strategy that is useful for this purpose is "Pretty Please Permission Seeking." In this strategy, the client is offered the behavioral symptom prescription that he or she asks others for permission to do whatever it is he or she wants to do (e.g., "Can I sit here?"). In this extreme form of seeking approval, the client is required to get a positive reply from others before he or she can proceed with even the simplest tasks (e.g., going shopping, going to the bathroom, watching television, going to sleep). The client's approval-seeking patterns are thus amplified to maximum intensity, and the difficulties associated with having to have one's own needs validated by others is quickly apparent and becomes framed negatively. The client is usually reacted to with variations of "Why are you asking me such ridiculous questions? Do what *you* want to do!", even by those who may previously have encouraged dependency. The client thus has the opportunity to experience firsthand that not only is excessive approval seeking a personal bother, it is also taxing to the others around him or her. The result is the establishment of a strong internal association that highlights approval-seeking behaviors that can then be noticed and altered appropriately. An internal frame of reference or validation of one's own needs must be offered simultaneously with this strategy in order for the person to successfully make the transition from being more other-oriented to more self-oriented relative to meeting one's needs.

D84   Dependency Plus

In a reversal of the previous strategy called "Dependency Plus," the other members of the client's social system may be assigned the task of asking the client for permission for all the things that they wish to do. Having to continually make decisions for others about such trivial matters as their bathroom visits gets very tedious very quickly. The feeling emerges quite congruently that it is better to let others make their own decisions responsibly and independently, reducing significantly the attempts to control others' lives.

Of course, the flip side to the need for approval is the fear of rejection. When one's self-esteem rests in the hands of others, it is an ongoing nightmare to try and keep everyone (of importance, that is) happy. If the person felt reasonably comfortable in his or her ability to competently manage confrontation or rejection, the impetus to seek approval so intently would be considerably less.

D85   Rejection Seeking

A directive strategy called "Rejection Seeking" may be used to help build a mechanism within the client for better managing rejection. The strategy involves having the client take a position on some issue he or she is not personally involved in, identifying a particular group that takes an opposite position, and then asking those opponents for monetary contributions to the cause. For example, a client who does not really have much of an opinion about homosexuality might take sides with a Gay Rights Tasks Force and then be told to call a Fundamentalist Church for a contribution. Similarly, a client may take sides with a real estate development program and then call the Sierra Club for a donation. The client is able to discover experientially where rejection comes from in a context that is impersonal. The client learns that each person judges others according to what he or she feels is right for him- or herself. Approval comes when one conforms to others' expectations and beliefs, and rejection comes from not conforming. The clinician can be quite deliberate in making the point that in the same ways groups reject positions that are opposite or different from their own, so do individuals. The basic affirmation that comes from this strategy is that others' rejections do not invalidate one's position.

The pattern of being a not-so-great judge of other people can certainly lead one into destructive, and therefore depressing, relationships. The recognition that depressed individuals tend to be internally absorbed carries with it the implication that the individual is less likely to be observant of externals, including other people. It carries the further implication that the individual is likely to use his or her own frame of reference to an even greater extent than others, assuming that what he or she experiences is similar to what others are experiencing. This assumption is what can lead to the often painful discovery that others do not feel the same way or value the same things. (This directive is described in clinical context in Case 4 of Appendix B.)

D86 Assessing Others

One directive that can be used in such cases is the task assignment simply called "Assessing Others," in which the client is asked to identify as best he or she can what variables he or she takes into account when making assessments of others. It is useful to give this directive to the client when he or she is missing the ability to assess significant patterns in others much to his or her detriment. Frequently, the client has little or no idea of how such assessments are made and will respond with something global like, "I guess I judge them according to how I feel when I'm with them—whether they make me feel good or not." The disadvantages of not having a more objective way to assess others can then be pointed out, leading into a discussion of different things one can take into account when with someone.

Significant criteria that seem central to the quality of one's relationship are how individuals deal with issues of responsibility, acceptance of inevitable differences, sense of commitment, ability to be honest, problem-solving abilities, ability to accept feedback, and knowledge of self (e.g., personal needs, values, and motivations). Providing the client with specific criteria for assessing others along with extremely concrete examples of such patterns can guide the client from a more global response to others to one that is more well defined. With a better means for assessing others' capabilities as they exist within those individuals instead of in terms of the way they make the client feel, the client can prevent him- or herself from getting caught up in impossible or destructive relationships. The cognitive distortion of "emotional reasoning" (Burns, 1980) is one in which the individual uses his or her feelings as the indicator of what to do. One's thoughts are accepted as accurate because they *feel* accurate ("I feel unloved, therefore I am unloved"). The problem, of course, is that feelings are easily manipulated and thus are not accurate reflectors of ongoing experience. Perhaps the most obvious way to exemplify this point is to consider how easily Hollywood manipulates our feelings, creating scenes and dialogue in television and movies that "push all the right buttons" to keep us coming back for more!

For the client who entrusts others to provide those things he or she wants, such as approval or support, the point needs to be made powerfully that the mere fact that he or she wants it does not mean the other person can provide it. When a client has been through a hurtful relationship that did not allow him or her access to what was desired (such as the example of the attorney still seeking his father's approval), a strategy needs to be used that will clarify to the client that his or her need was not the problem; rather, the other person's inability to meet that need was the problem. (This directive is described in clinical context in Case 3 of Appendix B.)

D87 Asking the Impossible

A strategy that serves this therapeutic need well is "Asking the Impossible." The client is directed to go to familiar others and ask them for things that he or she *knows* they do not have: "Can I borrow your yacht for the weekend?" "Can I borrow a million dollars?" "Would you please give me the property deed for Hawaii?" Such requests are obviously silly, but they make the exaggerated point of how ridiculous it is to ask people for things they do not have. With the added suggestion for carrying out the strategy that the client ask for what he or she wants as if the person really has it, it becomes easy to access the client's feelings that others are withholding and to address and resolve those feelings ("Imagine how you would have felt if you believed the person really had a million dollars and refused your request"). The point is again highlighted that before one entrusts one's needs to another to meet, it would be wise to know whether the person can "deliver the goods." If this is not the case, then one knows not to try and tap that source, preventing considerable frustration. If one knows that the person does have the resource and can share it, then one need not go through all kinds of manipulative tactics to get it. Hopefully, the client will assess that the person is open and giving of such desired resources.

Each of the strategies described in this section are meant, in one way or another, to increase the depressed client's sense of control within the boundaries of a positive relationship. Goals of greater self-awareness and other-awareness are tempered with the goal of acceptance. With acceptance comes a diminished need to control others, and since trying to control others is all too likely to lead to emotional pain, striving for acceptance is a much more satisfying goal.

INTERPERSONAL MANIFESTATIONS OF AMBIGUITY REGARDING RESPONSIBILITY

In Chapter 9, the issue of attributions regarding personal responsibility was addressed. Distortions regarding one's sense of responsibility for ongoing events (both internal and external) can lead one to make inappropriate and dysfunctional choices in a variety of ways, but perhaps especially so on the interpersonal dimension. The effect on one's relationships when one is unclear about issues of responsibility is to open the door to destructive manipulations and excessive dependency. If one is unaware of the limits of one's responsibilities, it becomes possible to assume one is responsible for more or less than one really is. The interesting thing about imbalances in an individual's personal sense of responsibility is how the person manages to attain balance in a relationship. If one tends to be generally irresponsible about one's life (i.e., making impulsive decisions, reacting rather than acting, letting others make the important decisions for oneself), the necessity for establishing a relationship with someone who can be responsible is quite clear. Likewise, when one is very responsible about one's life, one may be well able to manage personal affairs. The competence of such an individual can attract those less able to manage on their own.

If one is good-hearted enough to take someone "under one's wing" who is needy of a manager, one can get caught up in a trap of taking care of someone who is unable or unwilling to take care of him- or herself. In such instances, the individual's pattern of overresponsibility emerges in plain sight. The individual may feel it is up to him or her to make sure that the other person is well taken care of. A sense of obligation and commitment to another is not in and of itself unhealthy; however, the client must be made aware of the negative consequences of assuming too much responsibility for another. The overresponsible client experiences higher and higher levels of stress associated with more and more burdens being placed on him or her, while the other individual(s) in the relationship gets taken care of. Why continue in such a pattern? The overresponsible individual gets to control everything, which is what is desired in the first place. Furthermore, by being overresponsible relative to the other(s), the client maintains a sense of purpose and a feeling of being necessary when other things are a bit shaky inside. Finally, the manipulative quality of being overresponsible is evident, for when the person feels threatened in some way, he or she can assume the position of a martyr and ask in a most gut-wrenching way, "After all I've done for you, how could you do this to me?"

Reducing the overresponsible client's sense of responsibility for others can have some very dramatic consequences. First, dealing with guilt becomes an immediate priority, for once the person stops taking care of things he or she is used to taking care of, there is a strong sense of being irresponsible rather than the sense of relief one might expect. The clinician can anticipate this and can let the client know that guilt feelings are neither unexpected nor abnormal. Relief from the burdens one has been carrying usually follows fairly soon after. If the clinician chooses to, he or she can openly discuss the previous imbalance regarding responsibility in the relationship system, and then allow the client to more accurately perceive what a new shift in responsibilities will generate in terms of consequences for all involved. The excessive responsibilities that an individual takes on can be costly on many levels, but the single-minded determination to "make it all work" can be the most prominent pattern in a given individual's depression. The single-mindedness, however nobly motivated, precludes a recognition that when one is overresponsible, one is passively encouraging another to be irresponsible. A "hook" the clinician can use with some certainty of success involves relating to the overresponsible client how his or her advanced sense of responsibility actually precludes the growth of those who rely on it. The client's sense of responsibility can thus be utilized to allow the client to act less responsibly for the benefit of others.

The other side of the imbalanced sense of personal responsibility concerns the depressed, underresponsible individual. In such individuals, the tendency is to be less than responsible for oneself, sometimes because one wants to selfishly "let someone else worry about it," but more often simply because the depression has left little confidence that one can manage one's own life competently. Depression can leave one feeling weak and useless and lucky to have anyone around at all. Frequently, depression will cost one relationships because people leave. Trying to help somebody who seems unreachable, as depressed persons often seem, can get frustrating even for the most experienced clinicians, much less for friends and relatives. Depressed people are usually not much fun, and it's hard to be "up" around someone who is down without feeling guilty or somehow inappropriate. When the depressed person has been left alone, literally or figuratively speaking, he or she may come to depend on someone (anyone) willing to help, whether a clinician or a friend. The person may assume that the depression is clear evidence that he or she is not competent to deal with life's demands, leading to a reliance on the judgments of someone else. The excessive dependency on others shown by many depressed individuals is well known, and it should be apparent that without establishing a clear sense of responsibility for oneself in the client, such dependency can easily maintain a depressed lifestyle.

Satir (1972) described a number of different personality styles, two of which are the "placater" and the "blamer." The "placater" tries to make sure that everyone is happy with him or her regardless of the amount of pain he or she needs to go through to appease others. The "blamer" finds fault with everyone else and attributes whatever goes wrong to the errors of others. It seems remarkable that these people can find each other with such startling efficiency. The goal for the clinician, of course, is to balance the distribution of responsibilities within the relationship, empowering each person to make competent life decisions for him- or herself.

DIRECTIVES FOR RESOLVING ISSUES OF RESPONSIBILITY ON THE INTERPERSONAL DIMENSION

In intervening on the interpersonal dimension of the client's experience, the clinician has the opportunity to interrupt dysfunctional relationship patterns and establish functional ones. In order for a relationship to work well, the parties involved must achieve a balance of meeting personal needs and the needs of another. Every relationship involves give and take, but too much of one without enough of the other can quickly make a relationship a painful place to be. Directives may be used to shift the patterns of relating in a more positive direction.

D88 | Trust Walk

One relatively safe, nonthreatening, even enjoyable directive for discovering the limits of responsibility is the "Trust Walk." A well-known exercise to many in the human behavior field, the Trust Walk is a good way of amplifying the roles taken by each member of the relationship. Person A is blindfolded and then is led around by Person B, who is now totally responsible for A's guidance and well-being. Being totally responsible for someone in this way gets very tiresome very quickly. Being totally irresponsible for oneself also gets very tedious very fast. The clients should be encouraged by the clinician to keep the exercise going even after the point of fatigue, assuring a very strong memory of the experience to use later in therapy. The clinician can further require that the roles be reversed at another time of doing the exercise. This enables all parties to have a very easily referenced experience of over- and underresponsibility. There is something valuable to be learned from both vantage points.

D89 | Scapegoat of the Week

A strategy that directly brings issues of responsibility and blame into focus is "Scapegoat of the Week." This strategy is particularly effective with those who have a tendency toward martyrdom, that is, those who accept blame and guilt all too easily. When the clinician senses in the client an undercurrent of resentment at "always" being to blame, this directive can be quite useful. The individual is given the prescription of carrying out the role he or she is already in, even though he or she may not yet be conscious of being in such a role. By being assigned the role of scapegoat, what has been a naturally evolving role is now artificially encouraged, diminishing its power for the individual. Ideally, it can push the person to redefine responsibilities in a more realistic way, particularly when the person is blamed for ridiculous things he or she knows is not his or her responsibility.

This kind of prescription in which family members are instructed to continually blame the self-blaming client for whatever happens (e.g., rain, unemployment figures, a damaged wheat crop) can mobilize that person's resistance and lead him or her to assert blamelessness. Such assertion is a necessary step in recognizing the limits of one's responsibility since these are so often blurred when depression is present. In an example of this type of pattern, an attorney in his mid-40s, who was quite successful despite a chronic, moderate depression, was made the "scapegoat" for the family. He was all too experienced with being blamed for things, based on his having critical, rejecting parents. This was a pattern his family continued to carry out. Absurd blaming statements heaped on him by his family were to be met only with the reply, "Please forgive me." After a few days of experiencing this prescription that everyone initially found amusing, the client became enraged and firmly declared his inability to experience any more blame from anyone unless he either first acknowledged the blame as properly his or else was approached in a more neutral "let's talk about it" sort of manner. This was the start of a considerably more functional way of managing the issue of blame and all the related self-esteem factors.

D90 Relationship Sculpting

In another role play of sorts, one can assign roles to the members of a system and carry out "Relationship Sculpting," such as Satir has often done. Members are assigned the roles of placater, blamer, distracter, computer, and leveler (Satir, 1972). Each is then molded into the physical position that typifies his or her role. For example, the placater is down on one knee, desperately reaching out, while making self-effacing statements in a whiney voice. The blamer, as another example, stands full front with one arm extended and pointing harshly, looking angry and clearly blaming others. From these positions and demeanors, interactions are carried out, with the clinician in the role of facilitator. As is generally true with role play scenarios, what starts out as awkward and artificial soon becomes real and emotionally charged. Ventilation of feelings of being burdened or being controlled can emerge and thus be addressed. Whatever fears, doubts, or anxieties people have about their relationships can come out in most surprising ways, making this strategy a valuable means for facilitating changes in the way each member of the relationship handles the others.

D91 Reversing Roles

Another strategy that alters the dynamics of a relationship is one that involves "Reversing Roles." Recognizing that one individual's symptoms may be viewed as a metaphor for problems in his or her relationships, the clinician can offer the directive that members of the relationship switch or reverse roles. Madanes (1984) described an example of a severely depressed young woman whose father was asked to "take over her depression for a week so that she could be free to pursue other interests" (p. 173). The father complied and took on the role of a depressed individual, only to discover that his depression was quite genuine. Madanes (1984) explained it this way:

> The daughter had been helpful to him in that her depression had made him pull himself together in order to help her and had brought him to therapy. The depressed father, eager to help his daughter, offered no resistance to the idea of taking turns [with the problematic patterns]. (p. 174)

Suggesting a role reversal contains the implication that the symptomatic pattern is movable and bendable. When another person "assumes the depression," obviously a paradoxical prescription, the suggestion is accepted that one has control over what has previously been considered uncontrollable. The benefits for later interventions may be readily apparent.

SUMMARY

The strength of the interpersonal model of depression lies in its recognition that each of us lives in a world that brings us into contact with others who can help or hurt us, depending on how we manage our lives. The value of clarifying responsibilities, boundaries, roles, rules, patterns of communication, and other such systemic variables cannot be overstated in the treatment of depressed individuals. This chapter described strategies that may be useful in addressing these relational variables.

12

Inside Out and Outside In

The prevalence of depression presents a demanding challenge to the mental health professional. The recognition that depression is strongly implicated in some of the most troublesome problems our society faces — from drug abuse to violence against self or others — requires a strong response from clinicians. The message must clearly state that each person has the inherent capacity to make positive changes, however little or great, given the right internal and external environments. The internal world of the depressed client is a finely balanced system that has evolved over time, and before the client can emerge from the "inside out," he or she must have evolved a new internal frame of reference that permits new and better responses to life situations. Furthermore, the external world of the client (e.g., the relationships he or she has including the one with the clinician) is also an established system that is finely balanced. External situations inevitably require and get a response (since even no response is still a response) from the individual and thus can be used to facilitate changes from the "outside in."

The framework for the directives described in this book is obviously systemic, rooted in the recognition that all things are interrelated. How can one separate technique from context? How can one separate the words one speaks to another from the relationship they have? Psychotherapy is a curious blend of science and art and is often a subjectively conceived and practiced way of relating to another human being who is offered help on the basis of what the clinician "knows." Each of the hundreds of recognized psychotherapies work, which is why each approach has its devotees. The fact that each therapy has something valuable to offer can either rigidify one's thinking (through one's need to align with one methodology for the sake of maintaining some subjective clarity), or can allow one to evolve the flexibility that it takes to relate carefully to the subjective nature of each depressed person's reality.

The implicit message in the clinician's communications to the client may be considerably more powerful than the explicit one. Perhaps the most successful psychotherapeutic treatments developed thus far for depression are the cognitive and interpersonal approaches. The fact that each alters *patterns* of thinking and relating while simultaneously altering specific thoughts and interactions is undoubtedly the reason these approaches are so valuable. Such methodologies stand out in stark contrast to more psychodynamically oriented approaches that try and propel the individual forward by focusing backwards. The differences between altering the content of a person's problems and the structure of a person's problems are extensive. For example, one may get involved in a series of relationships with insensitive partners — the names and faces change (i.e., the content), but not the type of person one chooses (i.e., the structure). Until the structure of how one chooses partners is altered, the hurtful pattern is likely to repeat itself.

Therapy has been described in a most simple way in this book — as a process of pattern interruption and pattern building. To make use of a client's abilities, as well as the many contexts of his or her life, seems a much more comprehensive and individualized approach to treatment than does imposing the virtually arbitrary beliefs of the clinician onto the client. The directives that are described throughout this volume are appropriate to use only to the extent that the clinician observes specific dysfunctional patterns in the client according to the patterns of experience first described in Chapter 4. Thus, these patterns are not theory-bound, like a singular belief that says "depression is a reaction to loss" that sends the clinician off on the search for "the loss" that is assumed to be present. Rather, these patterns are atheoretical and thus can be incorporated into any treatment plan that has the basic structure of actively involving the client in the treatment process. Depression, perhaps more than any other human condition, demands action, for it is the lack of action that marks the downward spiral of deterioration. Furthermore, the more focused the actions taken at the earliest possible moment, the less chance there is for the problem becoming an ongoing way of life. Interventions in the acute phase are especially demanding for this reason.

Altering one's established patterns of doing things requires a measure of flexibility in one's makeup. Clinicians can easily become superstitious about their interventions, such that when one works, it is to be used again and again when conditions are similar. It was *not* the author's intention for the directives presented in this book to be used in this way. Rather, the author intended to describe a variety of ways of actively engaging the client both in the relationship with the clinician and with the many possibilities life has to offer. The author's hope is that the directives illustrate a way to utilize client patterns, whether for the interruption or the building of responses. The emphasis is on experiential learning, but not to the exclusion of the all important dialoguing and educating that goes on in the natural course of psychotherapy. Educating the client in the principles of many approaches to thinking and living provides as important a base for positive changes as do interventions on other dimensions of experience. The goal for the clinician remains one of evolving more ways of intervening therapeutically on more dimensions of client experience.

Can the reader imagine making use of directives in treatment, such as those described here? Does the reader have the flexibility to attempt solutions according to identified guidelines that lie outside the boundaries that may have been adhered to in the past? The author can remember the first reactions to reading about the unusual directive approaches to therapy employed by the late Milton H. Erickson, M.D. They were viewed as outrageous, preposterous, funny, and completely on-target in their own off-target sort of way. The influence of his and other strategic therapists' work is apparent in this book, with the emphasis on the recognition that change occurs when a new response emerges in a familiar context, whether the context is one's internal or external world. It was recognized that the approaches were and are viable, if only the author had the flexibility to make proper use of them.

Hypnosis can be an especially valuable tool in the clinician's work for its ability to help one set aside one's usual framework in order to respond differently. The emphasis is on creating effective strategies that alter the experiential dimension of one's life. It is often not enough to simply have the client in a "normal" waking state imagine an experience that will be helpful to him or her. The problem with such an approach lies in its potential for restricting the client to a mostly cognitive level, possibly increasing the person's effective reliance on "intellectualization." One way to consider how the world is experienced is to contrast the empirical (sensory-based) dimension with the symbolic (the way sensory experience is organized, stored, and communicated) dimension. The medium of exchange in the practice of verbal psychotherapy is the spoken word—a symbol. Yet, it is the empirical level (i.e., the actual experience) of the client's world that clinicians attempt to alter. The more one appreciates the relationship between words and the influence of subjective experience, which is the essence of hypnosis, the more one can make use of multidimensional communications like metaphors and task assignments in order to alter the client's subjective experience of him- or herself.

CONTRAINDICATIONS

Due to the serious nature of depression — especially the potential for suicide — the various directives that have been described in this book must be chosen and utilized only after careful consideration of the individual client's nature. Many of the directives are structured in such a way as to mobilize whatever resistances a client may have toward the demands of the clinician or to continuing a particular pattern. In order to effectively utilize resistance as a goal, one presupposes the existence of resistance within the individual. It is imprudent to simply assume the existence of resistance in the client, however. Depending on the individual client, the resistance one would hope to mobilize by engaging the client in a directive may be too weak or too deeply buried beneath depressive patterns to be effectively accessed and utilized.

In many instances, the client may require extensive supportive psychotherapy before interventions such as those described here can be utilized effectively. The reasons for this are twofold. First, the clinician is not in a position of influence until a sufficient degree of rapport has been developed. Some clients may require numerous sessions before feeling any sense of personal investment in working with the clinician; others may be highly responsive from the very start. Rapport is not so much contingent on the amount of contact as it is on the quality of the contact. The extent to which the clinician can demonstrate an understanding of the client's ongoing experience is the degree to which rapport will evolve. Second, much of what builds a positive progression in the way a therapy unfolds over time is the establishment of a "response set" in the client. A response set is a pattern of responding, and in the use of strategic therapies it is especially important to catalyze a mind set in the client that opens him or her to the benefits of actively carrying out task assignments and other forms of therapeutic "homework." Giving a directive with an air of certainty as to its capability to benefit the client makes it much more likely that the directive will be carried out. Without the belief system established that carrying out the directives will help, why would the client expend the energy necessary to participate meaningfully in the therapy? The reader may recall the more detailed discussion of the role of positive expectations in treatment presented in Chapter 6.

Unless rapport is adequate and a positive response set is established, the directives can be ignored, sabotaged, or otherwise resisted by the client. Rather than blame the client in such instances, however, the clinician can accept the responsibility for the client's feedback, which is saying in essence, "This assignment is unacceptable to me at some level." Perhaps it is too demanding, too threatening, too ambiguous, or too *something.* The best response for the clinician is to either reintroduce the assignment at a later, more appropriate time, or break down the assignment into smaller components that the client can better manage.

If the timing of these interventions is misjudged, these directives have the capacity to be antitherapeutic—after all, anything that can have a capacity to help can also have a capacity to hurt. *Care must be taken to introduce these directives at a time when rapport is good, motivation is positive, and perhaps most important, when the clinician is quite certain that out of all the responses to the directive that the client is likely to generate, ranging from good to bad, he or she can effectively utilize those responses for a therapeutic purpose.* If the clinician can anticipate that the client may generate a response that the clinician does not know how to use to therapeutic advantage, then it is most prudent to *not* employ the directive. Generally, the clinician can ask him- or herself, "What if this strategy generates a 'blow-up' of some sort? Can I legitimately find a way to make such a response an asset to the individual (perhaps by reframing it in some useful way)?" If the answer to the latter question is "no," then it is best to not offer the directive.

The absence of a sense of timing (i.e., the best time to introduce a directive) on the part of the clinician can yield negative consequences. Consider the following example. In a hospital setting, a clinician attempted a provocative "aggression training" therapy on a depressed patient. The clinician assumed that the client's depression was a consequence of "anger turned inwards." The goal of the intervention was to deliberately provoke the patient into a display of anger that would "release that inner rage" thought to be at the root of the depression. In this case, the clinician demanded that the patient scrub the hospital corridor with a toothbrush. The patient complied and got down on hands and knees to carry out the directive of the clinician. After a period of several hours had elapsed, the clinician returned to inspect the patient's work. The patient had worked continuously, although slowly, on the assigned task, and apparently expected to receive some approval for his efforts. Instead, the clinician began to defiantly and deliberately scuff the floor with his heels. Apparently, the clinician did not consider that the client might not be sufficiently provoked by the gesture, because all the patient did was take a deep sigh and withdraw even further into himself. The clinician was caught off-guard by the reaction, mumbled some words of explanation as to what was "supposed to" happen, and then left. The intervention was obviously inappropriate for that patient, a destructive miscalculation on the part of the clinician. The suggested principle governing the use of directives bears repeating: If there is any doubt as to whether an intervention is appropriate for a depressed client, or if a response might be generated from the client that cannot be utilized well as part of treatment, then it is more conservative and respectful to not use such an intervention. A directive may not help, but it should *never* harm.

CLOSURE

The future of psychotherapy is uncertain. There is little doubt that medical technology will have an increasing influence on our perception and treatment of many disorders. However, the artistry of successful psychotherapy will always be in high demand, since living skills and relationship skills are only teachable in the context of living and relating. Hopefully, the mental health profession will continuously strive to increase its own flexibility regarding the concepts and techniques of psychotherapy. A wide variety of interventions varying in degrees of directiveness and capable of addressing multiple dimensions of the client's experience are needed in order to address problems such as depression. Arguments about which theory is the better one to believe in about depression in particular or human personality in general are arguments that cannot be won. They just distract us from our larger goal of helping those who need our help.

As the stresses of people's lives continue to intensify in these complicated times of ours, it is predictable that episodes of depression will increase, manifesting in many different ways. The ability to identify and disrupt patterns that are hurtful to an individual, in conjunction with the ability to catalyze the discovery of better patterns, is needed to carry out psychotherapy successfully. Learning to plan and carry out therapies that allow for significant experiential learnings on the part of the client assumes an implicit promise that the clinician will actively do those things that he or she can to help. When deemed appropriate after careful consideration, the directives described here—and those that may have occurred to the reader while reading this book—can be most effective in facilitating escape from the chains of depression.

Appendix A:
Directives

Appendix B:
Case Narratives

The following case presentations illustrate applications of the methods described in this book. These cases involve clients for whom the primary presenting problem was depression, and in each of the cases the client had previously attempted therapy but was unsuccessful in overcoming the depression. The clients' subjective report of the absence of distress at the conclusion of therapy and at a later follow-up was the basis for considering treatment successful. Client names and other identifying data have been changed in order to protect confidentiality.

CASE 1*

Background

Charles entered therapy as a 54-year-old male presenting the problem of a moderate depression of approximately two years' duration. Charles experienced disrupted sleep, excessive anxiety, poor concentration, explosive outbursts of anger, extended periods of social isolation, and other less prominent but uncomfortable patterns related to depression. Charles was a highly intellectual, very well-read man who prided himself on his capacity for logic. He viewed himself as "apparently suffering a mid-life crisis." A hard-working architect, Charles was professionally isolated by choice, working on all of his projects at home alone. He had

---

*This case was included in a presentation on Ericksonian psychotherapy by Jeffrey K. Zeig, Ph.D., at the Evolution of Psychotherapy conference held in Phoenix, Arizona in December, 1985. It is also mentioned in the collected proceedings of the conference (Zeig, 1987, p. 401). In that presentation, the patient is called "John."

little interest in relationships beyond his immediate family, and described his disdain for the superficial nature of most social interaction. He much preferred the depth of reading books on philosophy, psychology, and the human condition. Originally from South America, he and his wife emigrated to America as young adults. He had two daughters. He described dissatisfaction with his marriage because of his wife's tendency toward simplicity, and with the American lifestyle because of its complexity.

Charles' family background was of particular importance in his presenting problems. Charles was born to and raised primarily by a devoutly religious but unsophisticated mother (his father died when he was very young). Charles' early interest was pursuing an education and career in art. Uncertain about her son's choice of career, Charles' mother sought the advice of a Church representative, who deemed such a pursuit "frivolous" and "a pathway to a life of sin." Charles was instead encouraged to study math and science, an ongoing source of frustration and resentment for him throughout his life.

Charles' emphasis on being well-read in the deeper philosophical questions of life eventually led to a withdrawal from all relationships, including that with his wife whom he viewed with disdain for her lack of interest in exploring the deeper issues of life. Charles' preoccupation with "finding answers" amplified his frustrations continuously when no such answers would be forthcoming, and eventually led to isolation.

In addressing Charles' problems, it seemed necessary to disrupt a number of patterns: the emphasis on logic to the point of being closed to emotional and social contact; the emphasis on searching to find answers to questions that are unanswerable in a definitive sense; the frustration over having a career and lifestyle that distanced him from his original passion, painting. Thus, the following goals evolved: 1) regaining control over the sleep disruptions and anxiety; 2) instilling a recognition of the value of superficiality on occasion and the ability to grow comfortable with it in many social contexts; 3) developing a respect for and acceptance of individual differences; and 4) the ability to pursue personal interests of a more expressive nature, particularly recreational and artistic ones.

Intervention

Therapy proceeded in stages, following the general flow described in this section.

The first stage of treatment involved building rapport and establishing positive expectations about the possibility of therapeutic changes. Instrumental to the attainment of these initial goals was accepting Charles' belief that all things are purposeful. This belief led easily to the reframing of depression as purposeful (directive 2) and the implication that this was an opportunity for a meaningful change. Charles had not thought of depression as having any positive purpose; rather he viewed it as a sign of personal failure (i.e., evidence of personal shortcomings).

In the second stage of treatment, Charles experienced formal hypnosis sessions aimed at solidifying positive expectations, learning to relax, accessing positive resources (such as the ability to *face challenges and succeed* evidenced in the move to America), and discovering creative parts of himself that had been suppressed. The formal hypnosis sessions had a relatively immediate impact of reducing anxiety and irritability, and enhancing restful sleep. These sessions involved directives 9, 10, and 62.

In the third stage of treatment, trance sessions involving metaphors relating to different types of relationships were offered, illustrating the principle that relationships can take many forms and can exist in varying degrees of closeness (unlike the "all-or-none" pattern Charles had been in). Homework assignments were given for Charles to engage people in *purposely* superficial conversations with the explicit instructions that he offer no opinions whatsoever. This served to interrupt his usual pattern of rigidly asserting his correctness regardless of context. The effect was eye-opening for him in terms of how judgmental and self-righteous he had been on the basis of his self-proclaimed superior knowledge. By being unable to express opinions of any type, Charles had much more opportunity to discover that other people can also use sound reasoning principles and yet arrive at virtually opposite conclusions. This learning had the greatest impact on his family relationships. Instead of Charles' critical reactions to his wife and two teenage daughters, his demeanor evolved into a more accepting one, which was eagerly supported by his family. These sessions involved variations of directives 15, 16, and 42.

In the fourth stage, Charles' suppression of his artistic interests was addressed as a metaphor for his own self-negation of inescapable personal qualities (emotions, the need for recreation and lightheartedness). Charles' perfectionism precluded his painting (he did not want to do artwork unless it could be excellent work), even though it seemed obvious he wanted to do so. Charles was directed to paint first thing every morning, but only to do three-quarters of a picture and then stop. He complied. Although Charles reported feeling very good about having begun to paint again after so long a period of abstinence, he reported being very frustrated about having to stop before completing his pictures. He was then allowed to complete the pictures, but not to sign them. In the next step he was directed to anonymously give the pictures to neighbors (leaving them at their door or in their mailbox). This he did with an enjoyable sense of mischief. Thus, he was able to complete drawings with no personal risk (since they were anonymous) and simultaneously was drawn into developing an awareness of his neighbors whom he had ignored. He went a step further on his own and began to initiate friendly encounters with them, curious about whether they would mention receiving anonymous pictures. In the last phase, Charles was to complete and sign his pictures and do with them as he wished. He entered several in local art competitions, and actually won prizes and earned recognition for his work!

Throughout this period, Charles' ability to accept others as well as himself to a greater extent than before proved to be critical in his recovery from depression. He learned to deal with others in a social and light way, and to express himself on other levels besides a purely intellectual one. Charles learned that even the deepest of relationships may start out on a most superficial basis. These sessions involved variations of directives 44, 45, 51, and 61.

In the final stage of treatment, Charles' evolving patterns of acceptance of self and others was stabilized, as were his new patterns of utilizing self-hypnosis in order to maintain control over anxiety and to enhance sleep. When Charles and the author agreed that his recovery had stabilized, therapy was terminated. Therapy was completed in 25 sessions over a nine-month period.

Discussion

Formal and informal trances, direct and indirect suggestions, reframing, and homework assignments were all used to catalyze Charles' recognition that the ultimate meaning of life is whatever he chose it to be. Because he rejected his own "illogical emotionalism" and thereby created an unrealistic expectation that his logic alone could govern his experience, his emotions escalated out of control in the form of depression. By learning to balance various dimensions of his world (logic vs. emotion, work vs. recreation, noncommunicativeness vs. openness, social vs. withdrawn), Charles was able to reach a much more satisfying level of living.

A confusion clearly existed for Charles regarding the controllability of aspects of his world. By trying to control others' opinions through the powerful assertion of his own, and by trying to control (i.e., deny) his emotional experiences, Charles was attempting to control things that cannot be controlled—other people and emotions (a basic unalterable part of all human beings' makeup). Through the use of hypnosis to facilitate a mind set receptive to discovering new possibilities, the seeding of positive expectations allowed for the discovery and acceptance of these ideas. Through the use of assignments that broke down the larger patterns to be learned into manageable steps, a progression of experiences unfolded over time, building a momentum toward recovery.

CASE 2

Background

Joan entered therapy as a 53-year-old female presenting the problem of a moderate to severe depression, which she described as lifelong but which had become worse in recent weeks, leading her to seek therapy. Joan's chronic depression was described as a way of life that she had accepted as normal. She did not have enough of a social network to make the kinds of comparisons with others that would have highlighted to her sooner that something was wrong. She assumed everyone fought the same emotional battles that she had been fighting all of her life.

Joan had been married twice and both marriages ended after a relatively short time. Single and living alone, she was a mother of two children, both of whom were living quite a distance away from her. Her relationship with them was amiable, with regular visits back and forth.

Joan had grown up in a very small town in Wyoming. At a relatively young age, the town's school closed and Joan was forced to move in with relatives in another town in order to attend school there. Thus, her family relationships were disrupted early on, and a genuine closeness with others did not seem possible to her. Joan's demeanor was matter-of-fact, and she described her personal history in a neutral way. It was apparent, however, that the lack of closeness and support she had experienced had left her feeling isolated. The lack of a support network currently was basically an extension of her mostly loner lifestyle.

Joan was well educated and was employed by a large company as a chemical engineer. She had been working for the company for nearly 20 years and viewed herself as trapped into staying with the company since other jobs in her field were extremely scarce.

Joan's job was the focal point of her life. It occupied the majority of her time, since she routinely worked overtime. It was central to her self-image as a competent, independent, professional woman. Thus, it also became central in her experience of depression. Joan felt she was being consistently underutilized in her work. Her job involved her working independently, and even her "superior" was generally quite unaware of her work responsibilities and the (low) level of demand placed on her. Joan had a very strong work ethic and, in order to justify her salary, would go out of her way to find additional projects to both help the company and better utilize her skills. She found it extremely stressful to have to find things to do; this stress was compounded by the fact that her requests for redefining her position received no response from those higher up in the company's hierarchy.

The depression that led Joan to seek treatment was apparently long-term, but it was the work situation that troubled her the most. It also was apparent that Joan's emphasis on work was problematic, since her work situation was negative, including a poorly defined set of responsibilities, underutilization of her skills, a lack of responsiveness to her needs and interests, and an objective inability to find similar work elsewhere. The fact that Joan experienced such high levels of guilt over her inability to justify her salary was strong evidence of how responsible Joan felt about the company's poor management of her position with them. Joan assumed that if she were a better employee, the company would be more responsive to her. The distortion in that line of thinking should be evident. Joan was attempting to exert influence on a system that was beyond her control, and instead of perceiving it as beyond her control, she attempted to do more of the same — that is, work even harder. Her attempted solution only had the effect of compounding the problem.

Intervention

The goals of treatment included: 1) redefining self-worth in terms other than the work ethic (i.e., the value Joan held that "one's worth is derived from one's work"); 2) developing a balance in her life between work and other interests; 3) developing clarity about the issues of guilt and responsibility such that Joan could let go of the guilt and depression she was experiencing associated with the company's mismanagement of her skills; 4) developing recognition of her inability to control the company's use of her skills; 5) developing greater sensitivity to her own needs and redefining depression as a warning signal indicating the necessity of a change somewhere, allowing her to respond more effectively to episodes of depression; and 6) preventing some episodes and minimizing the discomfort of others.

Therapy progressed rapidly through three distinct phases. In the first phase, the focus was on building rapport and building the expectancy of change. This was done in the first two sessions in which the problem's parameters were identified. Particular attention was paid to the sifting out of Joan's value that one's work defines one's worth even more than one's relationships with others. While the first session was primarily one of information gathering and rapport and expectancy building, the second session involved a formal hypnosis session regarding the need for diversity in Joan's life and the idea that being tied to one negative aspect of life (i.e., her job) does not preclude establishing positive ties to other activities that generate enjoyment. The need for diversity as described in directive 14 was followed by the task assignments described in directives 18 and 21.

In the next three sessions, open discussions were held regarding the strengths and limitations of a strong work ethic, the nature of wanting to control circumstances vital to one's life and dealing with the reality that Joan's efforts to control the system were misguided, and the need to shift her emphasis from being a model employee to recognizing that her managers were those ultimately responsible for best utilizing her resources. In addition to these discussions, hypnosis sessions were used emphasizing that while Joan might not be able to control the situation, she could very definitely control her reactions to the situation. Directives 22, 34, 46, and 62 were used in this phase of treatment.

Improvement for Joan was quite rapid. It was powerful learning for her to recognize the discrepancy between her professional ideals and the reality of her nonsupportive work environment, greatly easing the guilt and tendency to internalize responsibility for less-than-perfect outcomes.

In the final phase of treatment, a prescription for a scheduled relapse was given, which she carried out. Joan's reaction was one of delight to discover that she could easily experience a mock depression without any negative effects, and come out of it unhurt. In the subsequent two sessions, Joan was guided through future experiences while maintaining a high level of clarity about the issues of responsibility, control, and balance in her life. A one-year follow-up showed the maintenance of the therapeutic results. Therapy involved a total of nine sessions.

Discussion

Joan's integrity was a double-edged sword for her. Her sense of duty and commitment led her to internalize blame for circumstances affecting her, even when they were not in her direct control. She responded extremely well to hypnotic interventions, where her refined logic was irrelevant and her emotional needs could be better addressed. She focused on key words like "absorption," "depth of comfort," "balance," and "developing diverse interests," and found them useful in managing her experience.

The rapid nature of her recovery and the ongoing success in remaining essentially depression-free is attributed to the use of consciously directed restructuring of her ideas about control and responsibility, and the building of meaningful contact with parts of herself normally ignored in the hypnosis sessions. In discovering diversity within herself, Joan found it much easier to discover diversity outside herself as well in the form of new hobbies, providing a strong sense of relief to a previously troubled, one-dimensional life.

CASE 3

Background

Carol entered therapy as a 57-year-old female presenting the problem of severe depression, recently exacerbated by changes associated with her job. Carol worked for a construction company in an administrative position that primarily involved clerical work but also some training of employees in standards of safety on the job. When her position was altered (she was assigned to a new supervisor), Carol reacted intensely negatively and quickly slipped into a deep depression characterized by uncontrollable crying, high levels of agitation and anxiety, poor sleep, excessive alcohol intake, inability to concentrate, a sense of impending doom, and other depressive symptoms. Her reaction was excessive and was very much tied into the fact that she felt quite attached to her current supervisor.

Carol had been married for 23 years to a man whom she described as a "con artist." Extroverted and generally likable, he was a manipulative man who drew people into his self-serving illegal schemes to make money. This pattern eventually landed him in jail (convicted of embezzlement) and led to their divorce. Carol had been the stable, consistent partner in the marriage and almost single-handedly raised their two children. Passive to a fault, Carol was intimidated by her husband and basically asked "How high?" when he said "Jump!" Carol's self-esteem throughout her adult life had been extremely poor, and with one problem to face after another, she described herself as having lived a basically miserable life that was characterized by a seemingly ever-present depression. She had never been career-oriented and, when divorced at age 41, first faced the difficulties associated with entering the work world. Her level of confidence in her ability was extremely low, and she was always swimming upstream against a current of pessimism.

Her relationship with both her children was strained. Her son lived out of state, and contact with him was kept superficial in order to avoid his angry feelings simmering just beneath the surface. She and her daughter had been close at one time, but the daughter abruptly pulled away for reasons Carol did not understand. This estrangement was a central focus of Carol's emotional pain. Neither sibling was in contact with the other.

Carol was socially isolated. Other than her involvement with her job, Carol did not go anywhere or do anything with other people. The lack of a social support system was a key component of her inability to diversify (and balance) her interests, leaving her in a rut. She did not date, had not for years, and was convinced that no man would be interested in her.

A concern that Carol voiced from time to time was her financial future. She anticipated having to retire in the not-too-distant future and was worried that her retirement benefits would be inadequate for her needs. She also feared the loneliness of being old, retired, and isolated with too little financial security to compensate.

Therapy involved establishing and working toward a number of related goals: 1) regaining perspective in order to rapidly eliminate the most overt manifestations of her depression; 2) building a healthier self-esteem that would permit establishing social connections, more characterological flexibility, and enough of a future orientation to permit financial planning; 3) helping her reestablish a relationship with her estranged daughter; and 4) establishing a system of thought and behavior reflecting greater clarity in problem-solving skills and assessing the issues of personal responsibility and control.

Intervention

Carol was seen for a total of 31 sessions over a period of nine months. The chronic and pervasive nature of her depression required a slightly longer involvement in therapy. Use of many of the experiential directives was made in order to better establish a more functional frame of reference within her for making positive choices.

Early on in treatment, the goal was established of restoring normal sleep, stopping the uncontrolled crying, reducing drinking, and better adjusting to the current demands of her job. Directives 1, 2, 3, 9, and 10 were used in conjunction with formal hypnosis in order to facilitate relaxation and the flexibility needed to adjust to the changes at work. Each of the earliest sessions was tape-recorded, and Carol was given the tapes to work with in order to reinforce her learnings. She began to sleep better almost immediately, the crying stopped, and the passive feelings of being a victim of circumstances became transformed into feelings of anger with the company. The anger was a much more appropriate feeling given her situation, and was accepted and reframed as a potential catalyst to positive action on her own behalf. It was suggested to Carol that if she was more observant of the relationships of others at work, she might also be more politically savvy and better able to read people's tendencies and needs, creating greater stability at work.

This concept intrigued Carol and thus paved the way for the next phase of treatment, which focused on social relationships. As in nearly all other aspects of her life, Carol was intimidated by others and while she was not socially incompetent, neither was she skilled in managing others well. General discussions were held about people's relationships, including how people fit into socially defined roles, how they manipulate others to get the things they want, and so forth. Suggestions were given for the need for clarity about one's own needs. Suggestions were also offered about developing the ability to manage others well despite any negative feelings one might have about them. These suggestions highlighted the need to better understand others' beliefs in order to better understand their actions. Directives 30, 47, 48, 50, and 86 were used in these sessions in order to consolidate these learnings.

As Carol became more adept at drawing out others and tolerating differences between them, her level of social confidence rose substantially. She was feeling less like isolating, now that she was no longer overrun by others. She began asking co-workers to do things with her socially, and she was delighted to find out that "even much younger women make good company."

In riding the momentum of her evolving skills in building and managing relationships, the issues surrounding her daughter were addressed. There had been virtually no contact over a period of nearly a year, and very limited contact over the preceding three or four years. She described how she was desperate to resolve things, but every time she and her daughter did speak, it was an intense interaction.

Simultaneously with addressing the issue of her daughter, the issue of her financial future was dealt with. Carol confessed to the ambition of always having wanted to be an interior designer. She did not believe that at age 57, however, it would be worth her going to school in order to eventually work for herself as a consultant. She said that by the time she finished, she would be 59. Asked how old she would be in two years if she did not go, she sheepishly replied, "59." She was told to look into schools, talk with designers in order to assess income potential and the job market for designers, and so forth. Carol was excited to find a rapid and intensive program offered somewhere, and she enrolled enthusiastically. She was the oldest person in the class, a position she actually relished, particularly since the other classmates were openly admiring of her ambitious plans. She made new friends and was involved in an interest outside of home and her job. Directive 4 and a variation of directive 61 were used to facilitate these outcomes.

Carol was directed to call her daughter and to tell her that she no longer had much time for her since she was in school (as if the daughter was too demanding of her time!). She was directed to be abrupt in demeanor, but not impolite. Several days later, the daughter called and was clearly curious, but also abrupt. Contact was starting to be reestablished. An interruption of Carol's usual desperate demeanor was being replaced with a new pattern of her feeling she was important. She eventually felt important enough to think that the daughter (not just Carol) would be missing something valuable if there was no relationship between them.

Carol's depression was lifting dramatically as she developed more and better ways of problem solving. She developed social skills, ambition, ways of preventing herself from being manipulated by others and evolved a much more positive sense of her own capabilities than she had ever had before. The changes in her life were all woven into a metaphor delivered in trance mid-way through therapy that played on the theme of her interest in interior design. Talking about making changes in the way she felt and interpreted things was quite easy to relate to doing some "*interior* designing," taking what's old and drab and replacing it with things new and colorful and exciting. She used this type of metaphor a lot in helping herself maintain the momentum of her changes while she continued in school and with her future plans.

Discussion

The pervasive sense of helplessness and hopelessness in Carol was clearly a consequence of her inability to establish control over *any* dimension of her experience. The message continually given Carol was that each of the problems could be solved if she were to assume the personal power it would take to effectively address the problems. By passively pleading ignorance about what to do, Carol wallowed in the pain and desperation of her situation. So global was her thinking style that she could not identify *what* needed to be done, much less *how* to do it. So past-oriented was she that establishing goals and working toward them seemed impossible to her. The many directives used in her therapy were each aimed at helping her establish control over what she had perceived as uncontrollable situations and feelings, and building the expectations that her efforts would be rewarded. She learned to better distinguish what lay in her realm of responsibilities and what did not, and she learned to better problem solve when feeling "stuck." She learned to resist others' manipulations and to better relate to others through greater acceptance of their right to be who they are (including her daughter!). The Christmas card the author received from Carol six months after her therapy ended told him it was her best Christmas in 15 years, and that she had finally found some peace within herself.

CASE 4

Jeff entered therapy as a 43-year-old male presenting the problem of a moderate to severe depression. Jeff had been in therapy for approximately one year with a psychoanalytically oriented therapist, but felt he was not progressing and so wanted to pursue a different approach to his problems. Jeff gave a very intellectual type of self-report and described how he had recently gone through his second divorce after a marriage of 17 years. The marriage broke up when he began having an affair with the woman he currently lived with, although he was aware the marriage had been deteriorating for some time. Jeff was an electronics engineer by profession and placed a premium value on logic and rationality. He found many of the previous therapists' interpretations to be too subjective ("off the wall") to be credible and was more interested in getting some direct feedback on ways he could manage the behaviors that troubled him: "I'm a perfectionist, demanding, impatient, controlling, and generally irritable." Jeff described how he had a very clear sense of right and wrong, and how he would become very impatient and aggressive when others did not have the perceptiveness to share his wisdom. He had frequent arguments with his girlfriend and attributed the difficulties to her "lack of experience," as she had never been married. Jeff also described strained relationships with those he worked with, generally attributing the difficulties to their lack of organization, lesser ambitions, and lack of the work ethic he felt was necessary to be effective.

Jeff's understanding of depression was a surprisingly limited one, given the length of time he had previously been in treatment. He attributed the depression solely to the stresses of his work and his relationship with his girlfriend. He saw himself as "probably going through a mid-life crisis." Questioning about the long-term patterns in his behavior made it clear that the dominant, troublesome patterns were not recently acquired. He had been perfectionistic, controlling, and impatient for as long as he could remember. Family history information revealed that his relationship with both parents was distant and formal. Parental expectations of him were excessive and were not well recognized when they were met.

It became clear after the first two sessions that Jeff was living in a very concrete world of dichotomies, that is, the world is black and white with little or no gray. Jeff's ideas about the way things "should" be were firmly established by his parents, whom he viewed as positive role models for "what a little elbow grease can do." Jeff was generally very analytical about externals (situations or people), but not at all about internal experience. Consequently, he did not have much insight into the ways his parents' values were internalized by him, nor did he seem aware of ways in which his beliefs were limiting him.

The goals for Jeff's therapy were as follows: 1) establishing a greater sense of individuation through clarification of personal values, allowing Jeff the chance to discover the limitations of his parents' value system and thereby disengage from it wherever useful; 2) disrupting the tendency toward viewing the world in unrealistic extremes in order to evolve a greater tolerance for the ambiguities in life; 3) establishing clarity about the limits of his ability to control externals in order to build a greater acceptance of circumstances beyond his control; and 4) establishing a more effective and satisfying way of interacting with others.

Intervention

Jeff was seen for a total of 10 sessions over a three-month period. Jeff's initial presentation of his dissatisfaction with less than pragmatic interventions in combination with his acknowledgment of his impatience was a clear message that he was hurting enough to want some immediate direction and relief. In the second session, Jeff was asked to identify and describe his values regarding issues such as work, money, and relationships. His responses were quite dogmatic. Asked how his parents saw things, he responded, "Very much the same way, naturally." This led into a discussion of values in general and the many influences on the formation of one's value system. Also mentioned was the idea that children becoming adults reach a stage of questioning parental and societal values in order to establish themselves as unique individuals. At the close of this general discussion about values and subjective social realities, Jeff was given the task assignment of directive 21 to complete during the week between sessions.

Jeff found the assignment both stimulating and useful. He had not seen himself as significantly different than his parents, and "the prospect of emerging as a unique personality is intriguing to me, obvious as it may seem." Further discussion of the relationship between values, behavior, and self-image was held, and the point was introduced that "one would need to be quite flexible to accept that others' values are as real to them as yours are to you." Directives 8, 17, and 85 were used to facilitate an appreciation for his own values and those of others, seeding the possibilities for effective social changes later.

Jeff had not seen himself as dogmatic, but developed the realization from the assignments. He very much liked the concept of "flexibility" and saw it as quite a challenge to develop that characteristic. Directives 14, 35, and 60 were used in-session and in between sessions, catalyzing the recognition of a world that offers lots of possibilities and perspectives, and the realization that there can be many "right" ways, some of which at first glance seem entirely incongruous.

As Jeff evolved a greater awareness for the gray areas in life and the many diverse ways there are for responding to life episodes, his anxiety actually increased for a short time, which he insightfully interpreted was a result of "having less control over life than ever." It was the perfect time to introduce new ideas regarding the issue of control, contrasting overcontrolling tactics from undercontrolling tactics and identifying the need to be clear about what was and was not in his control. Jeff's highly controlling manner had been analyzed and interpreted but was never disrupted in any way, and he just assumed that he was "characterologically a 'Type A' personality." Directives 34 and 36 were used to catalyze awareness of controllability factors in a given context and to encourage greater acceptance when nothing he could do would make a difference.

Relief on a variety of levels was swift and dramatic, as if all had properly fallen into place. Jeff proudly reported on a variety of situations he simply walked away from that previously he would have gotten caught up in much to his own detriment. He reported a greatly improved ability to manage his overt disagreement with others, taking care to listen to them while trying to identify their values much as he had his own. By the eighth session, Jeff reported feeling "suspiciously well." Directives 3, 13, and 63 were used at this time to facilitate greater dissociation from the patterns of the past. The tenth session was a termination session, involving establishing patterns for maintaining the progress during the future that had been achieved in therapy. During a telephone contact almost 18 months later, Jeff confirmed that despite some tense moments in his relationship with his girlfriend, he was satisfied with his life and was "free of any significant depression."

Discussion

Jeff's need to control the events in his life reflected a less-than-secure sense of self. In general, when the client attempts to exert a high degree of control over his or her life in inappropriate realms (such as with other people), the person is unsuccessful simply because what is being attempted is not possible. The effect, however, is to convince the person that he or she is out of control. To disrupt this pattern, the client's dysfunctional assumption that "more control is better" must be questioned, and then a more functional pattern of learning to control *selectively* according to what *can* be controlled can be instilled.

Jeff's impatience was a wonderful catalyst for the therapy. Whereas a more traditionally oriented clinician might have been quick to attack the impatience as dysfunctional ("expecting too much too soon"), the author chose to utilize the impatience as a basis for introducing task assignments and getting compliance from Jeff in carrying them out. It may be apparent that the more effectively a clinician can utilize the various dimensions of a client's experience, the more multidimensional, and therefore complete, the intervention can be.

Bibliography

Abramson, L., Seligman, M., & Teasdale, J. (1979). Learned helplessness in humans: Critique and reformulation. *Journal of Abnormal Psychology, 87,* 49-74.

Alexander, L. (1982). Erickson's approach to hypnotic psychotherapy of depression. In J. Zeig (Ed.), *Ericksonian approaches to hypnosis and psychotherapy* (pp. 219-227). New York: Brunner/ Mazel.

American Psychiatric Association. (1987). *Diagnostic and statistical manual of mental disorders* (3rd. ed., revised). Washington, D.C.: American Psychiatric Association.

Araoz, D. (1985). *The new hypnosis.* New York: Brunner/Mazel.

Aronson, E. (1984). *The social animal* (4th. ed.). New York: Freeman.

Bandler, R., & Grinder, J. (1975). *The structure of magic* (Vol. I). Palo Alto, CA: Science and Behavior Books.

Bandler, R., & Grinder, J. (1979). *Frogs into princes.* Moab, UT: Real People Press.

Beck, A. (1967). *Depression.* New York: Harper & Row.

Beck, A. (1973). *The diagnosis and management of depression.* Philadelphia: University of Pennsylvania Press.

Beck, A. (1983). Negative cognitions. In E. Levitt, B. Lubin & J. Brooks (Eds.), *Depression: Concepts, controversies, and some new facts* (2nd. ed.) (pp. 86-92). Hillsdale, N.J.: Erlbaum.

Beck, A., Rush, J., Shaw, B., & Emery, G. (1979). *Cognitive therapy of depression.* New York: Guilford Press.

Beletsis, C. (1986). Balance: A central principle of the Ericksonian approach. In M. Yapko (Ed.), *Hypnotic and strategic interventions: Principles and practice* (pp. 57-73). New York: Irvington.

Burns, D. (1980). *Feeling good: The new mood therapy.* New York: Morrow.

213

Carter, P. (1983). *The parts model: A formula for integrity.* Unpublished doctoral dissertation. International College.

Clance, P. (1985). *The imposter phenomenon.* New York: Bantam Books.

Clayton, P. (1983). The prevalence and course of the affective disorders. In J. Davis & J. Maas (Eds.), *The affective disorders* (pp. 193-201). Washington, D.C.: American Psychiatric Press.

Davison, G., & Neale, J. (1986). *Abnormal psychology* (4th. ed.). New York: Wiley.

Erickson, M. (1954a). Special techniques of brief hypnotherapy. *Journal of Clinical and Experimental Hypnosis, 2,* 109-129.

Erickson, M. (1954b). Pseudo-orientation in time as a hypnotherapeutic procedure. *Journal of Clinical and Experimental Hypnosis, 2,* 261-283.

Erickson, M. (1980). The applications of hypnosis to psychiatry. In E. Rossi (Ed.), *The collected papers of Milton H. Erickson on hypnosis* (Vol. IV) (pp. 3-13). New York: Irvington.

Erickson, M., Rossi, E., & Rossi, S. (1976). *Hypnotic realities.* New York: Irvington.

Erickson, M., & Rossi, E. (1979). *Hypnotherapy: An exploratory casebook.* New York: Irvington.

Farrelly, F., & Brandsma, J. (1978). *Provocative therapy.* Cupertino, CA: Meta Publications.

Frankl, V. (1963). *Man's search for meaning.* New York: Washington Square Press.

Freud, S. (1917). Mourning and melancholia. In *Collected works of Sigmund Freud* (Vol. 4). London: Hogarth Press and the Institute of Psychoanalysis, 1950.

Gazzaniga, M. (1985). *The social brain.* New York: Basic Books.

Gibson, J. (1983). *Living: Human development through the lifespan.* Reading, MA: Addison-Wesley.

Gilligan, S. (1986). *Therapeutic trances: The cooperation principle in Ericksonian hypnotherapy.* New York: Brunner/Mazel.

Goldstein, J. (1980). *Social psychology.* New York: Academic Press.

Gordon, D. (1978). *Therapeutic metaphors.* Cupertino, CA: Meta Publications.

Grinder, J., & Bandler, R. (1981). *Trance-formations.* Moab, UT: Real People Press.

Haley, J. (1973). *Uncommon therapy.* New York: Norton.

Haley, J. (1984). *Ordeal therapy.* San Francisco: Jossey-Bass.

Harlow, H., & Suomi, S. (1974). Induced depression in monkeys. *Behavioral Biology, 12,* 273-296.

Hockenstein, B. (1986). Self-blame as a consequence of self-improvement programs. In M. Yapko (Ed.), *Hypnotic and strategic interventions: Principles and practice* (pp. 91-109). New York: Irvington.

Hollister, L. (1983). Treating depressed patients with medical problems. In J. Davis & J. Maas (Eds.), *The affective disorders* (pp. 393-408). Washington, D.C.: American Psychiatric Press.

Kleinmuntz, B. (1980). *Essentials of abnormal psychology* (2nd. ed.). San Francisco: Harper & Row.

Klerman, G., Weissman, M., Rounsaville, B., & Chevron, E. (1984). *Interpersonal psychotherapy of depression.* New York: Basic Books.

Kolb, L., & Brodie, H. (1982). *Modern clinical psychiatry* (10th. ed.). Philadelphia: W.B. Saunders.

Laliotis, D., & Grayson, J. (1985). Psychologist heal thyself. *American Psychologist, 40,* 84-96.

Lankton, S. (1980). *Practical magic.* Cupertino, CA: Meta Publications.

Lankton, S., & Lankton, C. (1983). *The answer within: A clinical framework of Ericksonian hypnotherapy.* New York: Brunner/Mazel.

Lankton, S., & Lankton, C. (1986). *Enchantment and intervention in family therapy.* New York: Brunner/Mazel.

Madanes, C. (1984). *Behind the one-way mirror.* San Francisco: Jossey-Bass.

Mahoney, M. (1980). *Abnormal psychology: Perspectives on human variance.* San Francisco: Harper & Row.

Massey, M. (1979). *The people puzzle.* Reston, VA: Reston Publishing Co.

McMullin, R. (1986). *Handbook of cognitive therapy techniques.* New York: Norton.

Miller, H. (1984). Depression: A specific cognitive pattern. In W. Webster (Ed.), *Clinical hypnosis: A multidisciplinary approach* (2nd. ed.) (pp. 421-458). Philadelphia: Lippincott.

Perls, F. (1969). *Gestalt therapy verbatim.* Moab, UT: Real People Press.

Phares, E. (1984). *Introduction to personality.* Columbus, OH: Charles Merrill.

Polster, E., & Polster, M. (1973). *Gestalt therapy integrated.* New York: Vintage Books.

Robbins, T. (1976). *Even cowgirls get the blues.* Boston: Houghton Mifflin.

Rosen, S. (1982). *My voice will go with you: The teaching tales of Milton H. Erickson.* New York: Norton.

Rossi, E. (1986). *The psychobiology of mind-body healing.* New York: Norton.

Rotter, J. (1966). Generalized expectations for internal versus external control of reinforcement. *Psychological Monographs, 80* (1, whole No. 609).

Samko, M. (1986). Rigidity and pattern interruption: Central issues underlying Milton Erickson's approach to psychotherapy. In M. Yapko (Ed.), *Hypnotic and strategic interventions: Principles and practice* (pp. 47-55). New York: Irvington.

Sarason, I., & Sarason, B. (1980). *Abnormal psychology* (3rd. ed.). Englewood Cliffs, N.J.: Prentice-Hall.

Satir, V. (1972). *Peoplemaking.* Palo Alto, CA: Science and Behavior Books.

Satir, V. (1983). *Satir: Step by step.* Palo Alto, CA: Science and Behavior Books.

Secunda, S., Friedman, R., & Schuyler, D. (1973). *The depressive disorders: Special report, 1973.* (DHEW Publication No. HSM-73-9157). Washington, D.C.: U.S. Government Printing Office.

Seligman, M. (1973, June). Fall into helplessness. *Psychology Today, 7,* 43-48.

Seligman, M. (1974). Depression and learned helplessness. In R. Friedman & M. Katz (Eds.), *The psychology of depression: Contemporary theory and research.* Washington, D.C.: Winston.

Seligman, M. (1975). *Helplessness: On depression, development, and health.* San Francisco: Freeman.

Seligman, M. (1983). Learned helplessness. In E. Levitt, B. Lubin, & J. Brooks (Eds.), *Depression: Concepts, controversies, and some new facts* (2nd. ed.) (pp. 64-72). Hillsdale, N.J.: Erlbaum.

Spiegel, H., & Spiegel, D. (1978). *Trance and treatment: Clinical uses of hypnosis.* New York: Basic Books.

Spiegel, D. (1986). Dissociating damage. *American Journal of Clinical Hypnosis, 29,* 123-131.

Suinn, R. (1984). *Fundamentals of abnormal psychology.* Chicago: Nelson-Hall.

Trotter, R. (1987, February). Stop blaming yourself. *Psychology Today, 21,* 31-39.

Watkins, J.G. (1971). The affect bridge: A hypnoanalytic technique. *International Journal of Clinical and Experimental Hypnosis, 19,* 21-27.

Watzlawick, P. (1976). *How real is real?* New York: Vintage Books.

Watzlawick, P. (1978). *The language of change.* New York: Basic Books.

Watzlawick, P. (1983). *The situation is hopeless, but not serious.* New York: Norton.

Yapko, M. (1981). The effect of matching primary representational system predicates on hypnotic relaxation. *American Journal of Clinical Hypnosis, 23,* 169-175.

Yapko, M. (1983). A comparative analysis of direct and indirect hypnotic communication styles. *American Journal of Clinical Hypnosis, 25,* 270-276.

Yapko, M. (1984a). *Trancework: An introduction to clinical hypnosis.* New York: Irvington.

Yapko, M. (1984b). Implications of the Ericksonian and Neuro-Linguistic Programming approaches for responsibility of therapeutic outcomes. *American Journal of Clinical Hypnosis, 27,* 137-143.

Yapko, M. (1985a). The Erickson hook: Values in Ericksonian approaches. In J. Zeig (Ed.), *Ericksonian psychotherapy* (Vol. I) (pp. 266-281). New York: Brunner/Mazel.

Yapko, M. (1985b). Therapeutic strategies for the treatment of depression. *Ericksonian Monographs, 1,* 89-110. New York: Brunner/Mazel.

Yapko, M. (1986). Depression: Diagnostic frameworks and therapeutic strategies. In M. Yapko (Ed.), *Hypnotic and strategic interventions: Principles and practice* (pp. 215-259). New York: Irvington.

Yapko, M. (in press). Individuation: Alone together. In J. Zeig & S. Lankton (Eds.), *Ericksonian psychotherapy: State of the art*. New York: Brunner/Mazel.

Zeig, J. (Ed.). (1980a). *A teaching seminar with Milton H. Erickson*. New York: Brunner/Mazel.

Zeig, J. (1980b). Symptom prescription techniques: Clinical applications using elements of communication. *American Journal of Clinical Hypnosis, 23*, 23-33.

Zeig, J. (Ed.). (1982). *Ericksonian approaches to hypnosis and psychotherapy*. New York: Brunner/Mazel.

Zeig, J. (1984, June). Personal communication.

Zeig, J. (Ed.). (1985). *Ericksonian psychotherapy* (2 Vols.). New York: Brunner/Mazel.

Zeig, J. (Ed.). (1987). *The evolution of psychotherapy*. New York: Brunner/Mazel.

Index

219